TOUR DE LANCE

TOUR DE LANCE

The Extraordinary Story of Lance Armstrong's Fight
to Reclaim the Tour de France

BILL STRICKLAND

HARMONY BOOKS | NEW YORK

Harmony Books is a registered trademark and the Harmony Books colophon is a trademark of Random House, Inc.

"Irresistible," from *Different Hours* by Stephen Dunn. Copyright © 2000 by Stephen
Dunn. Used by permission of W. W. Norton & Company, Inc.

Library of Congress Cataloging-in-Publication Data

Strickland, Bill, 1964–
    Tour de Lance: the extraordinary story of Lance Armstrong's fight to reclaim the
Tour De France / Bill Strickland.
        p. cm.
    1. Armstrong, Lance.   2. Cyclists—United States—Biography.   3. Tour de France
(Bicycle race) (2009)   I. Title.
    GV1051.A76S78 2010
    796.6'2092—dc22
    [B]   2010004504

ISBN 978-0-307-58984-2

Printed in the United States of America

Design by Gretchen Achilles

2009 Tour de France map courtesy of ASO (American Sports Organization)

Insert photographs copyright © James Startt

10 9 8 7 6 5 4 3 2 1

FIRST EDITION

For Beth,

my rhythm

CONTENTS

Character

on its way toward destiny—

my favorite kind of helplessness.

—STEPHEN DUNN, *"Irresistible"*

DATE	ÉTAPE	DÉPART	ARRIVÉE	
Samedi 4 juillet	1ère	**Monaco**	**Monaco**	C.l.m. individuel
Dimanche 5 juillet	2e	**Monaco**	**Brignoles**	
Lundi 6 juillet	3e	**Marseille**	**La Grande-Motte**	
Mardi 7 juillet	4e	**Montpellier**	**Montpellier**	C.l.m. par équipe
Mercredi 8 juillet	5e	**Le Cap d'Agde**	**Perpignan**	
Jeudi 9 juillet	6e	**Gérone**	**Barcelone**	
Vendredi 10 juillet	7e	**Barcelone**	**Andorre Arcalis**	
Samedi 11 juillet	8e	**Andorre-la-Vieille**	**Saint-Girons**	
Dimanche 12 juillet	9e	**Saint-Gaudens**	**Tarbes**	
Lundi 13 juillet		Repos à Limoges		
Mardi 14 juillet	10e	**Limoges**	**Issoudun**	
Mercredi 15 juillet	11e	**Vatan**	**Saint-Fargeau**	
Jeudi 16 juillet	12e	**Tonnerre**	**Vittel**	
Vendredi 17 juillet	13e	**Vittel**	**Colmar**	
Samedi 18 juillet	14e	**Colmar**	**Besançon**	
Dimanche 19 juillet	15e	**Pontarlier**	**Verbier**	
Lundi 20 juillet		Repos à Verbier		
Mardi 21 juillet	16e	**Martigny**	**Bourg-Saint-Maurice**	
Mercredi 22 juillet	17e	**Bourg-Saint-Maurice**	**Le Grand-Bornand**	
Jeudi 23 juillet	18e	**Annecy**	**Annecy**	C.l.m. individuel
Vendredi 24 juillet	19e	**Bourgoin-Jallieu**	**Aubenas**	
Samedi 25 juillet	20e	**Montélimar**	**Mont Ventoux**	
Dimanche 26 juillet	21e	**Montereau-Fault-Yonne**	**Paris – Champs-Élysées**	

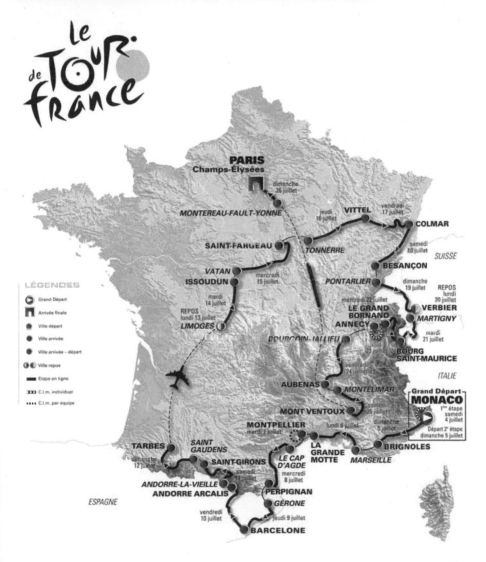

TOUR DE LANCE

TOUR DE FRANCE, STAGE 1
Individual Time Trial, 15.5 km, Monaco
JULY 4, 2009

Here he is, Lance Armstrong. And there he goes: a blue-and-yellow-and-white figure on a black-and-yellow bike streaking over the gray surface of a road in Monaco late on a summer morning, the sun's yellow pale in comparison to the shoulders of his jersey, the sky's blue like nothing more than the original idea for the magnificent tones that wrap around his back and legs. He is bent forward and low over the top of the bike, arcing himself butt to fingertips from the saddle to the handlebar like an airfoil, like a thing dreamed of and studied in prototypes and finally forged in perfection to round out the top profile of a bicycle in a way that makes it slippery against the forces of friction.

His feet each make a complete circle about 120 times a minute, or two revolutions a second, which is roughly the same cadence Usain Bolt maintains for 9.71 seconds to win a gold medal. Today, Armstrong will sustain this furious whirling of his feet for around 20 minutes. Some days he does it for six hours. This maelstrom occurs with a precision that if visible would surprise the untrained eye, and contains a daintiness that the sport's acolytes would find embarrassing. At the lowest point of a stroke Armstrong's foot lies almost flat on the pedal. As his leg begins to pull up on the pedal his foot starts to point down, and this oppositional change continues until his foot is almost vertical, a ballerina's pose that is imperceptible as it appears and vanishes in around one-eighth of a second. Then his foot comes over the top of the pedal stroke. His heel drops, and the muscles of his leg begin pushing the pedal forward with visible force. The calves have ripped themselves in half lengthwise by their own development, a deep V cut into their center in a muscle configuration peculiar to cyclists. Whatever tissue that was not useful for the execution of this pedal stroke has been eroded by years and years and years of miles and miles and miles of training. The thigh is its equal on a larger scale, the glutes and the hamstrings also, with everything extraneous scooped away. It is an act of violence and disregard, the way these muscles ram the foot forward then plunge it down to the lowest point of the revolution to start the whole stroke over. Twice a second Lance Armstrong does this with each leg, while its opposite leg in unthinking synchronicity performs the countermovement, the frightening muscular explosion on one side while the ballerina's pose is struck on the other.

His upper body betrays none of this effort. It floats placid above the dervish of his legs, covered in a skinsuit that appears more skin than suit in the way it ripples with every contour of his physique. The fabric of this suit draws sweat from his skin out to the air to be evaporated in seconds and cool him, and it also has been blended and tailored in such a way to soothe the swirling air into a smooth flow that diverges around his body instead of battering against it. The suit was custom-made, yet between the measuring and today's Stage 1 time trial of the 2009 Tour de France, Armstrong shed more weight than anyone could have guessed. He is lighter for this Tour than he has ever been, even in his prime from 1999 to 2005, and there are wrinkles around the armpits and the backs of his quads where the material sags a little, unable to conform to the new concavities Armstrong has carved into his body. The zipper of the skinsuit is undone a few inches, a casual act that doubtless breaks the hearts of the suit's designers and aerodynamic experts, who might have worked months to eliminate such minuscule amounts of drag. Snaking out of the unzipped collar is a black cord that leads to a radio earpiece taped into Armstrong's right ear with white medical tape gone a little greasy from some mechanic's fingertips. The pull tab of the zipper swings as Armstrong pedals, its metronomic motion coming not from his upper body, which remains still, but from a slight rocking of the entire bike itself.

This minor sway does not affect his steering. Any disruption it might cause is absorbed somewhere during its transmission from his torso through his arms, which are bent at the elbow nearly 90 degrees, then stretched out along aero bars that protrude in front of his bike. One black-gloved hand lies unmoving on each bar, and if you could touch these hands you would be startled by how relaxed they are. He is not clenching the bar but resting his fingers around it, the way someone might lightly palm but not grip a handrail on a set of familiar stairs. To clench would be to direct energy into something not necessary for propelling his bike forward. His hands move when the driver in the car behind him, his team director Johan Bruyneel, speaks to him through the earpiece and tells him to shift or to change his speed or set up for a corner or a climb or a long, straight flat section of the course. When this happens Armstrong's fingers snap forward and make a subtle but crisp movement that clicks a lever on the end of the bar, which pulls a twined steel cable that moves the rear derailleur either right or left, dragging the chain onto a different cog.

Right now, as I watch him, Armstrong's chain is meshed over a cog with thirteen teeth, one of ten cogs clustered onto the back wheel of his bike. The chain wraps around this cog, threads through the derailleur, and continues forward to pass around what is called the big chainring, which is one of the two toothed circles that are driven by the crankset attached to the pedals locked to Armstrong's shoes with cleats. The big chainring has fifty-three teeth, and in this gear combination (which in cycling jargon is identified simply as 53-13), one complete revolution of a pedal moves the bicycle forward a little more than 28 feet. At his cadence of 120 rpm that's just over 56 feet per second, which is somehow easiest to picture by imagining something impossible: Spider-Man climbing a six-story building in one tick of a clock's hand. More prosaically, that's about 38 mph, a figure unimpressive in the car-centric and sedentary context of mainstream America but staggering to anyone who has ever tried to ride a bicycle with ambition.

Inside Armstrong's body, an enormous amount of energy is being created—and wasted—to make this speed possible. More than sixty trillion mitochondria are firing inside his cells, turning sugar, oxygen, and other molecular substances into the force that contracts and expands the muscles that, unfortunately, deliver only about 23 percent of his power to the chain of the bicycle. Humans, even the most efficient ones like Lance Armstrong, are terrible engines, and most everything we produce is lost as heat. Even so, those sixty-trillion-plus intracellular explosions are at this moment managing to pump around 420 watts of power into the bicycle's drivetrain, nearly three times what a normal human could sustain over an extended period. Armstrong's heart pumps about nine gallons of blood per minute, not quite double an average man's. His lungs inhale and process about three liters of oxygen each minute— imagine inhaling the contents of three of those big plastic soda jugs in 60 seconds—about twice as much as typical.

His face is unremarkable. It is set in a grimace, but one not uncommon to his expressions off the bike. His lips look chapped, as they frequently do off the bike as well, and thin and pale. When his lungs bellow out carbon dioxide from his body, his mouth purses. If anything, age ravages his face more than the effort of riding. His nose is starting to sag at the point and recede at the nostrils, forming a hawkish look. There are half-oval wrinkles, once dimples, from his nose to his mouth. His eyes behind dark wraparound glasses are blue but a thinner blue than when he was young, and they appear flat these days, a little smeary at the edges where once they were sharp. He is thirty-seven years old, that's all his face says. It does not say he is going 38 mph.

He is thirty-seven and he has returned to the sport after a four-year absence to great acclaim and controversy. His fiercest and most bitter rival is on his own team. He has suffered in races in 2009 like never before and, for much of the season, he has appeared for the first time in anyone's memory to be human on a bicycle. Now, on this 15.5-kilometer course that each man rides alone against the clock, under a threat of rain he is pedaling his bicycle close to the riot fencing and fans that line the street. These spectators lean over as far as they can, and many thrust cameras out at him. When he cuts a corner tight, the heads, hands, and cameras seem about to hit his face, then are pulled away in a panic at the last possible second. Anyone standing there could reach out and touch him if they really wanted to—more like getting slapped as he hurtled past, but still: to touch him. Did any fan ever touch Michael Jordan as he dribbled? Babe Ruth as he swatted homers? Anyone could touch Lance Armstrong as he rides. No one does. Police stand inside the barriers in the corners, and here and there where the crowd is thickest, but as Lance Armstrong rides toward them the police watch him instead of the fans and they turn and watch him go, then remember they are supposed to be watching the crowd and do so after Lance is out of sight. The Astana team car follows Armstrong closer than anyone who is not a professional cyclist or a team director would judge prudent. Its wheels squeal as it tries to match his speed through the tight corners of narrow European roads. A motorcycle with a television cameraman buckled onto the back of the seat follows Armstrong, roars ahead of him, fades back to get a close-up from beside him. The cameraman tilts toward him. The fans pop flashes in his face. Bruyneel talks into his ear. Because the radios used in time trials are one-way devices, Armstrong can't reply.

I see all of this. But only because I understand and love cycling in a way few do. In truth, Lance Armstrong is a blur.

STAGE 1 RESULTS

1. Fabian Cancellara, Saxo Bank	19:32
2. Alberto Contador, Astana	+00:18
3. Bradley Wiggins, Garmin	+00:22
4. Andreas Kloden, Astana	+00:22
5. Cadel Evans, Silence-Lotto	+00:23
6. Levi Leipheimer, Astana	+00:30
10. Lance Armstrong, Astana	+00:40
17. Christian Vande Velde, Garmin	+00:57
18. Andy Schleck, Saxo Bank	+01:00
21. Carlos Sastre, Cervélo	+01:06
53. Denis Menchov, Rabobank	+01:31

THE COMEBACK BEGINS
SEPTEMBER 2008

The Biggest Secrets

I was sitting in the sunniest part of a lobby of a hotel in San Francisco when Chris Carmichael walked past me. I called out, "Hey," but Lance's coach didn't hear me. He kept walking. Around five foot eight, with straw-colored hair cut in a contemporary careful mess, he moves in public with the vague unease of the ever-so-slightly famous—he's not quite used to having people stare at him, but he also appreciates the attention. I stood and, raising my voice, said, "Chris," and when he turned his head toward me I waved him over.

Carmichael was the coach most popularly associated with Armstrong, the first to understand the superstar's potential and earn his loyalty. They met in 1990 when Carmichael, the new U.S. national team coach, promoted the eighteen-year-old amateur from the B to the A team, angering the older and more established members of the squad. In 1996, when Armstrong was diagnosed with testicular cancer that had migrated to his brain, lung, and abdomen and was considered by most in cycling to be a lost cause (his team, Cofidis, dropped him, and almost no others would return his calls), Carmichael stuck with him through the illness, recovery, and eventual return to the sport. Throughout his career, Armstrong has been coached by a cadre of trainers and physiologists, but Carmichael is the one the champion publicly credits with implementing the high-cadence pedaling style and the innovative training program that took advantage of his exceptional aerobic potential and helped turn him into a Tour de France winner post-cancer. Someone close to both Armstrong and Carmichael explained it to me this way: "Carmichael is Ringo Starr—good enough in his own right but damn lucky the greatest took a shine to him."

The association with Armstrong's seven Tour victories turned Carmichael into a marketable brand. He founded Carmichael Training Systems, an online-based coaching company with nearly seventy coaches on staff. He's written four books, including a *New York Times* bestseller, was inducted into the U.S. Bicycling Hall of Fame in 2003, and lists $30,000–$50,000 as his top speaking fee. He was there in San Francisco as one of the stars of the *Bicycling* Dream Ride, a four-day cycling vacation sponsored by the magazine I worked for. About twenty people had signed up for the chance to pedal through California's world-famous wine country alongside Carmichael and Bob Roll, a former pro racer now known mainly as a good friend of Armstrong's and an offbeat television commentator for the U.S. broadcasts of the Tour de France.

Instead of shaking Carmichael's hand when he came over, I reached out and patted his flat stomach. He'd lost around twenty pounds since the last time I'd seen him.

"I've been riding a lot," he said in explanation. Like everyone closest to Armstrong, during the Tour de France winning streak from 1999 to 2005 Carmichael had dedicated the entirety of each year to making sure three weeks in July went according to plan. In order to match Armstrong's relentless focus on the Tour de France and his daily drive to find something to improve or study or tinker with, his inner circle tended to put off most other interests, including their own fitness. Carmichael and I had talked in the past about the trade-offs that came with being part of Armstrong's success. I knew this one rankled him even more than some of the others because, before he'd become Lance's coach, Carmichael himself had been a world-class athlete, riding in the 1984 Olympics and the 1986 Tour de France.

Now, a full three years after Armstrong's retirement, Carmichael was finally starting to regain decent fitness. I looked at him there in the lobby and said, "I understand you're about to get fat again."

Carmichael shook his head no, puzzled. I didn't say anything else. I just watched his face and waited for him to unlock the coded meaning of what any bystander would have heard as nothing more than a lame bit of joking. Finally he squinted at me, squinted harder and took a step back, and gave a tentative smile. "Where'd you hear that?" he asked.

I shrugged, which was no answer, and, in a way, more telling than any answer I could have given him. He knew that I knew. I knew what just might have been one of the biggest secrets in sports at the time.

Lance Armstrong was coming out of retirement to ride the 2009 Tour de France.

It was about to not be a secret anymore. For weeks, rumors of Armstrong's return had been trickling out in the cycling media and on increasingly less-obscure blogs. A few websites had already predicted his comeback in variously inaccurate outlines, based mostly on vague leaks from employees at the companies that manufactured Armstrong's gear (who would have known in advance that he'd need new equipment). There had not yet been any confirmation from Armstrong, his longtime friend and team director Johan Bruyneel, or Carmichael.

I'd known for about a month.

Bruyneel had told me. I could have known much earlier, probably as soon as the first quiet rumor surfaced—toward the end of July of 2008, when I'd heard that the Tour victory of the well-liked but unspectacular Spanish racer named Carlos Sastre had provoked Armstrong into serious contemplation of a comeback. I'd co-written a book with Bruyneel, *We Might as Well Win*, an account of the incidents that shaped his life and his relationship with Lance. Over the two years we worked on the book, Bruyneel and I had talked probably hundreds of hours, e-mailed in sporadic but intense bursts, and come to be a peculiar sort of friends. We both understood that our relationship was professional, that he was the book-jacket celebrity and I was the writer helping him tell his story. But in the process of getting his story out, he'd confided more in me than either of us expected.

Some of these confidences were intimate remembrances that I sensed he was only fully uncovering as he spoke, passages of his life that he'd never widely—or at all—discussed in public, such as his father's death, his decision to drop out of school to pursue his cycling career, a bike wreck that had put him in a wheelchair when he was young. Sometimes he talked freely about other cyclists, told bawdy tales about the rookie hazing and practical jokes common to all sports, recounted slights, discussed the sport's infights and intrigues, and occasionally gave his take on what was really happening behind the day's headlines. Together we figured out what could go in the book without damaging his ability to operate in a sport that sometimes requires ad hoc cooperation between rivals, and the rest never got published anywhere. I'd also kept my mouth shut about some of the incidental details of Lance's life I'd by necessity learned. In a world in which the slightest news about Armstrong was tabloid worthy—Tour de France hero jogs shirtless with Matthew McConaughey!—even the picayune things I'd been told could have been blown up into giant, hollow news events.

And I'd sat on some more serious revelations, things Bruyneel told me about the inner workings of the sport but also things I'd heard from team directors, riders, coaches, and other people who assumed that because I was close to Bruyneel I must have already known what they were talking about. I was surprised to find out that this information was even easier to keep to myself. I knew things to be true that I wished I'd never been told. I knew many more things that could never be proved true or false, and I wanted even more to never have been told those. I didn't want to talk to anyone about such matters, and so it was that Bruyneel trusted me.

I could have asked at any time if Armstrong really was planning a comeback. But I hadn't wanted to know. I wasn't sure why. I just knew that I didn't want to. I thought that some of it might have been that, like the way Carmichael was finally regaining his fitness, I was starting to become just a fan again. I hadn't ever wanted to know which racer all the racers figured was doping and had only to get caught before everyone could talk about what a shame it was, what a crime. I hadn't wanted to know which rider paid off which other rider to help secure a win in the great one-day cobblestoned race Paris-Roubaix. I wanted to get back to the point when I watched people ride bicycles about as fast as they can ever be ridden and my breath would catch because I knew how much it took to go that fast, how much sacrifice there was in the training and how much danger there was in the race, and how much beauty there was in the danger and the sacrifice. I wanted to watch some skinny guy ride a two-wheeled toy under a banner on top of a mountain with a name I could barely pronounce and fight back tears because for whatever reason and for all the reasons we love sports, cycling speaks to me in ways so central to who I am that the depth of the feeling embarrasses me.

One day I was texting Bruyneel and he mentioned that he was in Texas. Bruyneel, a native Belgian, lived in Madrid at the time and vacationed most often in Europe. He was only ever in America for races, for training camps, or to visit Lance, who lived in Austin. It just seemed dumb to me to pretend to not know about the comeback, dumber than knowing, so I asked him: "Is it true?"

He wrote back immediately with a question mark: "?"

I wrote, "You know what."

There was no response.

"Come on," I wrote.

In a few minutes, he texted me back: "Yes!"

He was, he explained, sitting with Armstrong that second, going over the details.

In the lobby in San Francisco that September morning, realizing he'd run into someone else who knew the secret, Carmichael exhaled as if he'd been holding his breath a long time and let loose a torrent of conversation: when and where Lance had first brought up the idea to him, and wasn't it great, and some crazy ideas the two of them had cooked up about training in the superhigh mountains of Colombia, and wasn't it great? And I laughed when I was supposed to, and nodded at the right times, and said that, yes, it could turn out to be the greatest comeback in sports. Of our lifetime. Maybe ever.

But I was keeping another secret about the comeback of Lance Armstrong: I didn't think it was great at all.

A Sense of Destiny

I'd known Armstrong since 1994, when he was not a star or even a Tour de France star but simply a star bike racer, which for those who love the sport is like the difference between a movie star and a star of Shakespearean theater. He was an ignorant, gutsy, mouthy, and unpredictable kid who rode like a banging fist against the sophisticated chessboards of strategy and interlocked tactics that were European bike races. And we loved him for it—those of us who had heard of races such as the Trofeo Laigueglia (the first he won riding as a pro) or who cared that, as impressive as his 1993 world championship at age twenty-one had been, he was not, as frequently proclaimed, the youngest to wear the champ's rainbow stripes on his jersey. (It was a Belgian named Karel Kaers, who was twenty when he won it in 1934, then never delivered on such great promise, winning the Tour of Flanders five years later and a few of his country's national championships but not much else.)

There was already a sense of destiny about Armstrong, some indefinable quality that seemed to require that reality be improved to match the actual physical fact of him. That world championship, for instance—won after he crashed twice in the rain and held off a chase by the great five-time Tour de France winner Miguel Indurain—was so improbable that it felt as if some greater superlative must exist within it, and the unverified idea that Armstrong was the youngest to pull off such a feat was suggested somewhere, then referenced somewhere else, then repeated as gospel by most of the media and fans until it became part of his legend, with neither his encouragement nor his participation. The same phenomenon occurred when, at age twenty-one, he was widely hailed as the youngest to win a Tour de France stage, though record books clearly document nineteen-year-old Henri Cornet's triumph in 1904. Armstrong's only culpability in creating the myth of himself was that he was himself, that he rode the way only he could. And, as strong as he was and as unschooled as he was, whatever he accomplished seemed always to remain dwarfed by his potential. I think it was such promise that intoxicated those who knew better—who had, in fact, heard of Henri Cornet and perhaps even knew that his first name was spelled with an *i*—liberating us to assist in the creation of the Lance Armstrong we wanted to exist.

Our Lance Armstrong was never going to be a Tour de France winner. He was too muscled, too explosive, too volatile to meter out his performance over the course of a three-week race. Like many young riders, he didn't do well in the individual race against the clock that was known as a time trial, which was necessary to win a Tour. Even if he might one day learn to time-trial, more damning was his inability to stay with the pure climbers in the big mountains, a weakness that can be addressed by experience but almost never eliminated. He was going to be one of cycling's hard men, a gritty hero of the one-day Classics that evoked the spirit of the early 1900s, when professional bike racers were known as "prisoners of the road."

Our Lance Armstrong was never going to be a worldwide icon. Not only did that just not happen to cyclists, we wouldn't think to imagine it could. The greatest bike racer of all time was Eddy Merckx, "the Cannibal." The Belgian won five Tours de France, taking thirty-five stages and spending ninety-six days in the leader's yellow jersey (a total second only to Armstrong). His domination of the Tour was so complete that in 1969, when he rode his first one, he won the yellow jersey, the polka-dot jersey awarded to the best climber, and the green jersey given to the best sprinter. He also won the Giro d'Italia five times, wearing its pink jersey for seventy-six days, and the Vuelta a España once. The Tour, Giro, and Vuelta are known as cycling's Grand Tours; these three races, along with the world championship and five single-day races known as the Monuments, make up the sport's nine crown jewels. A single victory in any is sufficient to elevate a cyclist to revered status. In an American frame of reference, if the Super Bowl were the equal of a Grand Tour, then the equivalents to the Monuments might be the World Series, the NBA championship, the BCS title, the NCAA basketball championship, and maybe the Stanley Cup. Merckx won the amateur *and* pro world championships. He won every Monument—the only cyclist ever to do so—with seven victories at Milan–San Remo, three at Paris-Roubaix, five at Liège-Bastogne-Liège, three at Flèche Wallone, and two at the Tour of Flanders. He also set the hour record, won six-day races on velodromes in Ghent, Milan, Grenoble, Munich, Zurich, and Berlin, and in his twelve-year pro career from 1965 to 1977 won 445 total races, about thirty-seven a year. In his peak years he was victorious in one-third of all the races he entered, an unheard-of and still unmatched ratio in a sport in which four or five wins a year makes a rider one of the best there is. It's no stretch to argue that this cyclist ruled his sport in a way Michael Jordan and Roger Federer combined don't equal. For all of this, Eddy Merckx had a subway stop in Brussels named after him.

Our Lance Armstrong was never going to be an economic juggernaut, driving the market share of Trek, the company that makes the bike he rides (and of which he is a part owner), to the number-one spot in the United States, or raising around $50 million through sales of more than seventy million yellow Livestrong bracelets (each of which results in around 65–70 cents being donated to educational and grant programs for cancer survivors and research), or hitting number fifteen on the Forbes Top Celebrities ranking in 2005 thanks to estimated earnings of $28 million and more than one million significant media exposures. We accepted that he would make more money riding his bike than most of us could ever dream of—he'd already won a million-dollar bonus for sweeping the Thrift Drug Triple Crown in 1993—but we could be sure he'd never get so rich he'd stop being more like one of us than the amorphous them. Even in 2009, the minimum salary for a racer on a ProTour team (the highest designation, which guarantees entry into the most prestigious races) was slightly more than $46,000, barely one-tenth the NBA's $457,588. Cyclists had no security guards, did not arrive in limousines, practiced and played their sport on public roads instead of locked away in arenas, and afterward hung out on the streets of our towns instead of retreating to a locker room.

He was all ours, the Lance Armstrong of 1994. He was one for the purists.

Casual fans, the kind who follow only the Tour de France the way some people watch only the Super Bowl or check out the Final Four, would barely have recognized his name back then. He'd won one stage of the Tour the year before but dropped out before reaching the finish in Paris, and was on nobody's list of contenders. He wouldn't even complete a Tour until 1995, when he'd finally manage to hang on and finish in thirty-sixth place (but along the way to that modest result he would characteristically add another episode to his legend by pointing skyward as he won a stage in honor of his teammate Fabio Casartelli, who'd died on a mountain descent three stages earlier).

I got my first good look at Armstrong in that April of 1994 at the Tour DuPont, which was the biggest cycling event in America at the time. He was twenty-two, had finished second at DuPont the year before, and was on his way to another second place. The two-week race across the eastern part of the country was one that Armstrong could win (and would do so in '95). The shorter format favored him, the climbs in Virginia and North Carolina weren't as long or high as those of the Alps and Pyrenees, and because DuPont was early in the season, most of the top stage racers were not yet in peak condition.

I had a full-face motorcycle helmet on and was sitting on the back of a BMW moto that was being revved over a disengaged clutch by a guy in racing leathers. Just to my left, Armstrong was straddling his bike atop a ramp that was about shoulder high and sat in the middle of one of the main streets of downtown Wilmington, Delaware. I could hear neither the electronic speaker that was emitting low-pitched, monotone beeps one per second—when it sounded a final high note Armstrong would take off down the ramp—nor the shouts of the crowd behind the barriers just off my elbow. I'd talked my way onto the list for one of the precious spots on a follow moto, usually reserved for sponsors and VIPs, then was surprised to find out that no one had requested the moto that would track Armstrong through his time trial. Because the racers ride alone in a TT, as the time trial is called, the motorcycle can get closer than usual. As long as you don't drive directly in front of the rider (which would give him a speed-boosting draft by blocking the wind), you can generally buzz all around him and in fairly close proximity. There's no pack of other riders to watch out for.

The driver popped the clutch. We shot forward so hard my eyes rolled up. When my vision cleared, there, just in front of me, was Lance Armstrong. The speed was shocking, as it always is. The re-sults of a time trial will show that a rider averaged 27 or 28 mph or whatever, but the concept of an average speed is inadequate to the experience. Thinking of the ride as happening at a certain speed doesn't account for all the times the racer has to hit 43 mph to make up for the momentum he lost in the corners or on the slight rises. It doesn't convey how hard a motorcycle has to brake, how far over it has to lean, how the driver has to snap the throttle with whiplash intensity just to keep up with the cyclist. I knew to expect that, though. What shocked me about Armstrong was the visible excess of power pouring out of his body, so clearly there but not there, like watching the air shimmer over a hot driveway. This was years before he'd perfected his time-trialing. He was not smooth, not aerodynamic, not skilled at milking speed from the contours and peculiarities of the course. He rode his bike as if he were in a bar fight with it, punching the handlebar, kicking the pedals, throwing his weight against it. He was slugging his way through the race. What I witnessed was counter to almost everything I'd learned to appreciate about the art of the sport—one of the cherished qualities of a great rider is something called *souplesse*, the ability to spin the pedals so smoothly the action appears effortless—but I understood immediately that before me was one of the greatest cyclists who would ever live.

I tapped the driver on the shoulder and pointed up the road, and we moved forward so I could look over and see Armstrong's face. He was angry. There was no other word for it. The kid was in a rage, lips pursed, eyes cut to slits, his face all hard angles and grimaces and sneers. He seemed to me near berserk with fury at the road, at the race, at the bike that yielded under his assault, at the horizon, at his past, and at some part of himself.

Afterward, I was walking along a side street just past the finish line when I saw Armstrong sitting on a plastic lawn chair beside a car. There were no lavish team buses in those days, and there was no taped-off (let alone fenced-off) area to separate the riders from the spectators. I introduced myself and told him I had been on the moto that had followed his TT.

He nodded and studied me for a few seconds. He had, and still has, a way of considering people that lets them know they're being sized up; it is not so much an inadvertent transparency, in which you catch him judging you, as it is a transmission, in which he wants you to be aware that he is doing so. It was a trait that struck me as inborn but still too big for him. Like a puppy stumbling over his paws, Armstrong had not yet grown into the mannerism. He was twenty-two and closer to being the stubborn hellion of a struggling single mother in Plano, Texas, than he was to being the king of the Grand Tours of Europe. He had a cheap-looking, poofy, high-sitting haircut and the unseasoned arrogance of a high-school quarterback. There was some sort of silver bracelet, a little bigger than it ought to be, on his right wrist. He might have been sizing me up, the way he sized everyone up, but at this point in his life his conclusions didn't matter much to the world, or at least not as much as he believed they should and would. Something in his expression communicated as well that he seemed aware of this gap and resented it.

Finally he said, "It felt hard today," as if he'd ridden this course and I'd followed many times before and this particular ride had been different and he was daring me to try to win an argument about the veracity of his opinion. He still has this trait to this day, too, the ability to make any and sometimes every sentence in a conversation feel like something to be won or lost.

He's going to take the cycling world apart, I thought. We talked a little about Motorola (the team he was on) and some of the other riders, and I told him I believed he would be the greatest American one day and Classics rider ever, and he said thanks. He seemed happy I hadn't asked him if he'd ever win the Tour de France, or compared him to Greg LeMond. The three-time Tour champion LeMond was still racing then, though he was having a horrible season and would retire in December. He and Armstrong were still friendly—LeMond hadn't accused him of doping yet—and those of us in America who followed the sport closely were glad their careers had overlapped. The continuity seemed to say that we had arrived as a cycling nation, as did the fact that our two champions seemed destined to have such different sorts of greatness. The mainstream press and the casual fans had, of course, already dubbed Armstrong "the next LeMond." Armstrong's standard retort—"I'm not the next

Greg LeMond, I'm the first Lance Armstrong"—already seemed well worn, too, but I had no doubt it was true. They rode so differently, LeMond always projecting such joyful disbelief in his own exploits, and Armstrong in his rage.

"You look," I said to Lance, "like you're trying to chew the road out there."

He shrugged.

In two years he would retire from the sport the first time, to battle his cancer. In four years he would make his first comeback. In five he would win his first Tour de France. In eight years he would surpass LeMond's American record for Tour de France wins. In nine he would tie the outright record for Tour victories, joining Jacques Anquetil, Merckx, Bernard Hinault, and Indurain as five-time winners (and equaling Indurain's streak of consecutive victories). In ten years he would break the record, in eleven set it at seven titles and retire for the second time.

He would redefine what seemed possible in cycling, in those seven Tours never once being forced from the race by the most common frailty that plagued its champions: being too human. Armstrong would never get stung in the eye by a bee and be unable to continue, never run into a cat that darted into the street, never break a bone in a crash on a wet corner, never catch a cold that left him too weak to rise from bed, never brush against his own team car and get caught under its wheels, never eat a bad piece of food and quit the race after spending the night doubled over. When a spectator's bag caught his handlebar and threw him to the ground on Luz Ardiden in 2003, he would get back on his bike and chase the leaders down, and when it turned out that one of the tubes of his bike had been broken in the crash he would ride without stopping and go right through his opponents to win the stage by 40 seconds. That same year when, just inches in front of Armstrong, Joseba Beloki skidded on a patch of melting tar on the descent of the Côte de la Rochette and smeared himself onto the road in a crash that broke his elbow, wrist, and femur and effectively ended his career as a top rider, Armstrong would veer into the field beside the road, bump down the mountain, unclip from his bike to leap across a ditch, then rejoin the pack on the road. In 2002, when his team wasn't strong enough to control the race in the mountains, Armstrong would fade to the rear of the group on the way to the famous climb of Alpe d'Huez and pretend to be weak so his rival Jan Ullrich would send his own team to the front, hoping to burn Armstrong off but instead inadvertently assisting him by setting a pace high enough to keep all the major contenders in check—until, at the base of the mountain, Armstrong sprang away to gain nearly 2 minutes on Ullrich and win the stage. There would never again be any need to heighten the reality of Armstrong's life to equal his legend.

Through all of it, I never forgot the bike racer I met one day in 1994, the arrogance and ambition and aggression of him, but also the purity of how he rode, such naked power. I would have been surprised had Armstrong not defeated cancer. And once he was well, I was pretty sure that he would shock the cycling world by competing at a high level again. I was as astonished as anyone when the disease transformed him into a stage-race rider, remaking his body by stripping away so much muscle that it radically improved his power-to-weight ratio and long-term endurance. But once he won five Tours I was not surprised he won seven in a row. (I figured he had a shot at ten if he decided not to stop.) My belief in his innate greatness never wavered.

But my reaction to it did, as did my relationship with the possessor of it.

I had been at times an embarrassingly ardent fan (once owning a signed Lance Armstrong lunchbox). I had been what most people would consider a privileged insider—though only ever on the most outer rings of the inner circle. During some of the worst of cycling's performance-enhancing dope scandals, I had gone on *The News-Hour with Jim Lehrer* and other national media and put my reputation on the line by declaring Armstrong a clean rider. I had looked Armstrong in the eyes on a ride once as he told me he was looking me straight in the eye and telling me he'd never doped, and I'd told him that meant nothing, that plenty of people could look straight at others and lie. He'd agreed, but said it meant everything with him. I'd said maybe it did, but it still meant nothing to me—that I based my judgment on the sole fact we had before us, which was that he'd never tested positive. Yet at times I questioned my commitment to hinge my opinion solely on whether or not he failed a drug test. As racer after racer Armstrong had defeated turned up positive or was linked to doping scandals, and as increasing numbers of former teammates and staff accused him of doping or admitted to it themselves, I became a publicly silent apostate. When my wife was diagnosed with thyroid cancer, then defeated it, I was grateful for what he means to those who face the disease. I had once let a friend use my mobile phone to drunk-dial him. I had ridden at the front of a pack with him for thirty miles. I had lost a sprint to his agent, Bill Stapleton, on a ride and been given shit by Armstrong for the next five miles—"You got smoked! How'd you manage to lose that?" I'd been unable to get him on the phone to answer a single question during the height of his celebrity period, when he made more news than he ever had on a bike simply for showing up at parties with Bono or Jake Gyllenhaal, or making out in bars with Ashley Olsen, or dating Kate Hudson. I'd been at races, speeches, and publicity events where he stared so thoroughly through me I was sure he no longer recognized me and might not even know me by name.

After that original and miraculous Tour victory in 1999, I was the first journalist to interview Armstrong at length in the United States. I met him in Vail, where he'd gone to hide from the media and relax after a marketing campaign that had included a chat with David Letterman and an appearance before a near-riot-size crowd at the Niketown complex in New York City. We talked in an empty racquetball court for about two hours. He looked tired more than anything, more drawn than I'd ever seen him, taking long pauses after my questions, then pouring out answers in five- and ten-minute streams, more like he needed time not to formulate his answers but to process what I'd asked. He was limping a little. But when I asked him my first question—"What's it like?"—he laughed.

He said, "What's it like to be me, or what's it like to win the Tour de France? I'm not sure. And I'm not sure." He laughed again, a short barky laugh. Carmichael was standing there, and I looked at him and he shrugged—he wasn't sure, either.

"It's strange," Lance said. "Winning the Tour hasn't set in. Of course, I know I won the race. But this life—it's something I never led before. Or imagined. The schedule, the travel, the appearances, the TV, the interviews and photo shoots, the White House, the parade. You don't get that as a bike racer. I'm still trying to under-stand it. I know the Tour is a big race. We all do. But you have to—it sounds like a cliché—you have to be inside the win, looking out at the reaction, to truly feel its weight. I knew a Tour win was signifi-cant and far-reaching and huge. I knew it would mean something to the cancer world, to American cycling, to European cycling, to you. But you don't know, you can't anticipate, what it feels like to win."

I made fun of him for some gossip I'd heard, that he'd been photo-graphed nude by Annie Leibovitz for a feature in *Vanity Fair*. He smiled—he seemed to be done laughing, done using his energy that way—and said, "Buck naked. I was stretched across my bike, no clothes, there's smoke blowing everywhere and fifteen assistants and water spraying all over and I was thinking, *Whoa. How did this happen? Shouldn't I be at a race?* And the guy who shot me for *Interview* magazine had all this rock music blaring—boom! Boom! Boom! It was a scene, like I was a supermodel. Or a rock star. I'm a bike racer. I'm a bike racer."

He never stopped being a bike racer. But he became so much more like a rock star that I lost my appreciation of him as a bike racer. Where once he had belonged to us, he now belonged to *Us Weekly*. I never resented him for his popularity, or for the times I was temporarily out of even the farthest reaches of his circle; I had no doubt that he deserved the fame and money he'd gotten, and no matter how cavalierly he sometimes employed his celebrity,

I thought it was without question one of the leading developments in the battle against cancer in our era. His high profile was also a boon for cycling, from the level of professional racing (which got more worldwide exposure than ever) down to amateur racing in the United States (which was drawing bigger fields after years of declining participation), and also for nonsporting reasons—there were indications that more of the American public was riding bikes to work during Armstrong's reign, and anecdotally the roads seemed safer, as drivers who once might have edged weekend riders off the roads instead leaned out their windows and shouted, "Hey, Lance Armstrong!" And I thought it inarguable that when it came to Tour de France champions, Lance was the greatest. But in a way that made no sense even to me and sounded stupid whenever I tried to explain it, I missed what we'd never had—the simple racer Lance Armstrong had never become—and when he'd retired in 2005 I'd been happy to see him go.

It's Complicated

There was no way I could explain my conflicted ideas about Armstrong back in September of 2008, not while surrounded by cyclists who'd paid several thousand dollars for the chance to ride with Armstrong's coach and who, beyond that level of passion, had been driven visibly giddy at the proximity that lucky timing had granted them to what was becoming a worldwide news event. The rumors of Armstrong's return intensified every day, and the guests all wanted to talk about the chances that the comeback might be real.

I enjoyed riding along each day just off Carmichael's rear wheel and listening to him deflect the question with noncommittal replies. The ease with which people settled instead for Carmichael's versions of the classic stories about Lance made me think they'd never expected an answer anyway. They were also happy with answers about, in their words, what Armstrong was "really like."

"He likes art," Chris said to someone. And to others: "He's really into music. . . . He misses the sport. . . . He loves going to his kids' games and school events. . . . I've never met anyone so focused. . . . His hair is longer. . . . He's thought about going into politics, but it's complicated because, as he says, once you choose a party you lose half your support for cancer research. . . . Yes, he does like nachos."

It was easy to be accurate, I thought, without revealing any truths.

When Carmichael and I were alone, we would talk about the comeback. I asked him once how Armstrong's age would affect his training—not his performance, but his training. Until recently, those who studied, watched, and participated in sports took it as scientific fact that athletes could not compete at the highest levels past a certain age (which differed by sport but at its outermost boundary generally settled in somewhere around forty). Over the past few years, however, advances in both the study and training techniques of older athletes had demonstrated that someone like Dara Torres, after an eight-year layoff and at age forty-one, could win three silver medals in the Beijing Olympics. Sports scientists now believe— and the athletes are proving—that deteriorations formerly thought inevitable, such as the loss of muscle or an irreversible yearly reduction of VO_2 max, are caused by inactivity rather than physical aging, and that the nonnegotiable changes the body does undergo can sometimes be countered with training or nutrition. I didn't need to ask if it was possible for Armstrong to ride at the highest level of the sport at his age; I wanted to know what Carmichael thought Lance had to do to get to that point.

Some of his ideas were things available to any athlete. For instance, Carmichael said that to help his recovery Armstrong would probably drink more protein shakes than he had before (among other functions, protein repairs muscle tissue damaged by exercise) and also wear compression clothing or use compression devices after training. These are specially constructed socks, shirts, and leggings, or more elaborate inflatable boots or full-leg enclosures, that tightly squeeze muscles, a process that has been shown to enhance recovery. To prevent injury and reduce aches and twinges, Carmichael said, Armstrong would do more core exercises, which strengthen the abdominal muscles and the muscles that run along the spine and stabilize the body.

But he also mentioned a tool no one else has: ten years of training data on the greatest Tour de France rider who ever lived. "I have everything," Carmichael said. "Every test, every power measurement, every piece of information on every training ride he ever did, going back a decade. It's the most detailed model of any single bike racer that ever existed. I can find out exactly how his body should respond to each training stress we put on it, based on past performance, and determine almost instantly the success or failure of what we're doing now. We'll never have to guess if we're doing the right thing. We'll never waste a week on training that's not giving us exactly the benefit we need."

Sometimes I got a sense that Carmichael might have shared some of my doubts but didn't think he could express them even to me. Of the many ways to get on Armstrong's bad side, any sort or level of disloyalty was among the top.

"When Lance started talking about coming back," Carmichael said one day, "I did a lot of research on athletes who'd unretired. The ones who failed at it all said the same thing: 'It was harder than I remembered.' Lance was living the life of an elite athlete at age fifteen, when he was beating world-class triathletes before becoming a full-time cyclist. So from then until the age of thirty-three, when he retired—besides when he was ill—it was the only life he knew. Training at a high level and racing at a high level, getting his body to perform at intensities and durations unimaginable to most people, was simply a way of life. Like for most people the norm is that they wake up every day and go to work, Lance woke up every day and focused on turning his body into a machine—for almost twenty years. Then he retires. He takes three years off—it'll be four by the time he actually returns to the Tour de France—and sure, he stays fit, fitter than any average person, but he's not living that old life, where that high intensity and long duration is routine."

Despite his high-profile gadabouts with movie and music stars during his retirement, Armstrong had stayed at a level of fitness most people reach only in their best years. In 2006 he ran the New York Marathon in 2:59:36, then a year later returned and sheared 13 minutes off his time. In April of 2008 he ran the Boston Marathon in 2:50:58, and in August he finished more than 10 minutes ahead of the previous course record of the Leadville Trail 100 MTB, a mountain bike race in the high-altitude Rocky Mountains of Colorado (but had to settle for second place, nearly 2 minutes behind Dave Wiens, an ex-pro, Hall-of-Fame mountain biker and Colorado native who won it for the sixth time).

"When he comes back to that old life," Carmichael said, "will what once felt normal seem insane? Too insane? That's the question. I was out with Lance once when he was training for Leadville. He'd done a faster, longer ride, then met me afterward and we were cruising along, just talking, and Lance turns and says, 'This is a lot harder than I remembered.'"

Another day, I almost told Carmichael how I felt when the two of us happened to be riding by ourselves and he said, "You know, I tried to talk him out of it—coming back."

"What?"

"Yeah. It was when he was still trying to decide whether or not to one-hundred-percent commit. I wrote him, laying out the challenge, what we were getting back into, all the training we'd do, all the sacrifices, things he'd have to give up."

"What," I said, "like parties and movie premieres?"

"Freedom," Carmichael said. "Freedom. The guy's made enough money to do whatever he wants the rest of his life, and he worked hard enough and sacrificed enough, and had enough tough breaks"—I knew he was talking about cancer—"so that nobody can say he doesn't deserve to live how he wants. And, man, poof—all that is just going to be gone."

I was about to speak when Carmichael laughed.

"What?" I said.

"Ah. Well. Anyway. By the time I wrote that I knew it was just a gut check. I knew he wasn't going to quit."

We rode along in silence for a while, then I said, "Do you ever wish he'd listened to you?"

"What would be the point," Carmichael said, "of making a wish like that?"

Sorry That You Can't Dream Big

And I wondered, for the first time, what exactly was the point of wishing Armstrong wasn't coming back. Or, at least, why didn't I think it was as great as just about everybody else seemed to think?

For one thing, I believed he'd gotten his exit as close to perfect as anyone gets these days. He'd broken the record with his sixth win, in 2004, then did it one more time to show that he hadn't barely eked into history, that he could keep going if he wanted, that he was leaving not because he was afraid of losing but because he'd won enough. And he'd officially retired from the top of the podium in Paris, at the end of the 2005 Tour, just the way he'd promised at the start of the season. In our Rocky Balboa culture, in which diminishment by repeated resurrection has become routine, Armstrong seemed to have gone out more like Rocky Marciano.

The heavyweight boxing champion had retired in 1956, undefeated at 49–0, and never once reentered the ring to sully his legend with either a defeat or a deflating victory over a ham-and-egger. He'd reportedly considered a comeback three years after his retirement but after training for a month called it off. The closest he ever got to tarnishing his spotless record with a questionable return was in 1969 when, just three weeks before his death, he finished participating in a bizarre experiment dubbed "The Superfight," which overlaid movie footage of Muhammad Ali and him sparring, then edited the scenes into a movie that matched a computer simulation of what probably would have happened had the two champions met in their prime. (Marciano knocked Ali out in thirteen. But he'd had to wear a toupee for the filming.)

When Michael Jordan returned to basketball after a two-year layoff, his scoring average dropped by nearly ten points a game and in two seasons he failed to lead his new team to the playoffs. Björn Borg returned to tennis after a decade, losing in the first round of each tournament he played. Martina Navratilova took six years off, then, after six years of disappointing play, eventually squeaked out a mixed doubles title at age forty-nine at the U.S. Open (with doubles specialist Bob Bryan)—a career topper that in its way is more embarrassing than Marciano's toupee. George Foreman did regain the heavyweight title at age forty-four after a ten-year retirement, but in the process degraded from a lethal fighting machine to a tubby monolith—the beginning of his final transformation from toughest man in the world into infomercial salesman for a self-branded grilling machine.

I'd been happy to see Armstrong go, yes, but I'd been ecstatic that he'd gone out like the legend he was. His farewell fit the mythic truth of his life, one of those rare final acts that had made everything that came before it better and seemed to say that maybe we all had a chance, if not the obligation, to try to exit with the same spirit with which we'd lived. Nolan Ryan had pulled off the feat. Baseball's strikeout and no-hitter king announced his retirement before the start of the 1993 season (two years after pitching his record seventh no-hitter at the age of forty-four). In August of that year, when Robin Ventura charged the mound after being hit by a pitch, Ryan put the twenty-six-year-old in a headlock and punched him a few times. When Ryan blew out an elbow ligament with a pitch just a couple of starts before the end of the season, he tried one last throw before admitting he had to leave the mound. That ball, from the injured arm of a forty-six-year-old man, was clocked at 98 mph. The closest he ever came to a comeback was in 2007 when, at age sixty, he joked in a speech to a conference of sports editors that he would come back if he was offered a modern-day salary. "And I think my family would encourage me," he said.

Surveying the street he had reigned over for seven consecutive years, Armstrong had been granted an honor in 2005 never before allowed at the victory ceremony: permission to address the crowd from the top of the podium. He'd apologized that he had to speak in English because his French wasn't good enough, complimented the racers on the podium with him, thanked his team, and with a pugnacious graciousness that suited him and at the same time summed him up, he closed by saying, "But finally, the last thing, I'll say to the people who don't believe in cycling—the cynics and the skeptics: I'm sorry for you. I'm sorry that you can't dream big. I'm sorry you don't believe in miracles."

Those were perfect last words. But unlike Ryan's final fastball, which will always be 98 mph and come from a torn arm that in the same season had put an impetuous punk in his place, Armstrong's last words were in danger of becoming just another empty moment of modern sports. So that was one reason I didn't want to see him race again.

The second made even less sense but was no less real to me. Those "cynics and skeptics" Armstrong mentioned were his way of referencing people who believe he won thanks to the use of performance-enhancing drugs. It was significant, I believe, that the issue of doping had become so intrinsic to his career that he mentioned it in his farewell speech.

The allegations against Armstrong had begun as a sly whisper during his first victory in 1999, at the moment he did what he'd never been able to do before: destroy the Tour de France on its first mountain. The first anti-Armstrong intimation I heard was press-room buzz that a sportswriter from the premier French sports newspaper, *L'Equipe*, planned to allude to his suspicion that the transformation from Tour dropout to dominator was only possible with dope, by saying of Armstrong that "he is on another planet." The accusations grew more direct, more numerous, and more public as that Tour went on, with Armstrong eventually calling a press conference to state outright that, "I can emphatically say I am not on drugs." And in an effort to quell the controversy, Bruyneel told me, he instructed Armstrong to deliberately not win the stage that finished atop Alpe d'Huez. But the dispute would never become any quieter, or any simpler. For the rest of his career—and into his retirement—Armstrong was tested, investigated, observed, and accused like no other athlete. The fight to find the truth would result in three books focused on his alleged doping, at least four lawsuits, shattered friendships, and a public feud with LeMond that would ultimately end in the dissolution of the first American Tour champion's bicycle business with the market dominator, Trek. You could believe that Armstrong was a victim of a vindictive persecution, or believe he was the subject of a virtuous prosecution, but either way you could not deny that speaking of Armstrong and cycling was difficult, if not impossible, without also speaking of dope.

Dope controversies neither originated nor ended with Armstrong, of course.

The winner of the 1998 Tour, the one that preceded his streak, was Marco Pantani, the waifish, spectacular, and spectacularly troubled climbing specialist who also won the Giro d'Italia in 1998 and was on track for a repeat in Italy in 1999 when he was ejected from the race and suspended for two weeks after a blood test revealed a hematocrit above the sport's limit of 50 percent. (No test could detect the synthetic blood booster EPO back then, but there was one to monitor its effect—raising the hematocrit, the percentage of red blood cells, abnormally high.) He never made it to the Tour that year, then bounced in and out of the sport without ever officially testing positive for dope until he did so posthumously, overdosing on cocaine and dying in 2004 at the age of thirty-four.

The winner of the Tour that followed Armstrong's retirement was his former teammate Floyd Landis, the Mennonite-turned-bike-racer who rode one of the most stirring stages in the race's history. Landis fell apart on Stage 16 and lost the yellow jersey to Oscar Pereiro by what was considered to be an unbreachable gap of more than 8 minutes. The next day, in the kind of exploit Eddy Merckx once might have pulled off but no one expected in modern cycling, he attacked on the first of the stage's five climbs and stayed away from the peloton (as the main pack is called) to gain back all but 30 seconds of the loss. Everyone, including Pereiro, knew that Landis would eventually erase the remaining gap and seize the overall victory. ("He's the favorite now," Pereiro admitted after the stage.) Unfortunately, at the end of Stage 17, Landis submitted a urine sample that later tested positive for testosterone doping. Because the result of the test wasn't known until after the Tour ended, Landis actually stood on the podium in Paris. He then challenged the finding in court, beginning a legal battle that would become the longest and most expensive in anti-doping history, extending on final appeal to June of 2008—nearly two full years after he won. Tour organizers refused to recognize him as the winner, but second-place finisher Pereiro couldn't legally be named the official winner until Landis lost the first court battle in September of 2007—which meant that in July of 2007 the Tour started with nobody sure who had won the last one.

Yet none of that ever felt as bizarre as the hysteria that surrounded Armstrong, who was never legally convicted of or irrevocably implicated in the use of dope, who is taken on his word and on faith by literally millions of followers to be clean, but despite or because of that is attacked by journalists, fellow racers, and cycling fans with a crusading fervor that lies somewhere between obsession and hatred. Cycling always has been and always will be an impure sport. (More than a hundred years ago, the top four finishers in the Tour were disqualified for hopping on trains during some stages.) I can accept the Tour's cheats, and even appreciate them for making the race more representative of the ambiguities of real life. But for reasons beyond Armstrong's control, when he was racing, the impurity often seemed to get more attention than the sport.

I wanted my sport back.

And, most indefensibly of all, I wanted my sport back with new characters, simply because I felt it was time for change. I had become a fan in the era of the ferocious and confounding fights between five-time winner Bernard Hinault and LeMond, who in 1986 bludgeoned each other while on the same team, and between LeMond and two-time winner Laurent Fignon, who in 1989 famously lost to LeMond by eight seconds in the final stage's time trial (the closest Tour ever). Their generation's ceding in 1991 to Miguel Indurain felt not only natural but right on time. In turn, the six-foot-two Big Mig's dominion was so complete that its brevity felt justified, and his fall so severe that its end seemed fated. He was the first to win five in a row and did so with a ruthless but stoic, almost gentle riding style. Pedaling an enormous gear with a slow cadence, Indurain created unrecoverable gaps in the time trials—he won a 65-kilometer TT in 1992 by 3 minutes. Then in the mountains he sat among the leaders like an imperturbable giant who neither needed nor could be bothered to win those stages. (In fact, over those five years he won only two stages that weren't time trials.) There was no slow erosion of his greatness: he cracked apart on a climb in 1996, suddenly pedaling as if trying to yank his legs out of waist-deep hardening concrete, and would go on to finish 14 minutes off the podium and never again contend for a Tour or any other race. He retired at the end of the year. Then three riders won three Tours in the transition to Armstrong's era.

At least in my lifetime as a fan, the beginning and end of each of cycling's epochs had been clear and clean, and arrived with a sense of inevitability and, sometimes, urgency: it was time.

Armstrong was the first I'd known who had defined his end rather than having it imposed upon him by the race, but that made it no less absolute. A new age of cycling had begun—chaotic, still borderless at its far end, and, though to casual fans it might have appeared in Armstrong's absence to be a vacuum, transfixing. Landis broke our hearts—or else confirmed we'd been right to harden them. Carlos Sastre, who'd finished no better than eighth during Armstrong's Tours, was a quiet and patient racer who evoked a time when it was possible to still win the Tour de France then go home and eat a sandwich instead of jetting directly to Hollywood or using your winnings to hire a legal team. Andy and Frank Schleck, young brothers from Luxembourg who looked like whippets and climbed like starlings, always seemed as if they were twelve years old and out riding bikes in the street in front of their house, pretending their quiet lane was the greatest mountain of the Tour de France until their mother called them in to dinner.

And there was Alberto Contador, who just might turn out to be the greatest stage racer who ever lived.

The twenty-five-year-old Spaniard had been handpicked by Bruyneel to be Armstrong's successor. By the time Armstrong was considering a comeback, Contador had already won the Tour in 2007, then just ten months later the Giro d'Italia in May of 2008. In October of that year, he would win the Vuelta a España as well. He was one of only five riders in history to win all three Grand Tours, and one of only nine riders to win two Grand Tours in the same year—neither list of which includes Armstrong. "Contador," said the legendary team director and coach Cyrille Guimard, who led three different riders to Tour wins, "has an Armstrong in each leg."

Everyone knew that if Armstrong came back, he would do so only on Bruyneel's team—they were too close for either to accept anything else—and Contador would be his teammate. But everyone, even the two of them, knew they would also be rivals. That was another reason I didn't want Armstrong to come back. I liked Contador as a racer and had liked him personally when I'd spent a few hours with him after his Tour win. I thought he deserved what Armstrong had during his prime, the full support of a team built around him, and I was pretty sure that wouldn't happen once Armstrong returned. No matter what Armstrong, Bruyneel, Carmichael, or even Contador had already said and would say about teamwork and supporting whoever the strongest rider was come July, Armstrong would be there to win. But so would Contador.

And that was the last reason—and the hardest one to admit to myself—I didn't want Armstrong to come back. I'd seen Contador climb, and he really might have had the strength of two Armstrongs in his legs. People who hadn't watched the Tour much since Armstrong had retired might not know it, but in a head-to-head matchup it was clear that Contador would win. And no matter how conflicted I was about Armstrong's career and what he meant to the sport and to me and to everyone like me and even those not like me, who'd never appreciated him or who thought he was nothing but a cheater, in my heart I had to admit that I'd never stopped being a fan of his. I didn't want the man who'd been so full of miracles to come up one short.

Bring On the Next Miracle

On September 9, 2008, Lance Armstrong posted a 45-second video to his Livestrong website. He was wearing a wrinkled white T-shirt and appeared at least a day unshaven, and in the static screen shot that appeared before the play button was hit, he was looking not at the camera but downward, with half-lidded eyes. In seconds, he would be smiling for the camera, looking directly into the lens, and from then on he would never avert his eyes.

"Hey everybody," he said. "I know there's been a lot of reports in the media today about a possible return to racing. I just want to let you know that after long talks with my kids, the rest of my family, a close group of friends, I have decided to return to professional cycling in 2009. The reason for this is to launch an international cancer strategy based on the fact that we lose eight million people around the world to this disease, more than AIDS, malaria, tuberculosis combined. I will announce the entire initiative, along with other plans for the comeback, on September twenty-fourth, at the Clinton Global Initiative in New York City. So until then, take care and live strong."

His comeback would help his fight against cancer, and that had been one of his motivations. But there were others he didn't mention.

"I'd gone up to Santa Barbara to be with the kids the summer of 2008," he told me. His ex-wife, Kristin, was living in the area, "so I rented a house there to make it easier for the kids to go back and forth between us. I reconnected with an old trainer in the area, Peter Park, and when he saw me, I was probably a hundred and—my god—a hundred and ninety pounds, and he was like, 'Dude, what are you doing?'" That was twenty to thirty pounds over the racing weights he'd maintained from 1999 to 2005. "So we started training together," Lance said, "just to get fitter, and that morphed into wanting to run another marathon, and I pinpointed Chicago, which is in mid-October. So I was really training hard for that and trying to lose weight, and with time in the gym I was getting strength back, and flexibility, and I was also running. Then I went to Aspen, and I thought, 'I'll race Leadville for the heck of it.' I'd lost some weight, I was fit, I'd won a few mountain bike races around Aspen, so I trained for two weeks on the bike. That was after the Tour de France.

"There were certain things about that Tour that were troubling. I don't know if *depressed* is the right word, but I was just watching it and shaking my head. There was the performance part of it, how I felt I could have beaten the top riders, but also the way the story was being told about the sport. Every other commercial about the Tour was that slogan, 'Take back the Tour,' showing guys riding in reverse. That was ridiculous. We needed to reform things, we needed to tweak things, but to beat it into people's brains that the Tour needed to be taken back—that was terrible. It was nauseating. It was enough to make me . . . I didn't like that. There was that, and the combo of the training for Chicago getting me fitter than I had been in a long time and how I felt at Leadville. When I finally got on the start line there I had that feeling of looking around and going, 'Shit, I'm nervous, man, I'm anxious.' I had butterflies like I was at Plano East Senior High lining up for the cross-country district race. I called Johan and told him I was definitely coming back."

The best reaction came from Jan Ullrich. Retired since 2007, the thirty-four-year-old German had won the 1997 Tour when he was just twenty-three years old and seemed ordained to become the next great champion—until Armstrong showed up. Ullrich's succinct response to Armstrong's comeback could be unpacked like a suitcase stuffed for a long, unpredictable trip. It contained the common opinion that no matter how much Armstrong might pledge to support Contador, and perhaps even want to, he'd be unable to sublimate his own ambition. It communicated—by omission of any mention of philanthropy—that the creation of "an international cancer strategy" was not, as Armstrong claimed, the reason for his return and that he might just be, in fact, one more bored retired athlete. Ullrich's statement also came across as a commentary on his own career—which in a peculiar way itself had come to be understood as an acknowledgment of Armstrong's greatness, and of the existence of either destiny or the kind of pure dumb bad luck it takes to be Jan Ullrich in the era of Lance Armstrong. And it was funny, if you cared to consider it that way. The man who, thanks largely to Armstrong, had finished second in the Tour five times dryly noted, "He's not coming back to finish second."

Contador released a statement that theoretically said little more than that he admired Armstrong and "I look forward to the chance to work with him." The formal, polite, and restrained dispatch seethed with the opposite meaning. He seemed to already share an opinion voiced to me by one of Armstrong's insiders—after the fact pleading for anonymity—that the comeback occurred because "he's a killer, and he missed killing."

Some racers and team directors professed happiness that Armstrong's return would bring more publicity to the sport, or that they would get a chance to ride alongside a legendary racer. ("Most of us used to have his pictures on our walls," pointed out Ted King, an American pro who was twenty-five at the time of the announcement.) Others in the sport told me his return was "bizarre" and "surreal." And, as with any comeback, the reaction of the fans was polarized. There were some who found in this latest turn a whole new reason to hate him—his stalwart doping accusers, mainly, and some racers here and there who would rail about it off the record but clam up when it came to even anonymous attribution. There were more, by far, who were thrilled. The world's consensus was that Armstrong should bring on the next miracle.

TOUR DE FRANCE, STAGE 2

Monaco-Brignoles, 187 km

JULY 5, 2009

He stays in the pack, mostly near the front but not on the front, which is the place to be if you want to avoid wrecking your Tour. And there are wrecks today, because there are some every day in the Tour de France. There's a big pileup for no reason anyone could ever name, someone screaming and clutching at his shoulder as the pack rides away and the team cars drive by, and there's another catastrophe that will come right before the finish in a sweeping wide-open right-hand bend that should never cause a crash—but that's the Tour for you. Everyone wants to do well, and the pressure and the pushing and the fighting for position—even the meaningless fights for the meaningless positions, like elbowing some guy so you finish forty-seventh instead of forty-eighth—are bigger here than anywhere else, because the Tour is bigger than anything else in cycling and probably anything else in all of sports.

A popular way of trying to convey the magnitude of the Tour de France to a general audience is to compare it to the Super Bowl happening every day for a month. That's not a bad start. It's actually as if the Super Bowl were played for twenty-one straight days in the middle of the summer, starting each day in a new town and ending in another as it traveled across the United States like a barnstorming circus. And each Super Bowl would be held not in a stadium where only a lucky eighty thousand or so could attend and the athletes were

physically sequestered from the fans, but right out on the streets—
the players running their patterns close enough to the daily millions
lining the road to be smelled, heard, touched, doused with water, and
sprayed with beer, the fans able to leap out in the road and run beside their favorite players, screaming into their ears and patting their
backs. Occasionally, a player would catapult off the side of a cliff.

Live television coverage would be provided by four helicopters,
two airplanes, a wild bunch's worth of motorcycles, thirty-five to fifty
cars and trucks and vans, and twenty to twenty-five stationary cameras. More people would watch it than any other sporting event except the Summer Olympics and the World Cup of soccer (which are
able to build anticipation for four years). Traveling ahead of the
game every day would be a caravan of two hundred promotional
vehicles and floats from which smiling, dancing, costumed people
toss free shirts, jerseys, hats, toys, noisemakers, wristbands, neck-
laces, food, beverages, backpacks, photos, and other goodies to the
fans. This caravan, which stretches fifteen miles and can take up to
an hour to pass, gives away about eleven million freebies. Behind the
caravan comes a screaming, wailing brigade of the nation's most
elite motorcycle police, then incessantly honking cars and VIP vans
that reek of scorched engines and smoking brakes. Then the players themselves rocket through town, sometimes seen and gone in
30 seconds, other times—when the game is contested on steep
mountains—stretching perhaps 20 minutes from tip to tail. Then
another swarm of motorcycles, forty team cars that somehow manage to honk with more volume and frequency and urgency than the
lead cars. Behind them comes a curious vehicle, a bus with a broom
affixed to its grill. This is the dreaded broom wagon, the sweep vehicle into which exhausted or injured athletes climb upon quitting.
Then vehicles that include hopped-up six-figure luxury brands con-
veying race officials and celebrity guests, a busload of policemen,
and here and there a snowplow or a dump truck. Game over. Pack
up your picnic lunch and stroll home. Or stumble back into the bar
that's showing the finish live. Or jump in your camper van and join

the migration of the thousands of others driving to a spot that promises more great spectating somewhere on tomorrow's route.

Bruyneel likes to say that the Tour transcends sport and becomes life itself. Others have also described it to me as the only sporting event that lasts so long the participants have to get their hair cut. (I've actually had my head denuded by one of the official Tour barbers, a man who turned out to be vastly more interested in speed than style.) Then there is the opinion of the riders. "In a three-week stage race," says Michael Barry, who rode with Armstrong on the U.S. Postal Service team from 2002 to 2005, "the suffering is so intense it becomes spiritual." Simply to function, a racer must ingest up to nine thousand calories per day—that's the equivalent of what four typical adult men would eat in a day—and, on average, drink nearly seven liters of fluid just while riding. A landmark 1986 study by Dutch physiologists noted that the metabolic rate of Tour racers was higher than almost every animal known to man—about equal that of the hummingbird.

This madness began in 1903 as an event created to boost the sales of a struggling newspaper, L'Auto. World War I interrupted it for four years, and World War II for seven, but the Tour has run every year since, and after evolutions that include such elements as the formation of teams, the inclusion of mountains, and the use of support vehicles (early riders had to repair their bikes themselves or be disqualified), the race has more or less settled into its modern form. Each Tour travels about 3,500 kilometers (2,200 miles) in twenty-one days of racing (called stages) with two rest days that occur roughly before and after the second week. Twenty teams of nine riders each started the 2009 Tour de France, which covers 3,459.5 kilometers and travels a clockwise spiral from Monaco in the southeast down to the Mediterranean coast and into the Pyrenean border with Spain, then up through central France eastward to the Alps and the borders of Switzerland and Italy before going through Provence and over Mont Ventoux north to the finish in Paris.

This year's Tour includes three kinds of stages. In the mass-start stages, the entire pack departs at once and the first cyclist over the finish line wins. In time trials, riders leave one at a time and compete to see who can complete the course the quickest. Team time trials are similar races against the clock, but ridden with a squad's nine riders working together. The time it takes every rider to complete each stage is recorded, and the rider with the lowest cumulative time is the leader and, eventually, the winner—the wearer of the famous yellow jersey. (The ordering of the riders is known as the General Classification, or GC.) Riders also compete to win each stage, and for three other special jerseys. The white jersey is the simplest to understand; it goes to the cyclist twenty-six years old or under who has the lowest cumulative time. The green jersey is won by the rider who earns the most points in a competition that tracks the order in which riders sprint across designated spots on the course—usually at two to three sites on the course or at the finish. (The green jersey is commonly referred to as the "sprinter's jersey" or the "points jersey.") The polka-dot jersey goes to the rider who likewise tallies the most points on climbs (and it's called, of course, the "climber's jersey.") There's also a category for the highest-ranked team, which is determined by adding the times of each squad's three best-placed riders; there's no jersey for this, but the top team wears black-on-yellow numbers instead of black-on-white. And each stage's most combative rider—determined by a jury of eight—wears a red-on-white number the next day.

Cash—and prestige and fame—is bestowed for each of these honors, from 450,000 euros for the overall winner (and descending amounts for each lower placing) to 25,000 euros for winning one of the other jerseys and 8,000 euros for each stage win. With 180 riders vying for so many prizes and the GC determined not by who wins each day but by who maintains the lowest net time, new fans can struggle to comprehend the Tour. For instance, a rider can finish tenth in the stage but move into the yellow jersey of the overall leader—if the cyclists who were above him on the GC finish far enough behind him to blow their lead, and if the cyclists who finish the stage ahead of him still have a higher cumulative time. Even the timing can be confounding to the uninitiated: different finishing times are assigned only when there is a significant gap between riders, so if the pack finishes in a long, continuous string, as often happens on flat stages, the hundredth guy who crosses the line receives the same time as the first guy.

In general, most of the modern Tours are won by a rider who does well at time trials and in the mountain stages, where significant time gaps are easier to create. On the flat stages, the combined power of the pack typically ensures that overall contenders can't ride away from the group. A contender's team, or several cooperating together, will work to catch any breakaway that threatens their leader's GC position, taking turns doing the hard efforts in the wind, then tucking behind the others to rest. (Riders in the pack who draft, or hide from the wind behind other cyclists, use up to 40 percent less energy to go the same speed.) In addition, teams with the top sprinters will work to bring a break back and hope that in a pack finish their sprinter can burst ahead and take the win. Small groups of riders are sometimes strategically allowed to break away if they contain no one highly placed in the GC—and this, in fact, is usually beneficial for the top GC riders because once a break is established, the pack generally settles in at a constant speed for much of the race, monitoring the gap to keep it at a level they trust they can close in the final kilometers. Until a break is established, riders attack almost constantly, and the leader's team must work hard to bring each one back.

From there, the strategies become byzantine. For example, a team that has a rider in fifth place on the GC will gamble that if a break containing the rider in seventh place gets away, the team of the sixth-place rider will panic before they do and initiate the hard work of bridging the gap. But the break might also contain a rider who's second in polka-dot climbing points, so both the fifth- and sixth-place GC teams might gamble that the team of the first-place polka-dot rider will make the chase instead. Strategically, the race is a kind of cross between chess and mumblety-peg—at speeds exceeding 60 mph. No one ever lucks into a Tour de France win. There are not upsets so much as, once the brutality of the race strips the riders down to their essence, one who externally seemed weaker exhibits a core that, at least for the month of July, proves invulnerable.

Armstrong, who is hoping one more time to find that sort of core in himself, rides near the team for the most part today. Sometimes he sweeps out to one side and darts forward to have a look at what the racers call "the sharp end," or simply to put his nose to the wind and for a moment look as far down the asphalt as he can instead of at the backs of however many of the 179 other racers happen to be in front of him at any moment. He rides up beside and talks to Mark Cavendish, the compact sprinter from the Isle of Man who rides for Team Columbia and who Armstrong believes will win today's relatively flat stage. (Most of the racers who aren't sprinters set to go against Cav also believe this—and maybe even some of his rival sprinters do as well, secretly.) He rides over and talks to Tom Boonen, the twenty-eight-year-old Belgian superstar who is as famous in his homeland for driving a yellow Lamborghini and twice testing positive for cocaine (not a performance-enhancing drug but a recreational one) as for winning three times at Paris-Roubaix. Wherever he goes he is shadowed today by Gregory Rast, a big Swiss rider who has been assigned to the care and feeding of Lance Armstrong.

Everyone knows Astana's Tour is almost for sure going to come down to Contador or Armstrong, but this early in the race the team still has four riders who are capable of winning the whole thing—Contador and Armstrong plus Levi Leipheimer (who in four out of the five Tours he's ridden has finished third, sixth, eighth, and ninth) and Andreas Kloden (who in five Tours has finished second

twice—one of those a third place until Floyd Landis was disqualified and everyone moved up a spot). This leaves only five riders to
divide the support work: the fetching of bottles from the team car,
the transport between car and rider of vests or spare gloves, the
carriage of extra food, or in the worst case the sacrifice of a wheel
or bike. If a leader gets a flat or disables his bike in a crash, a support rider will sometimes hand over his own wheel or bike, then
wait beside the road until the team car arrives and supplies a spare.
Armstrong used to ride with eight riders in support.

That was a different era. One leader, eight *domestiques,* a single,
shared goal: Lance wins. The team would never try to win a stage
unless it was Lance doing the winning to gain more time on his
overall rivals; the individual stage victories never mattered, and
there was never any serious strategy set up to let one of the *domestiques* win a stage as a payoff for their selfless work. The team
never tried to win the polka-dot climber's jersey or the green
sprinter's jersey.

The Spanish rider Haimar Zubeldia will spend time riding in
direct support of Contador. So will Contador's frequent roommate
on the road, the Spanish-speaking Portuguese rider Sergio Paulinho.
Splitting the rest of the duties are Yaroslav Popovych, a Ukrainian
racer who Bruyneel once believed could be the next great Grand
Tour champion (and who did take a third in the Giro in 2003), and,
in his first Tour, Dmitriy Muravyev, a young Kazakh whose inclusion on the roster is widely believed to be part of an obligation to
the team's sponsor, an affiliation of companies representing the
country of Kazakhstan. (Astana is its capital city.)

On one of their trips through the pack, Armstrong and Rast drift
back past Fabian Cancellara, whose yellow jersey is soaked through
with sweat. The temperatures are rising above 100 degrees, and the
road is twisting across the French countryside on its way from
Monaco to Brignoles, and what is referred to in the guides and media
previews as a flat stage has too many rolling hills to keep track of.

Armstrong hates riding in the heat, and he just wants to get this day over, to get through without losing any time by crashing, getting drained by the sun, or getting caught out by any of the innumerable and unforeseeable routine disasters the Tour de France dispenses. Armstrong is in tenth. Most people would judge that a remarkable beginning to this comeback Tour, but, despite what he said to the media after yesterday's time trial was done, he is merely—barely—content with the result.

The problem isn't the 40 seconds he's down on Cancellara. The twenty-eight-year-old Saxo Bank racer won similar Tour openers in 2004 and 2007, won the world championship time trial three times, and is the reigning Olympic TT champ. But at six foot one and 180 pounds, he's too big to be a contender for the overall Tour victory. He was clearly the fastest man in the Tour on yesterday's roads, pounding over the 9.6 miles in just over 19½ minutes, for an average speed of 29.6 mph. But the muscle and skeletal structure that give him the nickname "Spartacus" and give his body so much raw power on the flats will turn against him in the mountains.

The problem is whom else Armstrong finished behind. There's Cadel Evans, an Australian tiny enough to climb well who can also time-trial, and who has used that combination to twice finish the Tour in second. He was only 23 seconds behind Cancellara yesterday, which puts him 17 seconds up on Armstrong. There's Bradley Wiggins, who rides for the American team Garmin and has everyone scared—not just because he finished third, 19 seconds behind Cancellara. The twenty-nine-year-old, six-foot-three Brit has always been able to produce winning speed on the flats, as evidenced by his three Olympic gold medals earned on velodromes. But he showed up at the Tour twenty pounds lighter than he was for those track victories, which means he now might be able to climb mountains as well as he could always time-trial. And of course there's Contador, who did some scaring of his own by finishing second, only 18 seconds behind the best time trialist of this era.

A pure, natural climber, Contador had reportedly been working hard to improve his time-trialing in the nine months since his last Grand Tour victory; on his way to winning the Vuelta a España in October of 2008, Contador had been embarrassed when Leipheimer, there to ride as a star super-*domestique,* had almost inadvertently stolen the victory from his teammate by gaining 31 seconds on Contador in just 10.6 miles in the final time trial. ("Levi could have won, and Contador knew it," a source on the Astana team told me. "He knew Levi backed off.") Contador had since won the Spanish time trial championship; national champions get the honor of riding the rest of the year in the colors of their country, so in Stage 1, Contador had raged across the roads in a fiery, custom red-and-yellow skinsuit instead of Astana's cool blue scheme. And as if to prove he'd truly become an all-around racer, Contador was the fastest to the top of the opening stage's only rated hill, earning first-place points in the contest for the polka-dot jersey, which he wears today.

Armstrong knows the Tour better than anyone else riding it. He knows that, mathematically, the time differences from yesterday's stage are insignificant. Last year's Tour, for instance, was 2,211 miles and Sastre won it with an accumulated riding time of 87 hours, 52 minutes, and 52 seconds. The 22 seconds separating Armstrong and Contador as they ride beside each other during Stage 2 is around 1/14,000 of the time it takes to win the Tour. He also knows Contador will not keep the polka-dot jersey, that others to whom this jersey matters more—because it is in their reach and, ultimately, the yellow jersey is not—will seek it on the three minor rated hills today, and even the small number of points they gain will be enough to take it.

Armstrong and Rast ride beside the polka-dot jersey, and Paulinho rides beside Armstrong just now, and Zubeldia says something to Contador, and Leipheimer and Kloden and Muravyev and Popovych are there as well, all of them sheltering on the right of the peloton, away from the wind driving crossways into it from the left. The problem, Armstrong knows, is that nothing much is likely to happen today in terms of the overall lead. The sprinters will contest for the stage win, and Cancellara will keep the yellow jersey because the pack will all finish together—there are no climbs tough enough to split the race apart. Tomorrow is supposed to be the same: nothing is supposed to happen again on Stage 3 except another astonishing sprint at the end.

And that is the problem—because Stage 4 is the team time trial. Every team sets off by itself, and every racer on the team gets the same time when they cross the line together. Armstrong is sure Astana has a chance of beating Saxo Bank. Though Cancellara is the world's best time trialist and will ride beyond exhaustion in a bid to keep the yellow jersey, the balance of his team isn't as strong against the clock as Astana. And if Astana wins the team time trial, the highest-placed rider on its team will almost certainly inherit the yellow jersey.

That's Contador.

Once Contador is in yellow, Armstrong knows—and accepts—that his own Tour ambitions will be meaningless. He'll have to do nothing more than ride to support Contador, sacrifice his own wheel for Contador if it ever comes down to that. There is no way even Armstrong, the legendary Armstrong, could ride against a yellow jersey on his own team. To do so would break one of the most sacred unwritten laws of cycling.

Only one other teammate had ever worn yellow while on the same team with Lance. In the 2003 Tour, a Colombian named Victor Hugo Peña was riding as a *domestique* for Armstrong's U.S. Postal Service team and finished the prologue one second faster. When Postal won the team time trial four days later, Peña became the race leader and wore the jersey for three days—but still returned to the car to gather water bottles like a *domestique*. Peña claimed it was a joke, but someone who was on the team at that time told me, "It was bullshit—the yellow jersey being sent back for bottles. You've never seen that. Maybe Peña volunteered it as a joke, but it should not have been allowed to happen. It was a stupid and mean reminder who was boss."

Unlike Hugo Peña, when Contador is in yellow he is not a rider who will go to the car for bottles. Contador in yellow is a rider who will be waiting for a bottle to be brought to him, who will be waiting for the mountains to start, for the long time trials that will decide the Tour, for the next day's yellow jersey and the one after that and the one after that and all the way to Paris. Armstrong rides hidden away from the wind on Stage 2, saving his energy for a chance it is hard to imagine will come but that he no doubt trusts eventually will. He knows the Tour better than anyone riding it, and what he knows is that the Tour is never what you expect.

STAGE 2 RESULTS

1. Mark Cavendish, Columbia	4:30:02
24. Andreas Kloden, Astana	Same time
38. Fabian Cancellara, Saxo Bank	
44. Christian Vande Velde, Garmin	
56. Cadel Evans, Silence-Lotto	
58. Alberto Contador, Astana	
80. Lance Armstrong, Astana	
82. Andy Schleck, Saxo Bank	
87. Denis Menchov, Rabobank	
103. Carlos Sastre, Cervélo	
105. Levi Leipheimer, Astana	
114. Bradley Wiggins, Garmin	

GENERAL CLASSIFICATION

1. Fabian Cancellara, Saxo Bank	04:49:34
2. Alberto Contador, Astana	+0:00:18
3. Bradley Wiggins, Garmin	+0:00:19
4. Andreas Kloden, Astana	+0:00:22
5. Cadel Evans, Silence-Lotto	+0:00:23
6. Levi Leipheimer, Astana	+0:00:30

10. Lance Armstrong, Astana   +0:00:40

17. Christian Vande Velde, Garmin   +0:00:57

18. Andy Schleck, Saxo Bank   +0:01:00

21. Carlos Sastre, Cervélo   +0:01:06

53. Denis Menchov, Rabobank   +0:01:31

TOUR OF CALIFORNIA
Sacramento-Escondido, 780 miles
FEBRUARY 14–22, 2009

Lance Won't Let Us Down

At 10:58 on a sunny California morning that kept trying to drizzle, or a drizzly California morning that kept trying for sun, a man wearing a purple rain jacket over black cycling tights was duckwalking across the promenade of San Jose's Center for the Performing Arts, the cleats on the bottom of his shoes tipping his feet back onto his heels and spreading them out with each step. An enormous, overstuffed backpack hung off his shoulders, not itself swaying but with its weight causing his upper body to sway with each step. The backpack carried a logo that identified it as having been manufactured by a cycling company, as did the rain jacket, the tights, the shoes, and, almost certainly, the socks hidden beneath the tights. For this man, as with about eight million others like him in the United States, cycling was not a mere hobby but a way of life. Though he had probably never competed in a single race, amateur or pro, according to the profile of American cyclists gathered by several industry sources, he almost certainly went out for a ride at least two times a week and owned four bikes. If you asked this man who he was—as a person, not as a name—in all likelihood he would tell you he was a cyclist before he got around to mentioning his profession. The bike industry would label him an "enthusiast." The general public would call him a fanatic.

At 10:59 a.m. the man almost imperceptibly but surely froze, for no more than a finger snap's time, midstep. Then he planted the left foot that had been hovering over the ground, only to lift it immediately and pivot awkwardly about on his other, at the same time bringing two fingers to his mouth to start a series of shrill, desperate whistles. This particular noise cut through all the other noises populating the block of Almaden Boulevard between Park and San Carlos—the idling buses, the yells of kids, the laughs of families (and bickering fights, too), the clicking of bicycle free-wheels, and the peculiar metal purring of the fixed-gear bikes that had lately become popular among the urban young and hip.

Here! Here! Here! the man whistled to no one in particular. To everyone in general. This fanatical enthusiast had just seen one of the most remarkable and unforgettable sights of his life: the yellow, blue, and black Astana team bus had rumbled along Almaden and was hissing to a stop in front of him.

The bus eased across to the curb and burbled for a second or two before shutting down. With that, a silence seemed to fall. The man was no longer whistling. The entire block seemed to be hold-ing its breath.

At 11 a.m., the cessation itself ended, and sound and air and movement rushed back into the street—and with it came the people.

There was, as if from nowhere, a man in an orange T-shirt im-printed "volunteer," who began fitting together sections of metal barrier fence that until that moment had sat unnoticed along the sidewalk. He was building three sides of a rectangle, the fourth of which would be the length of the bus. There was a fortysome-thing guy in sandals, towing along a boy of three or four, asking him, "You want to ride in Lance's car, huh?" There was a KIRO newsman who strode directly toward the bus, stopped, looked around, resumed his march, then stopped again and seemed to take a moment to consider his pattern, as if already his news story had gone in a direction he hadn't been able to anticipate. There was a Mexican gentleman in a brown, old, three-piece suit, damp from the morning's spatter of rain, climbing up onto one of the giant concrete flower pots that dot the promenade. There was, by the time the awning of the bus unrolled at 11:03, a crowd ten deep pushing against the first metal barriers.

On the second floor of the Performing Arts Center, on an outdoor walkway that curves elegantly up in a clockwise direction across the face of the building, seven people appeared, then sixteen, then too many to accurately count. Standing out somehow among them was a man wearing a black 1980s Bell bucket helmet. He was waving at the bus as if the Arts Center were departing out to sea for a long voyage and he would dearly miss Team Astana.

Bells were sounding, deep and melodic church bells from somewhere in the city, and the high, frantic cowbells carried by some of the fans.

Stage 3 of the Tour of California, the first race Lance Armstrong had done in America since his comeback officially began, was scheduled to start in just a few hours. Armstrong wasn't having a great race, but that barely seemed to matter to those who wanted to see him, talk to him, touch him, encourage him, pay homage to him. His presence, in fact, made how anyone was racing seem almost beside the point.

Yesterday's stage, for instance, had been won by Tom Peterson, a skinny—even by cycling standards—twenty-two-year-old American riding for Garmin who had been a pro for less than three years. His resume consisted of entries such as "tenth in Stage 2 of the Tour of Bahamas" and "eighth in Stage 3 of the Vuelta a Chihuahua Internacional." Late in the race, on a big climb called Bonny Doon, Levi Leipheimer had ridden away from the pack and Peterson alone had managed to match the two-time Tour of California defending champion's torrid pedaling, then hang on to his wheel through a hail-and-rain-battered descent, and finally somehow find the energy to sprint around him in a finish so close that the score-keepers gave the two riders the same time.

"Turn on your shower, as cold as it gets, and stand there for four hours" is how Leipheimer described that day's racing, at the end seeming shaken by the bitter conditions. That a kid like Peterson had won when so many of the sport's hardened veterans had been content to huddle together all day in the shelter of the pack was remarkable—and the kid knew it. In the post-race press conference Peterson was funny and self-deprecating. When asked if the win was the biggest of his career, Peterson said, "Yeah . . . and my only big win." Afterward, as he walked out to make his way to his team bus to finally clean off a bit, change out of his race clothes, and perhaps spend a minute or two thinking about the feat he'd pulled off, a few fans—two outside the door, one more at the sidewalk, three or so others around the corner—recognized him and wanted to talk, shake hands, maybe ask if he remembered riding with them at some point when he'd happened to be in their towns. Peterson was gracious and attentive, and smiled even after he had satisfied his new fans and was once again alone.

Armstrong had crashed on the rain-slicked road that day, then gotten up and rejoined the pack but ended up missing the race-deciding breakaway and finished innocuously, 21 seconds behind Peterson and Leipheimer, in a group of eighteen riders. Compared to Peterson's breakout performance, Armstrong's ride was an unremarkable and perhaps even slightly embarrassing result given the crash. But he'd been mobbed at the finish, barely able to push his bike through the crowd even with the help of a two-man security detail.

There was a hysteria surrounding Armstrong that was difficult for the cyclists, and the cycling fans, to comprehend. At every stop of the Tour of California, Floyd Landis—back racing after his doping suspension and without a doubt the second-best-known cyclist in the United States thanks to his Tour triumph turned downfall—was able to sign autographs one at a time, joking with the children who approached him and giving nods to the people who, in passing, shouted, "You rock!" or "Kick their asses, Floyd." Reigning Tour de France champion Carlos Sastre made his way through the crowds at the start line with the same kind of unassuming confidence and polite deference he'd ridden to victory with; he might be a winner of the greatest bicycle race on earth, but just about anyone could stop to chat with him and expect to get a minute or so of his attention. Armstrong was simply a whole different matter. It's not that he was trying to be aloof. He was just, in practical terms, too big and too popular—too much of a celebrity—to accommodate everyone who wanted to interview him, shake his hand, speak to him, get an auto-graph, or hand him a memento. At every start and finish, the crowd surrounding the Astana team bus would grow until it choked off traffic—foot, pedal, and vehicular. It was the kind of crowd that you could imagine one day losing its collective mind and tipping the bus over. For every person who managed to be at the front of that mo-rass, to push through and actually get an autograph or put a me-mento in Armstrong's hands (most often as a tribute for playing some inspirational part in their own or a loved one's fight with can-cer), hundreds stood behind, unable to reach him with anything but their voices—and sometimes even those shouts and calls did nothing more than blend into the buzz that encircled him.

On Almaden Boulevard that Tuesday morning, far outside the scrum squeezing ever tighter against the Astana bus, a father held his daughter's hand. He was in his late forties, just shy of obese. By no one's definition would he be considered in cycling terms either a fanatic or an enthusiast, yet topping his khaki shorts was a Dis-covery T-shirt—the last team Armstrong had ridden for before re-tiring. There was no wedding ring on the man's finger. The girl was maybe seven or eight, a little chubby in the way kids can get away with and still be cute, in bright pink pants, and in the hand not holding on to her father there was an easy-reader book about Lance.

"Find the page with the bike," her father said. "Find the page with the bike so it's ready for him."

She pulled her hand away and stopped walking, and he did, too, and people streamed past them, adding layers of half circles to the ever-growing crowd around the bus. The little girl flipped through the book. She paused on one of the first pages, and I was standing close enough behind father and daughter to read it: "Have you heard about Lance Armstrong," the book asked, "the bravest, strongest, toughest, and fastest bike rider ever?"

She kept riffling the pages, back and forth, and settled on one of the least busy, with a big blue sky. She looked up at her dad, and he smiled and took her hand again and said, "Let's go, Sarah. Let's go meet Lance Armstrong."

They took a few steps and stopped. There was barely anyplace to go. There was no more room to walk. The pavement in front of us had filled with people.

"Don't worry," the father said. He bent down, which seemed an intense operation for him, enormous forces at work simply to shift his center of gravity. When his face was level with hers, he said, "Don't worry, Sarah. Don't worry, honey." He still held her hand, and now with his other he patted it. "Lance won't let us down."

She looked into his eyes, and I didn't know whether I wanted more for her to believe in her father with all of her childish heart, or to know that there was no way in hell they were going to meet Lance that morning. I wanted to tell them that not getting let down by Lance was mostly a matter of knowing what to hope for—that in that strange way of the world it was reasonable to expect him to help you get over cancer but nearly impossible to speak to him at the Tour of California. I wanted to tell her father to never let her learn anything more about cycling than what she picked up from her book, so that she could go out that day and, somewhere outside of San Jose, stand beside the road and cheer and shout and remember it for the rest of her life, remember even the details she might make up later to fill in the dream—the way her father held her up on his shoulders so she could see the race streaking past, how Lance looked over at her amid the madness and smiled. I wanted her to never find out what I had over the past few days of racing, what the other riders knew, what even some of Lance's teammates would tell me: that he might not be the bravest, strongest, toughest, and fastest bike rider, at least not right now, and maybe not at all anymore.

There's No Shame in Not Being 100 Percent

I hadn't come to the Tour of California expecting to see Lance win. He wasn't even supposed to be the fastest guy on this team at this point in the season.

Levi Leipheimer was Astana's leader for the nine-day, 780-mile race. Not only had he won it the two previous years, but the race was going right through his hometown, Santa Rosa, which was proud enough of him to have set aside a Levi Leipheimer Day. (Leipheimer lives there with his wife, the former pro racer Odessa Gunn, who is a passionate animal rights activist and populates their home not only with pets—two dogs and six cats at my last count—but also with transitory animal rescue patients numbering in the hundreds as well. The Astana riders and staff aren't quite sure what to make of Odessa, who is quirky and energetic in equal measure. On a tough mountain climb of the 2002 Tour de France, when Levi was the top rider for Rabobank, she dressed like a cheerleader and jumped around the roadside yelling encouragement until one of her pom-poms accidentally became entangled in the wheel of Erik Dekker, one of Levi's teammates.)

The Tour of California was so important to Leipheimer that, as he had the previous year, he followed an extremely unusual training program, riding huge volumes and high intensities when most riders are easing off through the winter, so he could reach peak fitness in early February. Armstrong had pledged to ride in support of Leipheimer. Bruyneel had named him as the protected racer, and in early February, after Astana's training camp in Santa Rosa had ended, the eight riders chosen for the race had stayed on to ride some of the key climbs and sections of the course in anticipation of defending Leipheimer's title.

If Leipheimer wasn't able to win, it was unlikely Armstrong would step into his place. In the days leading up to the race, he, Bruyneel, and Carmichael had all said as much. Even Leipheimer, who unfailingly presents a positive outlook whenever questioned about his celebrity teammate, could not avoid admitting Lance was not ready. "There's no shame in him not being one hundred percent for the Tour of California," Leipheimer said.

Armstrong's training plan during his winning streak had been based on repetition and what was probably the most rigidly structured program in cycling. Since his comeback, however, his race schedule had resembled the sort of haphazard and impulsive lineup he'd once ordered riders new to the team to stop doing. The day after he announced his comeback, he won the Smuggler–Hunter Creek mountain bike race in Aspen (where he had been living and training for Leadville, and was awaiting completion of a $9 million home), the sort of small event that's barely known outside the region. Four days later he and two training partners won a team mountain bike race in Aspen, the Snowmass 12-hour. Ten days after that he stood on a stage with former president Bill Clinton in New York City and, as promised in his video, announced the details of his comeback, then left to fly to Nevada in time for CrossVegas, a pro cyclocross race held in conjunction with the bike industry's annual trade show. (Cyclocross is like a combination of road and mountain biking, held on a mix of surfaces from grass to pavement and featuring barriers that force riders to dismount and carry their bikes while running a short distance. "I slept on the plane," Armstrong said when asked after his twenty-second-place finish how he'd prepared for his first cyclocross race.) On November 1 and 2 he rode the Tour de Gruene, a time trial between Austin and San Antonio; the first day he won the solo division, and the second day he won the two-rider division with a longtime friend, John Korioth—nicknamed "College"—who for twelve years had been begging him to pair up.

"When he decided for sure he was going to come back, he said the one thing we had to make sure of was that we kept it fun this time," Carmichael told me. "So we did the mountain bike things, we did the cross race, he finally helped College out at Gruene. There was always a valid training aspect to it. Like at Snowmass, we knew he could do forty-minute laps, and about thirty of those minutes would be at threshold—the highest power output he can sustain for an extended period. Over the course of the race I calculated he'd do six laps, so six times thirty minutes is a lot of intensity. High-quality intensity, and more of it than he'd ever get in training over the same time period. But—and this is no knock on any of those guys he raced against in any of those races—those guys weren't Levi Leipheimer. They weren't Alberto Contador. They weren't Andy Schleck. They were guys who could hurt him a little, but nobody who could really knock him around. And that's what he needed."

His first chance to get knocked around had been toward the end of January at the Tour Down Under, a seven-day stage race in Adelaide, South Australia. It's the first important race of the cycling season, included on the ProTour calendar of the Union Cycliste Internationale (UCI), the sport's international governing body. Cycling's top riders go there thinking less of victory than of easing into the season in a warm climate—but no matter what they're there for, they're still there, guys like George Hincapie, the Classics specialist who'd ridden with Armstrong during every Tour victory then changed teams after their Discovery team broke up, and the sprinter Robbie McEwen, who won twelve stages of the Tour de France and three green jerseys, and 2006 Tour winner (via the Landis suspension) Oscar Pereiro, and 2007 Paris-Roubaix winner Stuart O'Grady. In such company Armstrong immediately took some of the knocks Carmichael wanted him to, finishing sixty-fourth in the first day's criterium, a type of race consisting of multiple laps on a loop about a mile long.

Australia itself was kinder to him. As at the Tour of California, his popularity had no correlation with his performance, and overshadowed the performances of everyone else. "Seven-time Tour de France winner Lance Armstrong of the U.S. holds a baby kangaroo," breathlessly reported Eurosport UK a few days into the race. The country's tourism office estimated that more than thirty-six thousand people traveled to the island just to see the race—more than double the previous year—and that event brought $39 million into the economy. Triple M, a nationwide syndicated radio network, played "Lance's Favorite 500 Hits," reportedly culled from his iPod. The Australian prime minister, Kevin Rudd, announced $3.8 million in new funding for cancer research, and the creation of the Livestrong Cancer Research Center, slated to open in 2011. On the final day of racing, January 25, native Australian Allan Davis rode to a decisive victory. The twenty-eight-year-old sprinter had won half the stages, repeatedly outdueling and outpowering McEwen and O'Grady and others in the finishing scrums that were as close and dangerous as brawls. When he clinched victory, Davis also became the only rider to ever complete the Tour Down Under in each of its eleven runnings. As he made the final circuits through the town of Adelaide, about 145,000 fans, among the biggest one-day crowds for any sporting event in Australian history, lined the street—to cheer for Armstrong, who finished twenty-ninth.

Armstrong's body, however, remained unawed by the celebrity inhabiting it and plodded along on its own methodical, unhurriable course. "His power numbers went up after that," Carmichael said. "They'd been rising after every big training load we put him under—he jumped about fifteen to twenty watts after two really hard weeks earlier in the season. And he was losing weight steadily. Everything was going in the right direction. But coming into California, I knew we were definitely not at the level we'd been at during the same time in his best years. We never talked about winning it. Not once."

The Edge That Had Been Lost

Levi's supremacy and Lance's relatively low fitness were understandable. What I could not believe, even seeing it, was how terrible Armstrong looked on the bike—at least alongside the other pros. Riding side by side with a weekend cyclist or even an experienced amateur racer like me, Armstrong as he appeared in California that February would in comparison look silky on a bike, smooth, unrushed, untroubled, full of effortless power and grace. But in a pack of the world's best racing cyclists, he looked nervous, timid, tight. Maybe even scared.

I wasn't the only one who thought so, but few would talk about it openly. "People are hesitant to criticize Lance," one racer told me, requesting anonymity for the exact issue we were discussing—he wanted to avoid the consequences that sometimes come to those who publicly disparage or even disagree with Armstrong. "I think the media is scared to criticize him because they're worried they'll get cut off from interviews with him in the future. There's also this feeling that if you say he shouldn't be trying to come back or that he doesn't look that great you get branded as being, you know, against the idea of defeating cancer or something. There's also this weird Keyser Söze feeling—that Lance will get you back through mysterious channels. There were a lot of rumors that Lance somehow got Frankie fired from Toyota."

Frankie Andreu, an American who'd ridden with Armstrong in his first two victories, had testified against Armstrong in a 2005 court case between the Tour winner and SCA Promotions, which contended that doping allegations surfacing against Armstrong constituted a valid reason not to pay a $5 million bonus the rider was to collect for winning the Tour. Andreu and his wife, Betsy, both testified that in October of 1996, while in the hospital during treatment for his cancer, Armstrong had admitted to doctors that he'd taken performance-enhancing drugs. (At the trial, none of the eight other people who had been in that hospital room, including Armstrong's primary cancer physician, backed up the Andreus' testimony, nor did Armstrong's written medical history. The case was settled out of court by an arbitrator, who awarded Armstrong $7.5 million.) In July of 2006, after the sealed testimony was made public—and two months before Andreu would admit to the *New York Times* that he himself had used EPO to train for the 1999 Tour—he was fired from his job as team director of the Toyota-United pro team.

At the Tour of California, I asked the racer who offered the anonymous criticism what the pack's general opinion of Lance was. "You can see he's heavy, but it's muscle and it'll come off," the racer said. "He's fast. But three years out of the peloton and you are going to get nervous and lose the edge. He looks like shit on a bike." Contrast that to one of the public statements from other racers, such as this one from George Hincapie: "He looked like he felt really comfortable. It doesn't look like he missed a step."

Figuring out which assessment was accurate wasn't tough.

Despite the tremendous power they create and the focus required to accomplish everything from diving into a downhill corner at 50 mph to anticipating an attack by a rival, cyclists keep their bodies relaxed to a degree that would seem unbelievable to those unfamiliar with the intricacies of the sport. Rather than trying to strangle the handlebar, their fingers often tap against it as if they are playing a soft melody on a piano. They wriggle their shoulders to avoid hunching, and yawn or flex their cheeks to make sure their jaws aren't clenched. They unclip their feet while riding and shake out their legs, let go of the handlebar completely and stretch their arms laterally across their bodies or, with their hands resting atop the brake hoods, they lightly flap their elbows like a bird settling in to sleep. Relaxed riders use less energy, which is important over the long term, but the immediate benefit is that they also have greater control.

When a rider's body is loose, it acts like a shock absorber—soaking up impacts from potholes, pebbles, uneven surfaces, and contact with other riders. (*Pack* is an apt name for a group of racers for many reasons, but a key one is that it connotes the claustrophobic density. Riders routinely bump elbows, hips, handlebars, shoulders, and wheels as they twine through the pack and the pack simultaneously twines around them. To an average person a typical pro pack would have the character of a wall; to the pros it is more like a school of fish, of which they are one.) A stiff body transmits or even magnifies the shocks. Tense riders wreck. They wreck other riders.

There was no doubt that Armstrong was fast and powerful. Even with his fitness lagging behind his own schedule, he finished tenth in the opening time trial, out of 136 racers. When Leipheimer—who'd finished second, just 1.2 seconds behind TT specialist Fabian Cancellara—took over the leader's jersey on the next stage, for the rest of the Tour Armstrong, as promised, played the role of world's richest and most famous *domestique*. "Lance took monster pulls," Levi said of Armstrong's turns at the front. "And he brought back a lot of guys on his own." This was against a field that was without a doubt the best the Tour of California had ever drawn. Besides Cancellara, there were Sastre, Landis, Tom Boonen, both Schleck brothers, the American Christian Vande Velde, who'd finished fifth in Paris the previous year, three-time world champion Oscar Freire, and 2006 Giro winner—and onetime Armstrong heir apparent—Ivan Basso.

But Armstrong wrecked. And he wrecked other riders. In Stage 2, he collided with a motorcycle that was carrying his personal photographer, Liz Kreutz. He got up quickly, remounted his bike, and rejoined the pack. The next day, he and Levi touched wheels and Leipheimer hit the pavement. (Levi got up and would go on to win his third TOC title, but a week afterward he'd be diagnosed with a broken sacrum—the triangular bone at the base of the spine—that would keep him out of racing until late March.)

In both cases other people took the blame.

"He hit a patch of mud," Armstrong said of the motorcycle driver. "The motorcycle started fishtailing and it went down in front of me. There wasn't much I could do."

Leipheimer himself said, "It was my fault," and explained that he'd lost concentration as the wind was causing the pack to swing from side to side. "The next thing I know I touched a wheel and went down on my ass."

But it seemed clear to me that the old Armstrong, the one with the edge, either wouldn't have gotten into those situations or would have routinely found a miraculous exit from each one. He was going for humor but I heard incredulity when, after the first crash, he said, "A year ago I was in St. Barts on a beach."

One day I saw Chechu Rubiera and I said, "Your boy is fit but, man, he looks terrible out there," and maybe because I was so direct he laughed. The quiet Spanish climbing specialist rode with Lance in five of his Tour victories and was often the last teammate with him on the big climbs—he was the rider who made the final attack that launched Armstrong up Alpe d'Huez during the famous bluff against Ullrich in the 2001 Tour de France. Chechu, who after squeezing his studies in among his racing obligations earned a degree in engineering during the 2004 season, is a thoughtful, introspective rider almost as different in personality from Lance as it's possible to get, yet the two of them are known to be not only teammates but friends. ("Maybe it is why we fit so well that he has a big big personality," Chechu said to me once, "and I can stand back in a room he is in.") He won two stages of the Giro d'Italia and, like Hincapie, might have been able to win more races if he'd decided to ride for himself instead of dedicating his best years to Lance. Just a year younger than Armstrong, the thirty-six-year-old Chechu had already announced his retirement in 2008 when Lance announced his comeback. Bruyneel told Chechu that Lance had asked if his favorite *domestique* could be talked into riding one more year, and that's how he found himself at the Tour of California. "I missed him," Chechu told me plainly and without any embarrassment.

Later in the year, he would tell me that I'd been right in California. "I could see in the first stages he was pretty scared to go in the group," Chechu said. "Always trying to go in the front but in the wind. That expends a lot of energy. You could see that he didn't like to stay in the middle of the group. After three years maybe your mind is really scared of crashes again. It is a different sensation to come back to the group and the guys so close to you. To fight for position, to try to even use the arms to fight as you ride, if you stay three years without that . . . I could see Lance was not confident at all."

Yaroslav Popovych was also on the Tour of California team, and when I told him what Chechu had said, he shook his head, looked down at the ground, and said, "I think I am seeing for the first time in the Tour of California Lance in really, really bad shape." A slender rider with a big engine—five foot nine and 140 pounds— Popo can sit on the front of a pack and drag it around for hours at a speed high enough to discourage attacks, or take off on long solo breakaways that force rival teams to expend energy chasing him down. The Ukrainian, who now lives in Italy, joined Armstrong's team in 2005 and while helping secure the seventh Tour earned the race's white jersey (for the top-ranked rider age twenty six or younger). Popo raised his hands to his face, looked at me, and opened his mouth in a silent howl, then said, "I see—agggghhhh— his face to suffer. I see him. And he go down."

Bruyneel was not as direct but, given the exponentially higher weight his words carry, his assessment struck me as harsher. "There's so much uncertainty in this year," he said at the end of the Tour of California. "We are constantly discovering. He's been so long out of the game. You have to be realistic. Three years out. That's very difficult. He's going to have to work a lot more than before, and he knows there are no guarantees. For me, that's probably the best thing I can say right now about this comeback."

Had that been the extent of his troubles in February of 2009, Armstrong might have considered himself lucky.

Crashing Down

Back in September, when he was winning mountain bike races and jetting from the Clinton Global Initiative to Las Vegas to race on a lark, everything seemed to be going right for Armstrong. His five-minute speech, given while sharing a stage with the former president, was concise and clear: he was coming back to save lives by racing. "I was just backstage talking with my good friend Bono," Armstrong said. "There's no difference. When Bono plays a concert in Buenos Aires he talks about his issue. When he plays a concert in New York City he talks about critical issues. This is a campaign."

Armstrong also announced that he would be racing for no salary, and that he was forming and funding a developmental team for young riders whose first signing was Taylor Phinney. The eighteen-year-old burgeoning superstar and junior world champion was the son of 1984 Olympic gold medal cyclist Connie Carpenter and Davis Phinney, who in 1986 became the first American to win a stage of the Tour de France and for the past decade had been fighting Parkinson's disease. Armstrong also said that to unequivocally resolve all doubts about performance-enhancing drugs, he would fund and create what he called "the most advanced anti-doping program in the world" with Don Catlin, a renowned sports scientist who founded and ran America's first anti-doping lab at UCLA for a quarter century before leaving to establish his own nonprofit lab, Anti-Doping Research.

Trek was busy creating custom-painted bicycles for the comeback. The first one, a black-and-yellow Madone road-racing bike for the Tour Down Under, had taken a painter thirty hours to finish. The number 1274 appeared on the seat tube; that was how many days it had been since Armstrong had competed in a pro road race. The seatstay (the part of the frame that extends diagonally from around the saddle to the rear wheel) had been painted with the number 27.5; that was how many million people had died of cancer during Armstrong's hiatus.

And for however much validity press conferences merit, after his initial icy reaction Contador had seemed to warm to the idea of racing with Armstrong. The two had attended a team training camp first in December in Tenerife, then later in Santa Rosa. "Now I'm very happy to share a team with Lance," Contador told the media. "Sometimes in the beginning some things seem negative, but turn into something positive. I'm certainly very happy that he's on my team and not on another team. And to be able to learn from his great spirit, that can only make me stronger in the future."

But by the time Armstrong unwittingly brought about Leipheimer's broken sacrum in California, all of these good turns had come crashing down, too—or at least suffered some scrapes and bruises.

Never-confirmed reports began floating around that the guy who was racing for no salary—for the love of the sport and solely for the good of the cancer community—was going to make more in appearance fees at races and related functions than most pros made in salary and sponsorships. This was no real scandal, nor remotely illegal; in cycling it is routine for race organizers to boost the prestige and visibility of their event by ensuring the attendance of star riders and sometimes even entire teams by offering them cash merely to show up. But the figures being mentioned were astronomical. There was a story I was never able to verify (and that was denied by Armstrong's team) that a retired teammate had accidentally run into Armstrong when he was there negotiating his Giro appearance and that while talking Armstrong had mentioned he could get 1 million euros for doing the race. Given what I know of race economics, even if the anecdote was mostly accurate, the figure wasn't correct. But the chatter tarnished the idea that Armstrong was racing with the purest of motives.

Likewise, his signing of Phinney, the brightest talent to emerge from America since Armstrong and who, like him, also came with a compelling backstory that made him a marketable figure, was suspected by some as a move less about promoting and nurturing a young star than about getting back at his rivals—the latest version of the Frankie-got-fired school of thought. Phinney had been part of the developmental team of Garmin, which was run by Jonathan Vaughters. In an instant-message exchange with Andreu, which was presented as evidence in the SCA court case and later leaked to the public, Vaughters could be interpreted to be claiming to have knowledge of blood doping by Armstrong's team, and also said that Landis (who was on the team at the time) had photos of bags of frozen blood stored in refrigerated motorcycle cases. Vaughters later retracted the statements, saying that he was repeating gossip and rumor rather than recounting facts. (And Landis denied having such photos.)

Once Armstrong got to the Tour Down Under and fans and media began documenting every possible detail of his life there, a photograph of his inspirational 1274/27.5 bike revealed another inscription, FSU 2009, tucked away under the bottom bracket. When asked if there was a deeper meaning, as with the numbers, Armstrong remained vague. On his Twitter account, he posted, "Florida State? Someone's initials? Or something else? It's personal to me, let's leave it at that. Thanks!" It wasn't left at that, and within a few days word spread that FSU stood for "fuck shit up"—a contention affirmed for me by people on Armstrong's team and by people who'd worked on the bike. More than many celebrities of his stature, especially those few aligned so closely with an authentically good cause, Armstrong lets bits of his true personality slip out and more admirably, at least in my estimation, doesn't apologize for those that run counter to his public image as a benevolent source of hope and

inspiration. For instance, though it's uncertain whether he's an agnostic or an atheist, numerous statements over the years make it
clear that he's not a devout follower of any religion or even an especially spiritual person. (In the funniest comment on religion attributed to him, and the closest to what I know of his nonpublic persona,
he is credited with having told *ET* magazine, "If there was a god, I'd
still have both nuts.") But for many, the idea of a guy who fucked
shit up before visiting children in a cancer ward proved disconcert-
ing.

Then, just three days before the Tour of California began, his
anti-doping program fell apart.

Though Catlin had appeared at two press conferences with
Armstrong to promote their collaboration, since the initial announcement in September few details had emerged, and sometimes
the information seemed contradictory. Catlin said he believed that to
achieve the total transparency and unquestionably clean record
Armstrong desired, he would need to test Armstrong every three
days, post the full results of each test online, and freeze blood
samples for future testing. "We want to eliminate any and all doubts,"
Armstrong said. But at the Tour Down Under in January, Armstrong
backtracked on the comprehensive online public posting of his results, saying the amount of information was more likely to confuse
people rather than reassure them. As an example, he said that a
highly technical factor such as the natural fluctuation in blood level
chemistry could show up, and "not everyone in this room is going to
say that means I must have cheated, but a few of you would say it
was suspicious." In February, Catlin said that after trying out the
planned program, the frequency was turning out to be unworkable.
Armstrong was also simultaneously subject to out-of-competition
testing by Astana's own internal anti-doping program (administered
by Rasmus Damsgaard, a Danish anti-doping scientist who also ran
Saxo Bank's program), by the UCI, by the U.S. Anti-Doping Agency
(USADA), and, during races, the usual round of random tests and
mandatory tests of the top riders. Armstrong was giving so many

samples, Catlin said, that collection couldn't be accomplished on time, and the results they did get could potentially be compromised. On February 11, he and Armstrong announced that the program that had never really gotten a solid start was finished. Armstrong immediately posted the results of seven of his blood tests online, and pointed out that he'd been subject to sixteen out-of-competition tests since August of 2008. (August 1 was when, during contemplation of his comeback, he'd put his name on the UCI's anti-doping register to meet a requirement that says a cyclist returning to the sport must be available for six months of testing before being eligible to race. This provision itself would become another controversy when the UCI granted a waiver so Armstrong could race in the Tour Down Under eleven days before the six-month span was complete.)

The dissolution of the program directly led to another controversy that put doping and Armstrong back in the news together again. The outspoken anti-doping journalist Paul Kimmage, a former racer who after his retirement in 1989 had written *Rough Ride*, a book that exposed the use of doping in cycling, said that, among other issues, Armstrong's failure to provide the promised transparency sparked him to travel to the Tour of California to ask the racer about doping. (Kimmage, who makes no secret of the fact that he believes Armstrong doped during his career, had requested an interview earlier and was turned down.) At the press conference the day before the Tour started, Kimmage asked Armstrong a question about the racer's acceptance of some who'd been convicted of doping and then returned to the sport, such as Basso and Landis, ending with "What is it about these dopers you seem to admire so much?"

Armstrong was expecting Kimmage to ask such a question, and he had a response he'd thought about. In a radio interview Kimmage had given about Armstrong's comeback, the journalist had said, "The great man who conquered cancer—well, he is the cancer in this sport. And for two years this sport has been in remission. And now the cancer's back."

After asking Kimmage his name, Armstrong glared at him from under the brim of a Livestrong baseball cap and launched into a response: "I just want to clear up one thing. When I decided to come back for what I think is a very noble reason, you said, 'Folks, the cancer has been in remission for four years, but our cancer has now returned,' meaning me. I am here to fight this disease. I am here so that I don't have to deal with it, you don't have to deal with it, none of us have to deal with it, my children don't have to deal with it. Yet you said that I am the cancer, and the cancer is out of remission. So I think it goes without saying, no, we're not going to sit down and do an interview. And I don't think anybody in this room would sit down for that interview. You are not worth the chair you are sitting on with a statement like that, with a disease that touches everybody around the world . . . I'm not sure I will ever forgive you for that statement, and I'm not sure anybody around the world that's been affected by this disease will forgive you."

Kimmage fired back a few sentences in retort, then the moderator cut in and moved to another reporter. The incident had lasted only six minutes, but it combined Armstrong, bike racing, doping, and cancer—lacking only a blond starlet to complete the perfect storm of Armstrong hysteria—and it instantly became bigger news than Carlos Sastre racing on American roads, bigger than Levi's attempt to win a third consecutive title, even bigger, for a few news cycles, anyway, than the comeback itself.

As if only to add to the circus atmosphere, the next night Armstrong's custom time trial bike was stolen from the back of the Astana truck parked at the team's Sacramento hotel. With a 1274/27.5 paint job identical to his road bike and prototype shifters, the bike might have been worth tens of thousands of dollars, but it would also be nearly impossible to pawn or ride around town. "Wtf?!?" Armstrong tweeted.

And as a topper, Contador checked in from Portugal, where he was opening his season at a small, five-day stage race called the Volta

ao Algarve, to say that he wanted to change the team's original plan
and ride with Armstrong in March at the Vuelta Castilla y León in
Spain. Bruyneel's schedule called for the two leaders to race separately until meeting at the Tour in July. Contador, who was on his
way to winning Algarve, told the Italian sports publication *Gazzetta
dello Sport* that, "I believe that Armstrong and I should race together
at the Castilla y León. I think that it would be good to share the team
at least one time during a race, because at the Tour we have to be a
united front." But unity was not his goal at all, according to one of
his teammates who would speak to me only anonymously. Contador
was telling friends he wanted a showdown. He wanted to beat Armstrong. He couldn't wait for his chance to bring the legend crashing
down.

Never Again in My Life

On the Thursday morning of Stage 5, I was standing right against
the cage of yellow tape and metal fencing that kept fans restricted to
the world while the Astana riders were free to roam in their protected rectangle of maybe five hundred square feet. Both doors to the
bus, the one in front and the one near the middle, were closed. The
curtains over the front windshield were pulled, and from the outside
occasional motion but no true shapes could be seen through the
dark tint of the passenger windows. No riders were out yet, but their
bikes were set in four slanted rows of two. The innermost bike of
each row leaned against the bus supported only by its rear wheel, a
feat of balance the team's mechanics perform without any thought
at all, and the second bike was propped against the first in reverse
direction so that, handlebar to saddle and front wheel to back, they
also supported each other. It was like a magic trick.

I was watching the crowd fixate on the doors and windows, as
if everyone here had all gotten together last night and agreed that

in the morning they would try to collectively will Lance Armstrong to appear in one of the openings.

The weather had finally turned sunny the previous day, warming up into the high fifties, though the riders had pedaled between snowbanks in the Sierra foothills on their way to the Central Valley. The race had traveled through rain and sometimes dense fog, with temperatures in the forties, since beginning in Sacramento, traveling west to Santa Rosa, then down the coast before cutting inland and south down to where we were today, Visalia. From the finish in Paso Robles, the racers would transfer by bus to Solvang for the final time trial, then south to Pasadena and the end of the Tour in Escondido. Leipheimer was in first by 24 seconds over Michael Rogers, an Australian riding for Team Columbia, and by 28 seconds over Dave Zabriskie, an American riding for Garmin. Armstrong was in fourth, 30 seconds back, followed by teammates Chris Horner and Jani Brajkovic, each 4 seconds farther back. Leipheimer was clearly the strongest rider at the race. Apart from the sprint finishes, which Columbia and Mark Cavendish were dominating, Astana was in control of the race, able to close gaps whenever they wanted to. As Zabriskie had told me, "They'd have to do something pretty stupid to lose, and they're not pretty stupid."

I wasn't sure what I'd learned by coming. I still didn't know what to make of Armstrong's comeback, not only whether it was good or bad for the sport—and for him—but why it might be happening in the first place. There was none of the promise I'd once felt when I'd watched him race, nor the grudging respect he'd commanded by the end of his career. There was only, it seemed, a crowd that followed Armstrong around for reasons that I suspected had almost nothing to do with the beauty of cycling or a yearning to believe in miracles. They wanted to see him mostly, I thought, because ordinary people were supposed to want to see famous people.

And though Armstrong was struggling, he was doing so in fourth place overall, and, anyway, in his struggle there seemed to be little at stake. He was making fun of Chris Horner, instead of exiling him, for eating a double-double with extra onions from In-N-Out Burger. Instead of fuming because the team might lose focus, Armstrong was laughing with the rest of them when they pulled pranks; Chechu and Popo had kidnapped Trevor, a garden gnome that one of the mechanics carries with him around the world, and posed in ski masks with a pistol to the gnome's head, leaving a photo and ransom note behind. Armstrong hadn't even seemed all that concerned about the stolen bike, which had already been found and returned. (When I saw the recovered bike it was in the care of Alex Wassmann, who works for the component company SRAM and had been assigned the job of following Lance around the world to make sure Lance's SRAM componentry was perfect. Trek had assigned a guy named Ben Coates the same job for the frame. Everyone at SRAM who worked closely with Armstrong operated under a non-disclosure agreement stipulating that they wouldn't reveal information to the media without Lance's approval. I said, "Hey, is the bike okay?" and Wassmann threw a quick look from side to side to make sure we would not be overheard, then leaned toward me and whispered, "The seat was lowered a couple centimeters.")

I was driving ahead of the race that day, so I left before the team came out of the bus. This was the longest stage of the Tour of California, just more than 134 miles, and roughly the first third of that distance was on long, flat stretches of farm road that made 90-degree right- or left-hand turns onto other farm roads. Irrigation ditches bordered many of the roads. Hay squeezers and balers and combines and tractors sat in the wide fields that ran out to the horizon. According to figures released by the organizers, more than 875,000 people had lined the roads to watch the first five days of the race. Today there were patches and spots of spectators, single figures sometimes sitting on a fence or waiting in a pickup parked nose-out on a dirt road. Most of them had come out from their farms because they had heard on the news or read in the paper that Lance Armstrong would be riding through their land.

After eight miles on a road that never required a single turn of the steering wheel, I came up on a right-hand corner cluttered with fifty or sixty people. There was even a police car there. I had a media pass on the windshield of my car, so when I slowed and pointed it out the cop let me pass through the line of people and park on the road that had been blocked off. I got out next to a white pickup with the tailgate open. Sitting on the tailgate was a woman in jeans and a belly shirt.

I said, "Come out to see Lance Armstrong?"

She said that she had. We talked a little more and she confessed to having never witnessed a bike race, and told me a little about the area, about the nearby town of Hanford, which was where most of these people had come from. I learned that the big building across the street was for storing harvested cotton, and that she was a dairy inspector.

"Any of your milk farmers out here?" I asked.

"Sure," she said, "right over there." She pointed to a group of older women, one of them in a wheelchair, and a man in a wheelchair sitting off a little ways from them but clearly with them. "The Giacomazzis. Their dairy's been in their family since 1893—the oldest family-owned dairy around."

I was still about half an hour in front of the race. I walked over and introduced myself to a woman in purple sweatpants and sweatshirt and white Crocs. "Are you the dairy farmer?" I asked.

"No, goodness," she said. "She is." And she pointed to the woman in the wheelchair, a blanket over her lap, her hair done up the way women of two generations ago did it for a special occasion. "That's Lilia Giacomazzi. She's ninety-five and a half. I'm Bel Bogan. And that's her son, Don." Bel pointed to the guy in the wheelchair, who looked nearly as old as his mother.

I nodded to Lilia and said, "Nice sunny day for a bike race." She stared at me, moving her lower lip as if trying to decide if my assessment of the day could be trusted. "They should be through here in about twenty minutes," I said. "There's a group of six in front of the main pack by about three minutes, but they won't win.

There's a guy named Mark Cavendish who's really good at sprinting, and his team will time it so they catch the riders right before the end so Cav can win."

"Is that Lance's team?" Bel asked.

"No," I said.

"I didn't pay attention to that Lance Armstrong until lately," Lilia said. "My son started telling me about him. I'd heard of the Tour de France, but it wasn't until lately I heard about Lance. My son got lymphoma and started telling me about Lance."

"Him?" I said, nodding over to the guy in the wheelchair.

"Yes," said Bel. "He left the hospital three days early to come out and see this. He has kidney failure now from all the dyes, from treatment, and was in for dialysis but wanted to be out here. We all want to see Lance. I had breast cancer five years ago. Lil had some."

"Well, I never like to admit to it because I had just a tiny bit," Lilia said. She'd contracted cancer of the uterus when she was eighty-seven.

"Listen," said Bel, "will you stay here with us and point out Lance when he comes by so we see him? I'm afraid he'll go right by."

So I stood there with them, and Don's wife, Jackie, came over, and his daughter, Cara. When the police cars and motos preceding the race came by with their sirens and lights going, I clapped along with the group. And when Bel mistook the Mavic neutral support car (which provides spare wheels or bikes to any riders stranded far from their team cars) for Lance's team car because it was yellow, I laughed and told her to look instead for Astana's blue car. Then the breakaway came through, and rushing behind it the six team cars, one each for the riders trying so desperately to pull off a victory. Farther down the long, straight, flat road we could see more flashing lights, and above them a helicopter, and I said, "Here he comes."

Here he comes. Not *Here it comes.* Not *Here comes the Tour of California.* But *Here comes Lance Armstrong, Bel, Lilia, Don.*

A bicycle race comes over a road like the world ending, all sirens and horns and dust and motorcycles buzzing up and down the length of the pack and overhead the chopping sound of helicopters and though you might wait hours to see it, it is gone in seconds. Amid all of this, I looked for Armstrong, and when I saw him I pointed and yelled, "There he is."

"Oh my god!" Bel said. "My god. I'll never see anything like this again. Never again in my life, never."

She was crying.

I was able to cut across the square-gridded roads of the farmland and get back in front of the race, and I stopped a few corners down and talked to an older married couple standing there, Bonnie and John. Five years ago she'd been told that she had cervical cancer and had six months to live. They'd taken a trip to Alaska and stood on a glacier, which they thought was pretty amazing, but the detail they most enthusiastically recounted was the ship's full buffet. "You never tasted prime rib like that in your life," John said. "And the breakfast, it wasn't one of those—what do you call them—conventional breakfasts. It was whatever you wanted. Hey, look—" He grabbed me by the shoulders and turned me around, and I thought the race was coming. But the road was empty. "The Sierras are usually fogged or smogged in," he said. "But look at them today. Look at them. Isn't this the most beautiful day?"

I stopped again at Shandon Elementary, Middle, and High School. Lance's Livestrong organization had been giving away packets of yellow chalk the entire race. The three hundred or so kids here had been let out of class to emblazon the road that ran in front of their school. (In Europe, cycling fans paint the roads with their heroes' names, but the Tour of California organizers had sent out a plea for its spectators to use chalk instead. "We're going to lose our permits to run the race through towns if we don't stop it," said the Tour's technical director, Chuck Hodge. "It's a great tradition in other parts of the world, but the public works departments here don't want it." The chalk created some problems of its own: it turned to dust under the riders' wheels, which was okay at the start when the riders left it behind, but put on too heavy at the end it caused the pack to finish in a choking yellow fog.) Most of the kids had written their names—Ana, Daisy Geira, Estefania. Some had gotten some chalk in other colors and, under the tutelage of a teacher, drawn flags from all the countries that had riders in the race. The principal had even sprung the detention kids for the afternoon, and it was presumably those kids who'd written, graffiti-style, words such as SCYCLE and SSSSICK. Some parents had set up a food stand to raise money for the PTA. The Frito boats were two dollars. It was the most beautiful day.

All a Part of It

Stage 7 began amid the malls and downtown-big-city-feeling boutique stores and upmarket food chains of Santa Clarita, the sort of neighborhood that overinflates the idea of a European village with the gases of the American dream. The street that passed under the start banner was, as always, lined along its length with linked sections of metal riot fencing that pinned the crowd to the sidewalk side of its curbs.

Hundreds of people? Thousands? Not too many to count, but too frenetic to count, as if someone had broken open an anthill and was trying to take a census.

The open ends of the street were patrolled by course marshals, and Mavic moto guys in motorcycle boots and zipped-up leathers, and arrogant yet unsure volunteers in orange T-shirts, and sometimes even actual police. If you weren't a racer or didn't have a plastic credential hanging around your neck, you weren't supposed to be able to enter the hallowed ground of the open street.

Except the last hundred feet of the Santa Clarita start was buzzing with kids. Kids on their knees, on their hands and knees, or squatting, or jumping, shouting kid shouts (or those shrill girly shrieks), kids smacking each other for no reason except that they're kids, teenagers, toddlers, some still in strollers, a few leashed to their parents, some standing in one place and turning circles as if to wind the whole experience around themselves, and others leaning with self-conscious casualness against a fence while talking to someone stranded outside its metal bars. All of them were dusted with yellow on their hands, hair, shoes, or knees.

The street beneath them was yellow, too. I looked down and saw that I was standing on someone's scrawl. I moved my feet.

Uncle Sam We Miss You Xoxo

I looked around me.

Grandpa Abbey
Mom & Dad miss you Love Sandy
My Mom Sybil 6-25-88

I started walking, head down, in a haphazard procession from one chalked message to the next, my feet sometimes at odd angles, my legs twisted about or splayed apart to keep my shoes from scuffing what I now understood to be tributes. And wishes, and prayers, and sometimes a challenge. Sometimes a promise.

In Mickey's absence we live on
go Dorothy In Memory In Heart Go Levi
Mimi: You are not forgotten.
Jason you are a survivor Love you
Miss you Shirley mom
Grammy
Jason Hang in There
In Memory of Helen Nestor
In Memory of Jeannie
To Dad Thank U for not giving up
This is for Boom Boom Shirley Joe

Mom Rincon Keep Living Strong
We love you Mickey
In Memory of Ed, Ride Hard
In Memory of Ann
Kristyne will KO cancer
Livestrong Lynn
Livestrong for Aunt Debbie and Ed McKeon
We love you Makenna Marie
Livestrong Liz
4 Uncle Steve Makenna
Livestrong Tom
Livestrong Richard
Livestrong Misti's Mom
In Memory Miriam
Katie '07 Live strong Be strong

By the time I got to the end of the tributes, the cops and volunteers down there were beginning to blow their whistles and hustle people from the street back behind the barriers. I turned around to look down the street I'd just walked, unlike any street I'd ever walked, and right there behind me stood a little girl, maybe as tall as my waist, wearing ruby-red slippers, pink socks high up over her ankles, a plain gray dress, and a pink and purple plastic tiara with red jewels. She was holding a black Mavic bell and a golden-haired doll, and she looked at me with the complete self-assurance of the very young, with more poise than any of the strutting volunteers who were trying to shoo her away.

She was covered with yellow chalk marks.

"Hi," I said. "Do you want Lance to win?"

She smiled as a courtesy.

"Do you know who Lance Armstrong is?" I asked.

She shook her head with that slow and deliberate motion children can pull off. She looked past my shoulder.

"She doesn't," said the girl's mother, sounding almost apologetic.

Tara Olsen, from Santa Clarita, had just driven down to the mall this morning to take Alexa, four, and her other daughter, Ava, two, for some shopping. "And we saw this," Tara said.

"I guess you wrote something," I said to Tara, pointing a finger at her yellow-flecked daughter. Tara laughed. Alexa held her doll up and said, "Goldilocks."

Tara said, "We wrote, 'Keep Fighting Papa Rick—Livestrong.'" There was a pause, and she said, "He's my father."

I said, "Oh." I did not know what to say. I thought about asking Alexa something about her doll.

"He has prostate cancer," said Tara.

"I didn't see it," I said, sort of turning and gesturing out along the road.

They had to go. Cops, volunteers, and TV crews were crowding into the open space. "In the corner," said Tara, and she and Alexa and Ava were squeezed off the road and toward the sidewalk. "Right at the start."

I flashed my credential and walked back along the yellow-chalked street. The hum of the crowd behind the barriers seemed almost as solid as the metal of the fencing, and the loudspeakered voices of the announcers communicated excitement even if you didn't listen to their words. I walked and looked out at the crowd and down at the chalk and back out at the crowd, and in the corner, the farthest left corner, there was the little piece of hope Papa Rick's family had created for him.

I just stood for a while looking down at it.

Lance's comeback didn't belong to him. Not only to him, anyway. It belonged to Papa Rick and Tara and Alexa and Ava, and Bel and Lilia and Don and Cara. It belonged to all of us. It belonged to the sixty-two thousand or so licensed amateur bike racers in the United States, plus the eight million people in this country who get out for a ride at least twice a week, the estimated million or so who will stand beside the roads in France daily for three weeks in July, and the immeasurable but probably accurately claimed worldwide *billions* of fans (and equally committed anti-fans) who track Lance Armstrong's exploits via television, newspapers, magazines, radio, streaming video, daily blogs, and his own Twitter posts ("Went whale watching today. Had about 7–8 humpbacks around. Amazing. Makes you feel real small").

It belonged, also, to the chip-munching, couch-bound legions of ESPN addicts who hadn't watched the Tour de France since Lance rode his last in 2005, and the fame-worshipping celebrity-mag readers who'd soaked themselves in Lance's dalliances with stars from twenty-two-year-old Ashley Olsen to forty-six-year-old Sheryl Crow. And for that matter it belonged to the celebrities themselves, like his fellow philanthropist Bono, or his riding pals Matthew McConaughey and Jake Gyllenhaal. It belonged to our society's economic stars, too—such as the COO of Apple (a self-professed Lance fanatic) and the Wall Streeters who, despite historic financial losses, would once again buy brand-new $9,000 Trek Madones for the privilege of being able to say they rode the same bike as Lance Armstrong. Yet it also belonged to the teenager in a tattered, grease-stained Livestrong T-shirt who spun wrenches for $6.55 an hour in every neighborhood bike shop. And to all the five-year-olds who, inspired by a thirty-seven-year-old man wearing a yellow spandex shirt, were going to set aside their Wii this summer and go outside and learn to ride without training wheels.

It even belonged to Contador.

We were all a part of it, and it had become a part of all of us.

A security officer stepped on the first letter of Papa Rick's name as he walked past, kicking up a little scuff of chalk dust. In four minutes, these were the people who walked on it: a local race official, seven photographers, a UCI *commissaire*, someone who'd obviously borrowed a media pass, a Mavic support guy, a three-person TV crew, and Tweety Bird.

Tweety was part of a six-character entertainment troupe that was running all over shaking hands and posing for pictures. Daffy Duck hit me on the top of the head with a Lance Armstrong Foundation HOPE RIDES AGAIN placard.

Papa Rick's name was starting to disappear. I walked away, and I didn't stick around to watch the start. I didn't want to stand there and watch it all turn into dust.

TOUR DE FRANCE, STAGE 3

Marseille–La Grande-Motte, 196.5 km

JULY 6, 2009

What he senses he will later be unable to explain, and when he is asked to, the words that he will come up with accomplish nothing except making him appear arrogant or dismissive. He will force the moment into the confines of a declarative statement of fact. This is no surprise, because this is his way, but it is a deep disappointment because the mystery of what happened out there in the changing wind will be lost.

The pack is 164 kilometers into the day when, maybe, the sea smell of the wind swirls in his nostrils with a different note. Or maybe amid the enveloping hum of 179 chains pulling around 179 cogs (the pack is minus one already, Jurgen van de Walle, who didn't show this morning after crashing yesterday and still managing to reach the finish with a punctured lung and a fractured collarbone) his ear collects the tick of eight or nine bikes being shifted into higher gears. Or maybe what moves him is something more basic, yet for that harder to categorize let alone define, an awareness more instinctual than sensory. He possesses a gift the other racers respect in part because acknowledging its existence feels something very much like faith and in part because, bottom line, intangible or not it determines everyone's paychecks. He has what riders call "a feel for the race." He knows where to go.

Where he goes, with just about 30 kilometers left to pedal on this hot, windy, day, is up through the pack and into what could be con-sidered the back of the front of the group. Gregory Rast, who is sup-posed to shadow him as long as he can and as far as he can every day of the Tour de France, happens not to be around when Armstrong makes his move, but Popo and Haimar Zubeldia see him go and fall in with him, and the three of them slot up at the back of the front and wait, as Armstrong will say later, "for something to happen."

The day has not been easy although, strictly according to the course profile printed in the race bible that's given to each rider and each team director, it should have been. From Marseille the route would travel northwest over rolling terrain with only two minor climbs. After the second of these, the race would turn southwest and head to the coast for the finish in La Grande-Motte. The last 80 kilometers would be nearly dead flat across marshland roads that on this day were going to be ripped from the side by crosswinds.

Crosswinds always make a race harder. When a pack is riding straight into a headwind, it is easy for the entire peloton to tuck in directly behind the lead riders; they just assemble into neat rows (one reason the word *peloton*, French for "platoon," is such an apt term). In this formation, all but the riders on the front get an energy-saving draft. In a crosswind, however, the draft can only be found by riding to one side of the lead rider, and in a slightly overlapped position. For instance, in a crosswind from the left, a drafting rider will go not behind the lead rider but on his right side, and the draft-ing rider's front wheel will be even with or slightly ahead of the lead rider's rear wheel. The second rider drafting will assume this posi-tion off the first drafter, and so on. This staggered formation is called an echelon. The draft is good, but the positions are limited; unlike a peloton, which can stretch as far down the road as it needs to, an echelon's dimensions are confined to the width of the road. Eventu-ally there will be no more room on someone's right and the unfor-tunate rider who can't tuck in becomes what is known as guttered—stuck behind a rider and battered by the crosswind in-stead of sheltered on the side. (Getting guttered is one of the most demoralizing acts in the sport; I have been guttered in crosswinds so bad that the sheltered rider inches in front of me was coasting and taking sips from his water bottle between chats with the guy to his left while I pedaled so furiously against the wind that my lungs felt as if they were crawling up my throat to escape the burning environment of my body.) Eventually—ideally—guttered riders will organize and form a second echelon behind the first, but it takes some time and cooperation. Sometimes, however, for reasons that probably have to do with the correlation between suffering and the ability to form a sensible thought, even such skilled and experienced riders as the pros are never able to get out of the gutter, and a long line of them hangs back there in unsheltered single-file misery until one by one they explode and lose contact with the group.

Within the stage's first kilometer, four riders had attacked and got a gap, and the pack seemed content to let them go. The highest-placed rider of the four was Maxime Bouet, who was seventy-fourth overall. Neither he nor the other three riders with him were considered a great threat to the leaders or such deep powerhouses that they would be able to resist the pack's efforts to chase them down once such a decision had been made. (Certain riders, such as Jens Voigt, are known for their uncanny ability to somehow hold off an entire pack if allowed to get in a breakaway, and these riders are rarely allowed to make the breaks. If Voigt attacks and does get in one, many of the powerful teams will attempt over and over to pull the pack up to the break. Giving him any chance to steal a stage is too risky, yet despite the extra vigilance he still sometimes pulls off just such a caper.) With about 100 kilometers to go, the four riders were 13 minutes up and Saxo Bank had gone to the front of the main pack and increased the speed. Two minutes came off the gap quickly, and Saxo stayed at the front, drilling away until with 65 kilometers to go the gap was 6 minutes. Generally, a pack in closing-speed mode will pull back 1 minute per 10 kilometers toward the end of a flat stage, so Cancellara's yellow jersey appeared to be nearly safe. Sure that the teams with top sprinters would close the rest of the gap before the finish—it's in their interest to share the work so they all arrive at the last kilometer together and their fastest riders can then slug it out for the win—Saxo Bank had peeled off the front and gone into the pack to rest up from their effort. The teams with the top sprinters moved forward. And that's when everything started to go wrong.

Columbia, working to give Stage 2 sprint winner Cavendish another chance, had been happy to take the first turn, and put seven riders up front. But one by one the other sprinter teams there—Française des Jeux, Rabobank, Garmin, and Cervélo—had refused to take their turns at the front and remained in Columbia's slipstream. They didn't want to give any help to Cavendish—who earlier in the year had also won two sprints at the Tour of California and three at the Giro d'Italia and was generally considered the fastest man on earth over 200 meters. With 45 kilometers to go, Columbia on its own had brought the gap down to four minutes. With 35 kilometers, the gap was 2:30. Columbia had been at the front nearly an hour and, as George Hincapie said later, "We got mad because none of the other teams would work."

It is at this exact moment that Armstrong gets himself to where he senses he needs to be and is waiting for something to happen.

All nine Columbia riders draw tightly together, and as soon as the road turns right and the crosswind abruptly changes from north to south, they accelerate as if sprinting for a finish line and at the same time form a new echelon that provides drafts right to left instead of left to right, the way it had just a second ago. Behind them, the pack shatters.

Riders who'd been sheltered suddenly find themselves battered by wind, and as they take time to get reorganized Columbia rides away. There is a mad scrabbling implosion in the pack as some riders jump into the open road after Columbia and some try to form a second echelon and some are guttered and some are simply lost. Teams fall apart, leaders are isolated, directors are screaming into the earpieces, horns are honking, and the riders hunker down and grit their teeth and pour themselves into their pedals and the wind blows sand against their faces.

Back in Hanford, California, at just this moment Don Giacomazzi is sitting down at one of the dialysis stations at the clinic. Each has its own little television, so Don flicks around until he finds the Tour de France. Nobody else there is watching the bike race. He can hear that. He sees the split happen and can see Lance Armstrong in what looks like the front, but the camera keeps jumping around and showing someone else on Lance's team who is behind him in another bunch. When the television shows a shot from overhead, the two groups don't look like they're very far apart, but the announcers seem agitated and one of them is almost screaming. Maybe, Don thinks, it's because Lance is riding right next to the guy who is winning—the guy who's wearing the yellow jersey, which everyone, even Don, who can't understand a goddamn thing about what's happening in the race, knows is given to the leader. He sees some racers he guesses he recognizes but can't name—the Italian guy in the light green, who rode right by him close enough to touch back on that street corner in February, and the little bald guy who's friends with Lance and won the whole Tour of California, and that tiny muscled-up kid who won a bunch of the stages. At home on the computer that sits on the desk pushed against the kitchen table there's a whole roll of photos from that day, and sometimes Don looks through them because that was something, the top goddamn riders in the world right there in Hanford. Lance Armstrong. Lance. Armstrong. You can't kill that guy.

The dialysis takes 8.8 pounds of shit out of him—he keeps track even though he gets caught up in the race. When he's done and he puts his pants on, they'll likely fall off him. And he'll by god be able to swing his leg up into the truck for once. But he knows he'll pay for that by being wiped out exhausted once he's home. He wonders if they're that tired or worse when they're all done, the bike racers, if this is what it's like for them. But he thinks probably not. It's a whole other thing to be empty when you're young and strong.

On that forsaken road in France, only twenty racers are able to go with Columbia. Armstrong is one of them, and Popo and Zubeldia both go with him. Cancellara, in the yellow jersey, made the jump, but no one else from Saxo did. Stuck in the pack, 20 seconds behind, are overall contenders Carlos Sastre, Andy Schleck, Cadel Evans, Bradley Wiggins, Denis Menchov, and Christian Vande Velde. And Alberto Contador.

Columbia drives the pace and the four breakaway riders come into sight, are caught and absorbed. Back in the pack, the curious math of the Tour de France comes into play and Saxo Bank takes the front to power the chase; they have Cancellara in the lead group—which means if the gap remains, the yellow jersey would gain time on all of the overall contenders except Armstrong—but they don't want Andy Schleck, who in actuality is their best shot at winning the Tour, to lose time to Armstrong. It is just such complexities that make bike racing impenetrable to casual viewers.

But in an effort that Hincapie (who has all seven Tours he rode with Armstrong as reference) calls "the greatest collective team performance I've ever been a part of," Columbia gains ten more seconds on the Saxo-led pack.

Of course, Don can't rest that much once he does get home, because the visiting nurse is coming over to check out the wound VAC and flush the fucking hole in his foot. Because of complications from the diabetes, he got a toe and a finger amputated a while back. The diabetes and the kidney failure and the problem with the oxygen getting to his heart all being complications themselves of a long string of complications that have to do, as far as he can tell or care, with getting lymphoma in 2001 and generally running into, when it came to his health, a long string of bad breaks.

While the nurse unpacks the wound and clears the suction tube and trims away some of his foot to make sure the hole is filling in before it closes over, he eats a pink Rice Krispies treat Jackie gave him. It's their anniversary today. They've been married forty-six years.

The kitchen radio is playing softly enough that Don can hear it but not discern what it is playing. The window is cracked open, and coming in on the airflow is the olfactory equivalent of the radio, the smell of the fields for the alfalfa and the corn and the wheat, and the big piles of silage and the cows, of course the cows, the nine hundred they're milking a day, and diesel and gas and probably sweat, cumulative sweat, and turned-up dirt, and wet dirt and cow shit and piss, all of it making up the smell of Giacomazzi Dairy that Don is barely aware of but would miss instantly and acutely if it were to suddenly vanish—and which he will, he knows, miss almost most dearly among all the things he will miss when he is gone.

In France, Lance Armstrong raises his hand—a simple motion with a complex mix of motivation and result. Armstrong has a kind of animal intelligence that breaks down almost every situation into winning or losing. His intellect is not to be underestimated for being cast in such basic terms. To win or not is a simpler question than, say, *Why are we here?* or *How can we fly this space vehicle to the surface of Mars?* but the sheer force Armstrong brings to bear on the central question of his life is no less formidable than that of a rocket scientist charting a course to another planet, or of the endless searching of great philosophers. He is a bike-race-winning genius, and this is why he not only was the sole Tour de France contender to make the break but also why, with 24 kilometers to go and the gap dipping just above and below 30 seconds, he raises his hand and motions for Popo and Zubeldia to go to the front and increase the pace. He wants more time.

It is quintessential Armstrong, immediately polarizing and afterward open to ongoing interpretation as either the only suitable action under the circumstances or as an arrogant display of his power. Bruyneel is telling him to stay in the front, and under normal circumstances, on a team without divided loyalties, any tactical analysis of the situation would lead to the same conclusion: gaining time here means that Contador's rivals will have to mark Armstrong if he attacks in upcoming stages, and thus waste energy they would otherwise save to defeat Contador—or, at the least, if Armstrong can never attack and get away, the rivals will waste energy worrying about such a possibility. Yet, in the opposing view, Armstrong could have helped Astana more by being less worried about himself and instead looking out for Contador—making sure his younger and less-experienced teammate got in the split or, after it occurred, dropping back to pace him up.

Armstrong is a master at identifying and taking advantage of situations that produce dual or even multiple gains. For instance, he told the American television channel covering this year's race, Versus, that he would only give live interviews to one of their commentators: Frankie Andreu.

A source who was there as Bruyneel and Armstrong discussed forcing the banished friend to perform the interviews says that Bruyneel advised against it but Armstrong laughed and said, "No, it'll be great. It'll be great." Was it great because the relationship could start to be mended in this way, or was it great because Armstrong could demonstrate to his rivals that he had the power to make those who crossed him submit to his will? With Armstrong, the answer is probably both: each outcome is beneficial for him.

About Stage 3, he will admit to wanting more time on Schleck, and on Wiggins, Sastre, Evans, and Menchov. He will say it was unfortunate that this also meant he took more time on Contador. He will communicate without actually saying so that Contador should have been there, and insult Contador without expressly insulting him by explaining, "When you see what the wind is doing and you have a turn coming up, it doesn't take a rocket scientist to figure out that you have to go to the front. I have won the Tour de France seven times. Why wouldn't we ride at the front?"

Don ends up driving around the farm a little. He doesn't get out of the truck much because he doesn't want to have to unload the walker from the back. Before it happens to you, he thinks, you'd sure as shit figure something like all the time needing a walker or that damned scooter wheelchair would be nothing except humiliation.

But two days ago, for Hanford's Fourth of July celebration, he was in the scooter, so he and Jackie and some of the kids couldn't sit up in the bleachers at the school the way they always had, and not knowing what else to do, they went out in the field and lay down, and it was the goddamnedest thing of his life, being right under the fireworks like that.

You never know what's going to take a hold of you.

After the Tour of California went by that day in February, he got on the computer and looked at the whole route the racers had ridden from Visalia past Hanford all the way to Paso Robles. He wanted to see that route for himself. He couldn't explain why to anyone, but he kept on it and got one of his sons-in-law, Nagi, to drive him the whole way at the end of May. Then he and Jackie did it in June, going off course a little on their own but getting there in the end. He's heard some people think Lance Armstrong should never have come out of retirement, but he figures the guy's comeback might be like him wanting to see that race route before he dies.

He drives past the calf pens and a field of alfalfa and the twenty-five-ton mounds of additional feed he buys at $350 a ton, rolled corn and canola and mill run in giant, three-sided bins. He stops at the hay and rolls down the window and puts his head out and inhales as deep as he can, which isn't much these days but still draws in enough of his dairy farm's fragrance to nearly intoxicate him.

After the stage is over and Cavendish has won (showing off as he crosses the line by putting his right hand to his ear as if making a phone call, and with his left pointing to the logo of the team's newest sponsor, the cell phone manufacturer HTC), the General Classification reshuffles and shows Armstrong in third, 19 seconds ahead of Contador. Bruyneel tries to keep peace on his team by saying, "We would have ridden the same if it had been Levi or Kloden or Alberto in the lead group. The idea was for our team to put time into the other contenders and make it hard for them." Contador says only, "I don't want to judge the tactics of the team. I will let everyone make up their own minds."

Don and Jackie go out into Hanford, and they stop in at the Superior Dairy. He's missed coming here. He can't eat ice cream anymore—there's too much calcium in it for his body to clear, and it could get into his veins and make sure he died some kind of horrible death. The Superior is a big-windowed place with two long, old Formica counters at which sit spinner stools mounted to the floor. The men in here look stove in but strong, lifelong farmers and laborers wearing feed and co-op caps and cowboy hats dirty and crinkled. The women, even the young women, have wide hips and strong torsos and open faces. The children have ice cream on their shirt fronts.

The scoops are enormous, a single one the equal of five or six at most other places, the banana splits towering up level with the eater's head. The servings aren't some kind of big-city gimmick, some novelty of marketing that someone decided was a way to make a name for the place. It's just the way the Superior started serving ice cream in 1929, with no reason to skimp in such a dairy-rich county. And with the taste just as overwhelming as the serving size—a single spoonful delivers the sensory wallop of a fresh lemon or a habanero pepper—getting all the way through a Superior Dairy ice cream is, like lying in a field under fireworks, the goddamnedest thing.

Rocky road used to be Don's favorite back when he could still eat some, and that's what Jackie orders, one for the two of them. When the waitress sets the dish clinking down onto their table, Don picks up one of the spoons and peers around the ice cream at Jackie in a way he didn't have to because he could see her plainly the whole time.

"It's amazing," he says, and he shakes his spoon at the ice cream a couple of times, then digs it in and brings it into his mouth. If anyone could imagine a tough-ass old farmer like Don Giacomazzi crying, you could maybe say that he almost cries right then.

Jackie is nodding as she moves her spoon in and out for her first bite.

Don swallows and does the peering thing again, and he is smiling when he says, "We have been married forty-six years and we have four children and those children have grandchildren, and one day I am just going to not be here anymore. That's amazing, isn't it?"

He goes for another spoonful. It is amazing to Don Giacomazzi that one day he will just be gone. But he reckons it more amazing that he was ever here, that he ever got a chance to taste Superior Dairy's rocky road ice cream, that he was lucky enough to smell his hay all his life, and that he was on the street corner when that goddamn Lance Armstrong rode by.

Tomorrow is the team time trial. When Armstrong last competed in one in the Tour de France, in 2005, his squad won with an average speed of 35.54 mph, the fastest in Tour history. If Astana can beat Saxo Bank by 41 seconds, for the first time in four years Lance Armstrong will pull on a yellow jersey.

STAGE 3 RESULTS

1. Mark Cavendish, Columbia	5:01:24
6. Fabian Cancellara, Saxo Bank	Same time
19. Lance Armstrong, Astana	
32. Cadel Evans, Silence-Lotto	+0:00:41
35. Bradley Wiggins, Garmin	
41. Christian Vande Velde, Garmin	
49. Alberto Contador, Astana	
52. Denis Menchov, Rabobank	
54. Andy Schleck, Saxo Bank	
88. Levi Leipheimer, Astana	
93. Andreas Kloden, Astana	
94. Carlos Sastre, Cervélo	

GENERAL CLASSIFICATION

1. Fabian Cancellara, Saxo Bank	09:50:58
2. Tony Martin, Columbia	+0:00:33

3. Lance Armstrong, Astana   +0:00:40

4. Alberto Contador, Astana   +0:00:59

5. Bradley Wiggins, Garmin   +0:01:00

6. Andreas Kloden, Astana   +0:01:03

8. Cadel Evans, Silence-Lotto   +0:01:04

10. Levi Leipheimer, Astana   +0:01:11

22. Christian Vande Velde, Garmin   +0:01:38

24. Andy Schleck, Saxo Bank   +0:01:41

26. Carlos Sastre, Cervélo   +0:01:47

56. Denis Menchov, Rabobank   +0:02:12

VUELTA CASTILLA Y LEÓN

Paredes de Nava–Valladolid, Spain, 651 km

MARCH 23–27, 2009

The Worst Thing About Being on This Road

The road was bad. It was narrow enough to be termed a lane except for the circumstance of its being laid down here in a part of northern Spain where anything not a dusty field or a distant mountain was eligible for consideration as a major thoroughfare. It was potholed, pitted, and cracked, bordered on both sides by dry irrigation ditches, and sifted with gray dust, and wracked with stones. None of that was the worst thing about being on this road. The late winter Spanish sun was thick on the backs of the riders, but the wind that yowled across the open, colorless land was bitter cold, so there was no way to dress right, to neither sweat nor freeze, even amid the usually stable rolling microclimate of humid breath and body heat that exists at the center of a pack of cyclists. That was also not the worst thing about being on this road. The worst thing about being on this road was being on it with this pack.

The group of 136 riders was tense, nervous, eager, anxious, desperate, pushy, excited, with far too many of them willing to ignore the condition of the road, the unpredictable push of the wind, and the draining effect of the counterpunching sun and the cold.

They were not all like this. Among the seventeen teams were several composed of seasoned pros and true stars for whom the five-day

Vuelta Castilla y León was just another chance to get in good training miles, another prelude to the big races of the year. There were some of the gods of the sport, such as Carlos Sastre with Cervélo, Christian Vande Velde with Garmin, Denis Menchov with Rabobank, and Alejandro Valverde of Caisse d'Epargne, and some of the steady paycheck riders, most keenly typified by Victor Hugo Peña running down the final days of his long career, with Rock Racing.

The character of the pack was defined not by its leaders this time, however, but by its fodder, the full squads of tiny continental teams such as Andalucía CajaSur, Barbot-Siper, and Burgos Monumental. For the Spanish and Portuguese riders on these teams (Burgos, in an expansive move, did have one rider from Ecuador), this year's Vuelta Castilla was their best shot ever at getting noticed by the big European teams. They knew the world was watching the race this year. It was the first official showdown between Lance Armstrong and Alberto Contador.

Both of them had attended Astana's December training camp in Tenerife, but they didn't ride together there. They were on different programs, Bruyneel explained, Armstrong getting ready for the Tour Down Under in January, while Contador wouldn't start racing until February. It was true, but it was also a convenient excuse to keep the wary superstars apart. By statement of fact they had pedaled alongside each other at the next training camp, in Santa Rosa in February, and Contador had dropped Armstrong on one climb, but they had still not ridden long, hard miles together in the way teammates do. Both had been circumspect, noticeably "careful," as an Astana rider said to me, "not to face off, not to test the other" in a way that would really count. It was as if neither wanted to take the chance of losing the leadership of the team five months before the Tour began. Contador, says the Astana rider who spoke to me about the camp, seemed to be trying to find out if Armstrong would stick to what he promised—to support the strongest rider in July no matter what. And Armstrong seemed in his cagey way to be doing his best to live up to his promise while still being able to win the Tour: if he was the strongest of the two come July, he would not have lied. He would be riding for himself.

Bruyneel wanted to keep the two of them apart to lessen the chances of a feud fracturing the team. The original schedule had called for Armstrong to spend March racing in Belgium and France while Contador did the Vuelta Castilla. Then—in what Bruyneel says were concurrent but separate decisions—Contador demanded a chance to race with Armstrong before July, and Armstrong decided he would benefit from the rhythm of stage racing more than from the knockout punches of the one-day races.

Most observers rated the mere appearance of Armstrong at the race as a victory for Contador, who appeared to have more or less ordered the two to meet, almost certainly had better form, and was on home turf in respect to not only the country but also the specific race, which he'd won the two previous years. I didn't think the calculations were so simple. I figured Armstrong had agreed to meet either because he thought he could come in with surprising fitness and shake up Contador by beating him in a time trial or because he planned to bury himself working to help Contador as proof of self-lessness (which would then be reserved for reference later in the year when he needed to demonstrate he held no grudges) At the same time, Armstrong knew he'd be getting in the high-quality miles he needed if he wanted to make the question of selflessness moot in July. I wasn't sure Contador had ever run into anyone who could think like that, who would not cease poring over a situation until he found a winning circumstance.

Whatever their reasons, they were here. On the first stage, the pack had been riding as if the entire Vuelta Castilla—or an entire career—could be won on these 168 kilometers. There were ceaseless, desperate attacks and, once those were caught, immediate counterattacks, then counters to the counter. Most of the maneuvers seemed as if they were timed to take place on the worst stretches of road, but the reality was that many stretches of road could be equally termed the worst. As a solo attacking rider or a group of two or three threaded between potholes, those in the pack rode blindly into the rough. The handlebars felt like jackhammers in their hands.

Contador watched Armstrong as if most intent on trying to decide what it meant that the American had his arm warmers rolled down to his wrists, exposing his arms: was he tough, or was he working so hard he was overheating? Riders leaped forward out of the pack, fell back into it, others leaped and came back, and the sides of the pack frayed and fell inward. Rocks skittered under wheels. The wind continued to blow against all of this, and with about 20 kilometers to go there was yet one more leap and fray and another falling inward, except this time the falling was actual and the left side of the race began running over itself.

It was a crash.

Red and blue and yellow and orange jerseys disappeared over the fronts of the bikes that had an instant ago been carrying them, and the colors strobed as the riders somersaulted, or slid along the pavement until they ran into someone else who had just finished sliding along the pavement and were, in turn, slid into or run over. The left was a clot, and what remained of the race streamed to the right and passed around it. Some of the cyclists were off their bikes and running all crooked on their cleats, one hand on the saddle or handlebar. The team cars were coming up on the scene now, and also the motorcycles with their engines searing hot and as loud as they were hot and exposed out where they could peel the skin right off a rider if the drivers weren't careful. Riders were walking stiff-legged in circles, or holding their wrists, or already back on their bikes without fully realizing they had risen from the ground, and mechanics were jumping out of the backseats of the team cars and unlocking new bikes from the roof racks and pushing them under riders. It was absolute chaos, and it was pretty ordinary for a bike race.

Over on the right, there was one figure sitting in the ditch. He was far from his bike, which was lying prone on the dusty broken shoulder of the road. His knees were drawn up, and he was looking not at the madness behind him but at a wall of loose-piled rocks that for some reason existed between the ditch and the emptiness beyond it. He stared at the rock wall.

Tomas Vaitkus, a Lithuanian who was riding for Astana, coasted into the mess and began picking his way through the cars and the fallen riders and abandoned bikes. He looked to his right, and as soon as he did he braked and swung sideways, dropped his bike to the road, and walked swiftly back to where Lance Armstrong was sitting.

Vaitkus put a hand on Armstrong's right shoulder. Armstrong waved him away.

By then Chris Van Roosbroeck, one of Astana's mechanics, had jumped out of the car and run up to Armstrong, carrying a spare front and spare rear wheel. He crouched and, seeing that Armstrong would not be getting back on his bike, stood, walked over to Vaitkus, and took Armstrong's bike.

A race doctor was beside Armstrong then, touching his right arm, talking to him. Armstrong was hunched over, rocking a bit now, his legs spread wide. His right arm was propped on his thigh. His helmet was still on his head, but cracked. The doctor was speaking to him in Spanish and English. Chris was carrying his bike to the team car, racking it up on the roof with the spares. A helicopter chopped up the air directly overhead. The honking of the cars came less frequently, less loudly. Armstrong's glasses were still on, against the sun and dust. His two water bottles lay out on the road.

Lance Armstrong was thirty-seven years old. He was going to become a father again in June—in December he'd announced the pregnancy of his girlfriend, Anna Hansen, a manager for a cancer outreach program he'd met through some of his charity work. The child had been conceived naturally, which he'd thought impossible following his chemotherapy treatments, and so conception felt like a miracle rather than a mistake. In the last race he'd done, Milan–San Remo, European oddsmakers had put the chance of him winning at 100–1. He'd finished 125th. He had crashed twice already this year. His legs were pale against the dust and dry grass. Chris came back.

He took Lance's helmet off. Lance dropped his head and looked down into the dirt, and thought: *What the hell am I doing here?*

Very Very

Earlier that morning, a couple of workmen had just begun inflating the arch that would span the start line of the race when the Astana bus came up a little hill and around a corner and paused, rocking back and forth between the gas pedal and the brakes, at the mouth of the square that had been taped off as a team parking area.

Two television crews winked into existence outside the Astana bus as it hissed to a stop just inside the square. There was one team car pulling around the bus and braking to a halt, then another roofed full of bikes, and a third. Legendary race photographer Graham Watson strolled over, as if by happenstance. A tall woman, in jean shorts cut so high the bottom curves of her butt swung free, stalked over to the bus, projecting great intent. Seven girls broke from the line that had formed around the Cervélo bus, which had arrived much earlier, and began running toward Astana; the youngest was maybe ten, the oldest perhaps twenty, but despite these differences they ran in a tight though swirling circle, giggling and waving their arms over their heads, some of them holding little autograph books, one of them holding a stuffed beast that was neither bear nor lion nor any species easily named. They all had long, dark hair, and boots that clunked against the stones of the square. Then in the flood of fans that came it was hard to describe anything singly but the streaming flow.

In ten minutes or so, the crowd had settled thickly and completely around the Astana bus, marooning it from the other teams and their scatters of admirers. Out at the farthest edge of this swamp of people, two women held up a bedsheet between them. There was a Spanish flag painted on it, and two words: Pinto Contador. The women were chanting, over and over, a three-part refrain made up of a single word: "Conta-dorrr, Conta-dorrrr, Contadorcontadorconta-dorrr-or-or!"

They were from Alberto Contador's hometown—Pinto, Spain—and while the women understood that Lance Armstrong was one of the world's great heroes, they explained in as much English as they possessed that Alberto Contador was *their* great hero. One of them said, as if divulging something a tarot card had told her, that Contador's girlfriend was from this town, Paredes de Nava. A young man orbiting the women, one of their sons, perhaps, a twentyish kid with sharp features and low-slung, faded jeans over boots, summed up all of this: "Contador," he said, "he is very very."

The door to the Astana bus swung open.

Alberto Contador paused for a second or so on the last step still inside the bus, taking a good look at the people coming through the tape the team mechanics had strung up to create a feeble safe zone. The first impression he gives is that of leanness, but not in the way the word is typically visualized; he looked somehow simple in shape, his form communicating his purpose in the manner of a knife blade or a sharpened stick. His face and arms and legs were dark against the Easter egg blue of the Astana uniform he wore, and his eyes flickered darker still. He smiled, and though it was dazzling white and unwavering there was something shy and unbelieving to it as well. And from even the least movements of his body—as one hand trailed against the side of the doorway and he stepped down into the crowd, his foot despite being strapped into a cleated, carbon-soled cycling shoe falling soft onto the hard, sun-drenched stones of the square—there exuded the unthinking, untrained pure grace possessed by humankind's greatest natural athletes, dancers, beauties.

The women warbled and fluttered their shared bedsheet, and Contador reached and took his bike from a mechanic and swung his leg over it and—still all of this in one fluid motion—pushed off against the ground with his aft foot rather than pedaling. The crowd veed open for him and in an odd visual effect, as children pushed closer to him as adults fell back, it appeared as if the parting crowd was also bowing before him. Contador stopped at the women, kissed each singer on her cheek, and said a few words. Back in a shadowed veranda, gone shy, the predatory short-shorts woman watched, her mouth open, red blotches on each cheek. Contador was surrounded now completely by children, and little hands reached to touch his jersey, the handlebar of his bike, the water bottle on the down tube. He somehow neither noticed nor ignored this, some indefinable thing in his manner granting these littlest admirers permission while establishing that there was to be no grabbing, no plucking, no offense or annoyance. I thought that the kid had been right: Alberto Contador could best be described as very very.

Then the door to the Astana bus opened again.

In as simple and seamless an action as the swing of the door, Armstrong stepped down out of the dim rectangle and onto the square. His charisma was more majesty than grace—a beauty not sublime but terrible, and made not of his movements nor his expressions but our own cumulative memory of all he had vanquished. Everyone—except for the singing ladies and the children—twisted to regard this new wonder. Above head level, on almost every arm that now stuck up to blindly click a camera aimed at the center of the mob, there was a yellow Livestrong bracelet. The cameras of the TV crews swam toward Armstrong like leeches going for a host. The ass-pants woman licked her lips.

In the little time I'd gotten to spend with Contador and the occasions I'd seen him compete, I'd concluded that he had no less fire than Armstrong, though it manifested itself differently. When it came to racing, Contador was an unpredictable lightning strike that might slash at any time, then vanish, while Armstrong at his best was like a wildfire beyond control. When it came to fans, Contador was more likely to inspire warmth than heat. He was a nice boy.

He always has been, as far as I could tell. I got to know him for the first time in 2007, at an industry trade show in Las Vegas just a little more than a month after he won his first Tour. His chaperones, expense-account executives from one of the companies that sponsored him, kept suggesting forays into discos and strip clubs, and Alberto kept demurring. He just wanted to find a quiet bar. He was uncomfortable, though not tense—he was too self-possessed for that. I got the sense that this night was one more thing he knew he could simply outlast. At one point, as we finally sat and talked, he told me in broken English and through a translator about his childhood, growing up with his mother, father, and two brothers and sister in an apartment in Pinto, a little town outside of Madrid. They were happy but not without difficulties: his younger brother had cerebral palsy. The winner of the most grueling sporting event in the world, he told me without any hint of embarrassment that it was true what I'd heard—that when he was a kid he used to run home from school as fast as he could, dash out onto the balcony, and whistle for the doves that he knew would come down to be fed by hand. (And he still tends to canaries to this day.)

His older brother Fran, who's now his manager, got him into cycling at age fourteen, and he began racing a year later. When he began winning some of Spain's biggest amateur races, at age sixteen he dropped out of school to devote his life to cycling. In 2003 he turned pro with ONCE, and though everyone who saw him and knew anything about cycling could tell his potential was immense, he didn't win much. In May of 2004, during a rainy race in Spain, he began having convulsions while riding and crashed. He'd had a stroke, caused, as it was later diagnosed, by a congenital blood clot. In emergency surgery, the clot was removed from his brain, leaving a scar that runs atop his head from ear to ear. He told me that during the surgery he dreamed of riding the Tour de France and that when he awoke with his family standing over him he struggled for hours to speak until finally he was able to coax out a single sentence: "Where there's a will there's a way." His mother knew he was talking about returning to pro cycling and, he said, "she cried."

Eight months later he won a stage of the Tour Down Under, racing for essentially the same team under the new name of Liberty

Seguros after a change of sponsors. It was this team that was caught up in Operación Puerto, a doping investigation that began in 2006 and, as it continued, resulted in the exclusion of stars such as Ullrich and Basso from that year's Tour de France just days before the start. Five of Contador's teammates were on the list of riders excluded for suspicion of involvement in the case, which meant the squad couldn't meet the requirement of fielding at least six riders and had to withdraw from the Tour entirely. Contador's team director, Manolo Saiz, had been arrested and charged with administering a doping program along with Eufemiano Fuentes, the doctor at the center of the investigation, and the initials *AC* were on a handwritten document seized from Fuentes. But Contador was never directly linked to Puerto, and in July of 2006 he was cleared of involvement by the Spanish courts and later that year by the UCI as well. In 2007, he was signed by Bruyneel to the Discovery team. By October of 2008 he had won all three Grand Tours; he was twenty-five years old, two years younger than Armstrong had been when he won his first Tour.

The mainstream media were already portraying Contador as the villain to Armstrong's hero. I thought that cheated them both—and all of us—by reducing to a zero-sum game what was in reality a complex and passionate theater of sport. In that Spanish square in the early morning of March 23, Contador lingered a moment more with the two middle-aged women from his hometown, and with a downward tip of his chin he acknowledged once again the painted bedsheet they held. He reached out and touched one of the children on the head. Then, with the square open before him and the crowd trailing him growing bigger each moment, he rode off to the start.

The Story We All Know

Lance had no doubt that he'd broken his collarbone.

The bone is so close to your ear that you can hear it snap when your shoulder hits the road. When you're done tumbling and make your first tentative movements, the splintered ends of bone grind against each other and the pain makes your vision go white. Then once you've gotten yourself up, either sitting or standing, your arm sags and your whole body lists to the injured side as if you're trying to tip downward to pour the boiling liquid heat of the pain out of your busted shoulder.

Bound to happen, Armstrong thought as he sat in the ditch and the doctor talked to him. Aside from sprains, aches, and the skin abrasions that racers call "road rash," a broken collarbone is the sport's most common crash-related ailment, yet Armstrong had gone his entire seventeen-year career without a single fractured clavicle, a feat that at the pro level was nearly as unthinkable as his seven Tour wins. His pristine collarbones had been two more small proofs of his ability to rise above the ordinary human experience.

Viatcheslav Ekimov, one of Astana's team directors and a long-time friend of Armstrong's—he'd ridden with him in five of the seven Tour wins—had gotten out of the team car and was with him, along with Dean Golich, a coach who worked with Carmichael and was there to oversee Armstrong's training.

"I broke my collarbone," Armstrong told them, though he didn't need to. Golich could see the telltale bumps on Armstrong's shoulder where detached pieces of bone were pushing up against the skin.

"It's broken," said Armstrong.

An ambulance arrived.

I was standing just past the finish line in Baltanás, waiting for the race to end and knowing nothing of the crash, when Sean Yates drove past in Astana's second team car, pulled in beside their bus, and parked. I walked over and nodded to him from a distance as he got out of the car. As with Armstrong, I'd originally gotten to know Yates back in the 1990s, when he was riding for Motorola. He'd been one of cycling's hard men, a tough *domestique* who made more wins possible than he won himself and was considered one of the sport's most fearless and skilled descenders ever. He'd won a stage of the Tour in 1988 and wore the yellow jersey for one day in

1994, but was most famous for being one of Armstrong's mentors. When they rode together from 1992 to 1996, the hardened veteran taught the fresh kid how to scream down mountains. I'd run into Yates at the opening time trial of this year's Tour of California—he had an Astana T-shirt on and after escorting some riders to the ramp he asked to look at the start list I had in my hand—but I hadn't seen him in so long I didn't recognize him.

"You work for Astana?" I'd said.

He'd nodded. His hair was cut short to his scalp without being a buzz, and though he looked his mid-forties age, he also looked chiseled instead of soft. He was the kind of person who you knew was somebody even if you had no idea who he was.

"What's your name?" I'd said.

He'd looked at me more or less sideways, intent on watching the rider he'd just brought over, Rast, to make sure nothing went wrong as he queued up in the start chute—a dropped chain at the last second, a flat tire, any of the innumerable bits of mundane bad luck that in the moments before a time trial become disasters. In deep, drawn-out syllables, he said his name.

"Oh," I'd said. "I'm sorry. I didn't—I know who you are. Of course. I used to know you, sort of." Then as if I could prove this, I said, "You rode twelve Tours and finished nine."

Yates had smirked and walked away. But when I saw him again later he said, "You thought I was some plonker, didn't you?" And I saw that the smirk was just his smile. "Well," he said, "I guess I am, anyway." We shook hands.

In Spain, before I could get close enough to talk to him, two French journalists rushed up and began asking him about Armstrong. The questions were formal, journalist inquiries—*Can you comment on the crash?*—and Yates gave precise answers limited to the few facts he possessed: that he'd driven by the crash and seen Armstrong but had to follow the group in case Contador or Levi Leipheimer needed support; that Eki and Golich had stopped; that

Armstrong and Golich both said the injury was a broken collarbone but it was unconfirmed by doctors.

The journalists ran off to get more quotes and I looked at Yates.
"Goddamn," I said. "Sean, what's the story?"

He said, "It's the story we all know, isn't it?"

I stared at him, stunned by the news but also because what he'd
just said seemed in some important way to explain more than all
the facts he'd given in response to the journalists' questions.

Beside us, the big blue wall of the bus shook as the engine kicked
over, then rumbled in neutral. "I guess we're going," Yates said. "I
guess we need to leave right now." He got in the car and left and the
bus followed him, and I turned around and saw parked almost in
the ditch a small panel truck that had been hidden by the bus. There
was a picture of Lance on the side along with the words ZYCIE IN-
SPIROWANE PRZEZ LANCE'A ARMSTRONGA. I walked over, and on the
other side of the bus there was a tall, doughy man staring down at
the ground and shaking his head.

"Do you speak English?" I said.

He looked up at me and said, "Certainly."

"What do those words say?" I pointed, and he looked at the
truck and squinted.

"These words?" he asked.

"Yes, on the truck," I said.

" 'Life inspired by Lance Armstrong.' This is a Livestrong truck
from Poland. I drove it here myself. I am Martin Cieslik, and I
drove it here for it to be here. Now . . ." He took a step away from
me, then a step toward me and some more backward, then some
toward the truck and one back toward me, sometimes looking at
the words on his truck as if he'd just discovered them, sometimes
as if studying them for a test, and sometimes he looked back down
into the dirt as he shuffled around, and in this way over the course
of two or three minutes he wandered off out of sight.

A teenage kid in a red T-shirt, faded jeans, and black Converse walked by, pumping a fist in the air and singing the Contador chant. He was wearing a necklace of sausages and carrying a hand-lettered sign that said CONTADOR TE CAMBIA TU MAILLOT PAR UN SASTE DE CORIZO CASERA. He'd been hoping to trade some of his homemade chorizo for a yellow jersey or, I thought, to at least make his hero smile. The kid stopped, turned and faced the truck, and sang and punched his fist skyward. Life inspired by Lance Armstrong.

Martin Cieslik was gone, and the Livestrong truck sat silent in the weeds.

It Hurts a Lot

The ambulance took Armstrong to a nearby hospital, where X-rays confirmed the racer's own roadside diagnosis. He was given pain-killers and a sling and driven back to the team hotel in Palencia. By the time he was in his room and had changed out of the grimy race shorts he'd been wearing all day and taken a shower, then re-wrapped his bandages, it was evening. In a few hours someone on the team would drive him to Bruyneel's house in Madrid, where he'd rest for a day before flying home to Austin to have the collar-bone examined by his own doctors.

"I feel miserable right now," he said on his way out of the hospi-tal. "It hurts a lot."

The Giro d'Italia was five weeks away. Elite cyclists generally race again within four to six weeks after breaking a collarbone, and can begin training on the road within ten days. As Bruyneel said, "He hit the ground so hard that his helmet cracked, so a col-larbone is not a bad outcome. It's one of the breaks that takes the least time to heal." For most professional bike racers, that would be true. But for Armstrong, the fact of the crash itself seemed some-how more damning than the physical damage.

"For seven years he won the Tour," the mechanic Chris told me, seeming like a person shaken into candidness by a trauma, "with not one bad crash, not—" He gestured to his stomach and roiled his hand around, indicating stomach distress. "And not a bad cold, nothing. It is a thing, to do that. It is something, right? And now? Already it was in his head that he might crash, that's been the problem. And now after this? Phew!"

Chris is a Belgian native who raced a little himself—like almost all of his countrymen did—but quickly realized he didn't have enough talent to turn the sport into a career. When he was fourteen, he began helping his uncle, who wrenched for a Dutch pro team, and he discovered that what he lacked in natural cycling ability he had in mechanical aptitude. In 1988 he worked his first Tour de France, and this year's would be his twentieth. He was as much at the top of his profession as Leipheimer was of his. He has a round, open face, and laughs a lot but is prone to the Belgian frown and head shake, and has a certain way of standing and gesturing with his hands that identify his place of birth. One day I asked him to spell his last name.

"Oh, man, I'm pink pants," he said. He had the Belgian scowl.

"What?"

"My last name, Roosbroeck, it translates to 'rose pants,' 'pink pants.' My nickname on the team is 'Pink Pants.'"

"Jeez," I said. "How do you feel about that?"

"Oh, it's okay, you know." Now he smiled, and he seemed almost proud. "Lance gave it to me. It's Lance's nickname for me."

Such is Armstrong's charisma that even to be chided or needled by him can seem a momentous personal event. This is a quality that doesn't come across in his portrayals in the media or in film clips, a curious magnetism that he possessed long before he became a celebrity, and which isn't often mentioned because it's so hard to pinpoint, but which even his harshest critics can't deny—though they experience it as an overwhelming negative force.

At a press conference, Levi would say that the broken collarbone was just bad luck. But in private he told some of the team members that Lance could have avoided the crash. "We were together, working up front chasing," he said, "and Lance just started going away. He came off. He wasn't there. He went backward, then he got caught behind a crash."

Other riders, seeming to sense the first real weakness Armstrong had shown since 1999, began to dig into him in ways he would not miss but the public likely would.

Armstrong had insulted Carlos Sastre, saying in various ways and with various degrees of confidentiality that one of his inspirations for coming back was Sastre's 2008 Tour victory. I had heard from multiple people in his inner circle that Lance had been watching the Tour on TV the day Sastre made his race-winning move on Alpe d'Huez and, in a state somewhere between disgust and disbelief, had said that if he'd been riding he would have "kicked all their asses," and that the performances of the Tour contenders were "bullshit" and "weak." Sastre would have heard similar leaks. (The tenor of Armstrong's belief, if not the specific words, would be confirmed in June 2009 when John Wilcockson's book *Lance: The Making of the World's Greatest Champion* quoted him as referencing Sastre and Christian Vande Velde by name when he termed the 2008 Tour "a bit of a joke.") Speaking to several reporters after the crash, Sastre called Armstrong's injury "a shame" and, in his understated, near-deferential way of speaking about almost anyone or anything, dismissed the stage's riskiness by saying, "I always kept more or less safe, and always protected by my colleagues." The meaning was clear to cycling insiders: *It's too bad he couldn't ride at the front.*

Contador said, "It is a pity to lose Lance," seeming to relish the chance to feel bad for his rival. Earlier in the month, Contador had been on track to win the eight-day stage race Paris-Nice for the second time when, on the next-to-last day, he bonked—ran out of energy after neglecting to take in enough food and water—and lost about 3 minutes in the final 4 kilometers. "Amazing talent," Armstrong had commented on Twitter that day, "but still a lot to learn." He followed that up a few days later by calling Contador "too nervous" in an interview in *L'Equipe*. "He is too strong to be so nervous," Armstrong said, embedding his put-down in a compliment. "He has a good team manager and a strong team. Why get nervous?" Spanish newspapers were reporting that although the two riders sat across from each other at the team dinner table the night before the first stage, they had not spoken, and that Armstrong had repeatedly delayed showing up for a joint photo shoot with Contador until the appointment had been cancelled. Now, with Armstrong sipping wine in Bruyneel's kitchen to top off painkillers, Contador hit back with his own artful insult, what to the public would sound like an innocuous comment but in cycling was known to be the champion's classic dismissal of an also-ran: "I didn't see the crash because it happened behind me."

You Get Used to That

The race rolled on without Armstrong.

Leipheimer, fully recovered from the broken bone he'd suffered in the crash with Armstrong at the Tour of California, won the Stage 2 time trial by 16 seconds over Contador, moved into the leader's spot, and would hold it all the way to the end despite incessant attacks from the Spanish teams and a vicious ride from Dave Zabriskie in the mountains of the penultimate stage.

Most of the challenges were shut down by Contador. He accepted with grace the chance to show he could play the noble champion and ride in support of a lesser teammate—especially one whose loyalty to Armstrong might be nice to shake—and he stated as much every day of the race. "I will work for Levi as he worked hard for me in the past," he said after the time trial. After the final stage, he proclaimed, "It was an honor and a pleasure to work for Levi. Levi has worked so much for me in the past."

He granted his favor in this way each day, progressively becoming more humble until he could no longer give up anything more of himself and assumed a kind of imperious charm—"the king of

Spain," Chris the mechanic said to me once as we watched him ride off across a playground to a start, a tail of fans a hundred yards long trailing after him, crying his name.

One day after a stage I was standing by a team car with Yates. He was waiting for Contador to finish up with dope control or a television interview or something so they could drive to that night's hotel. A middle-aged man in a dark denim jacket and matching jeans walked up and asked Yates for an Astana cap. Yates shook his head, and the man stepped aside and gestured a girl forward, his daughter, perhaps fourteen years old and wearing a light green Puma sweat jacket and matching pants over bright white Puma sneakers. She had dark, deep-set eyes and thick eyebrows, freckles, was lovely but not yet beautiful, and all the more beautiful for not yet being in full possession of what was destined to be hers. The man raised a palm as if to ask how this could even be questioned, that his daughter deserved a cap. But there was nothing to be done; Yates could not give out a cap to just anyone who asked. "No, I'm sorry," he said. Suddenly there came Contador, surrounded by Spanish police in their green uniforms and a swell of admirers washing out before him as the cops broke through the crowd. He handed his bike to Yates, who turned to rack it, and the father stepped forward and in Spanish implored Contador for a picture. He assented and stood next to the girl, and she broke into a small, retreating smile rather than the radiant one that was expected and this put the final shine on Contador and he stood resplendent and lean, and I said to Yates, who had turned around, "the king of Spain." I was embarrassed to have said it, because I felt it so deeply.

The race rolled on without Armstrong, across rippling plains with mountains in the distance, then into the mountains and back down. Dogs sat in the road and scratched themselves before the race came and after it left. Statues of saints and the Savior watched the race pass from atop far hills. There were smoky cafés where children of three or four sat up on the bar while their fathers drank glasses of Mahou beer. The podium announcers kept calling Levi

"Levy." In contrast to the spectators at American races, who are principally cyclists and dress as if they have to be ready to break into sporting mode at any moment, and to the throngs that line the roads at every Tour de France, who are essentially the European equivalent of a NASCAR crowd, many of the Spanish racing fans dressed as if they regarded the race as an occasion of much import. There was a man in a brown tweed beret and checkered black-and-blue-and-green slip-ons with gray slacks and a black dress coat. He was missing a thumb and the first two fingers of his left hand, but he carried a kerchief in his pocket. There was a man in green corduroy with a blue cardigan over a black shirt, riding a bicycle with his walking cane lashed to the tubes. There was a man with a brilliant red cashmere sweater tied around his waist, and a man in a light brown suit with a yellow button-down shirt.

The race rolled on without Armstrong, with music and banners everywhere it went, and a stage and a tireless announcer narrating your enjoyment, a voice-over for your day to help you understand the history and future of the drama you found yourself a part of. Young girls leaned into one another as they walked and boys punched each other out of sheer ebullience. A stage race coming to your town was how a birthday party must have felt when you were six years old.

The motorcycle drivers were lean or fat, grizzled or sharply young, but they all had the same bearing. They were the race's underappreciated outlaws, and off their motorcycles they carried their helmets with them not like purses or small dogs but somehow like sidearms. The race officials, the many judges and timekeepers and logisticians and bureaucrats, all had a shared bearing as well, much impressed with themselves in their polos, but to their continual dismay they were received by the public with the same second-rate regard given to umpires at a major league baseball game. Some of the press tried as hard as possible to project the attitude of lifers in prison, hanging out bored in cars at the finish with the doors open and their feet propped on the dash; some walked around telling more interesting stories than they would ever file, some used their press passes to strut along the barricaded stretches as if on a fashion runway, and some were truly hardworking journalists who equaled what all the other types lacked in drive and ethic but were so blinkered by their sense of mission that they never would write about children sitting on bar tops or dogs scratching themselves in the road. All of these citizens of the stage race were rendered invisible when even the lowliest, worst-placed rider entered town. They were not merely the stars. They were the substance of it all. Each town was a milieu constructed especially for them and would be torn down when they left and another would be erected in front of them and then destroyed in their absence while the next was constructed only to be disassembled. The racers were not confined to a stadium or a field. The world of traffic, stop signs, stoplights, deliveries, business hours, and school days made way for them, parting to let them play. Seeing one of them was like being in one of those drive-through zoos and spotting, amid the other tourists and the guides and the maintenance workers and the souvenir vendors, one of the beasts.

The race rolled on without Armstrong, and one day I stood just past the finish line with Ryszard Kielpinski, one of Astana's *soigneurs*—a catchall term that covers masseuse, valet, psychologist, short-order cook and waiter, laundry worker, and whatever else might need to be done. Richard, as he's called, was there with a Livestrong backpack, a big soft-sided cooler, and an Astana *musette*—the food bag that's handed off to riders on the fly at designated feed zones on long stages—with ARRIVO written on it in black marker. There were drinks and foods in the cooler, and towels, hats, jackets, long-sleeved jerseys, and other things in the backpack. Richard was there to meet each rider as he came across the line, immediately give him a drink or something to eat, wipe him off and dress him warmly, then tell him where the bus was parked so he could ride there without getting lost.

We found out we both knew some people who'd ridden on

Montgomery Bell, which had been the predecessor of the U.S. Postal Service team with which Lance had won his first six Tours, and we caught each other up. We talked about the reign of the enigmatic cycling coach, Eddie B., who'd brought American cycling to world-class level in the 1980s but also advised things such as eating horse meat. For at least half an hour we talked about crashes we had seen, our favorite old races, the weather, Spanish food, and the funny or striking spectators we saw around us. Then I said, "Do you think Contador is really okay with Levi winning this?"

Richard shut down. He pursed his lips and shook his head and said, "It depends," then turned his shoulder to me and for the rest of the time watched down the road for the riders to come.

The teams headed up by Bruyneel and Armstrong have always had a reputation for being impenetrable, secretive, unfriendly. I could hang around all I wanted and talk, and most anyone was happy to shoot the breeze with me. But as soon as I asked a direct question about Armstrong or team dynamics, the conversation would either end or shift into a formal mode I found useless. The entire team, and Lance especially, were practiced enough with the media to simply ignore questions, or else speak for minutes at a time either without saying much or saying only what they had already determined they wanted to communicate even if it didn't address what had been asked. You could fill up a notebook with their answers and not learn anything important about the team.

I was never going to understand Armstrong's comeback, or my own fascination with it, by asking questions. This was not only because of the reluctance of those close to Armstrong to fully and truthfully answer questions. It was also, I thought, at least when it came to Lance himself, because of an inability to think too much about himself. One of the people closest to him in all the world had said to me something I'd heard about him before: when it came to asking Lance to elucidate who he was, "you might as well interview a shark about why it's biting you."

Yates had said, "It's the story we all know," and he was right.

But that story never got told because it was easier to get a quick quote and write down the finish order and time splits. If I wanted the story, the real story instead of the official one, I would need to follow him around the world all season without brick by brick erecting between us a wall built of stock questions.

And I needed, as much as I could, to avoid supplying my own stock answers. One day I'd been hanging out at the team bus with Philippe Maertens, the team's press manager, when he told me that he raised pigeons back at his home in Belgium.

"For sport?" I asked.

"No, no. I got a few racing pigeons to start, but I had no time to work with them and they had young ones, so I began eating the young ones. I eat them."

I don't think I spoke, but my face must have communicated something. Philippe said, "It was very difficult, at first—to eat something you know." He paused a second or two, shrugged and said, "But you get used to that."

A reporter who'd spent only a few minutes or even a few days around Astana might have spun that anecdote into a piece about the ability of the cold Astana machine to eat the young when necessary. But having spent time with Philippe the day after Lance broke his collarbone, seeing how through his exhaustion he still politely told disappointed fans he couldn't get them Lance's autograph, I was equally inclined to guess that maybe he just really liked the taste of pigeon and was frugal.

The race rolled on, and even without Armstrong there I was learning so much about his comeback that I followed it to the end.

We Don't Have Many Options

He began to think that maybe he liked it that way, the race rolling on without him.

Armstrong flew home from Madrid on Tuesday and, still in the same T-shirt and warm-up pants he'd worn on the flight, wasted no time in getting to Doug Elenz, an orthopedic surgeon at Austin Sports Medicine. Elenz examined Armstrong and took new X-rays, then delivered some bad news: the injury was not a simple break that divided the bone in two, as the doctors in the Spanish hospital had thought. Elenz hung his X-ray next to the dimmer, fuzzier Spanish one on a wall-mounted lightbox and pointed out to Armstrong how his collarbone had fractured into four pieces. As Elenz explained his recommendation of aggressive surgery, Armstrong, who was sitting in a chair against the wall, rested his head in his good hand, and stared down and to the left, away from the negative images of his shattered bone.

Elenz operated the next day, screwing a five-inch stainless-steel plate into Armstrong's clavicle in ten places and using two more screws to stabilize the bone in other spots. The three-hour process was "like putting a jigsaw puzzle back together," Elenz said.

Within six hours Armstrong was home and playing with nine-year-old Luke and seven-year-old twins Grace and Bella, his kids from his first marriage. About an hour later he called Bruyneel. "He sounded good," Bruyneel said. "He sounded tired but he sounded like Lance, so I wasn't worried about him. We'd been through harder situations together, and he'd been through much more serious health issues, obviously."

The next morning, Armstrong woke before 6 a.m. He felt, he said, destroyed by the combination of the crash, the 200-kilometer drive to Bruyneel's house followed by the flight, then the surgery and the combo hangover of anesthesia and jet lag. He posted a two-minute video to his website that started off by thanking his doctors and saying that everything had gone smoothly. He looked no more tired or drawn than any of the world's best stage racers sometimes do. But a little more than halfway through, as he sighed and took deep breaths between phrases, he said, "This is a new experience for me. There's a lot of questions that are left to be answered. In almost twenty years of pro cycling I very rarely had crashes. I've been very lucky, I've been very blessed when it comes to that. And for this to happen now is a new experience for me, so we don't know how my recovery will go. We'll just take it day by day and ultimately get back on the bike and try to sort things out."

The next day he said he felt better, and he hung around his house and watched a couple of movies. He had a stationary bike out in the part of the garage that he'd converted into a home gym, but he didn't get on it; Elenz had advised him to take a week completely off. But the following morning—just two days after the surgery—he went to Luke's flag football game, then got on the bike in his garage and did a thirty-minute spin. That sounded exactly like something Armstrong would do, and everything seemed to be on track.

But Bruyneel began getting phone calls from Armstrong's friends and staff, who said they were worried about him—that he didn't have his usual intensity when he talked about getting back into shape in time for the Giro, that he just seemed to be going through the motions on the bike, and that his heart didn't seem to be into the comeback anymore. A few people told Bruyneel that Armstrong had mentioned that "he didn't know if he should be doing this anymore."

Bruyneel called Armstrong—not to ask if he was quitting but to get his own read. "He was quiet," Bruyneel says. "He wasn't giving the responses I expected. He had no desire to race. He avoided some subjects such as training and plans for races."

Armstrong kept up a happy, energetic front on his Twitter posts, and he kept riding, however much by rote it might have been, eventually going on a real road ride after a week had passed. In the meantime, he went to Luke's pinewood derby race, took the kids to school, hosted play dates for them, dug up a photo from 1980 of his own pinewood derby car to show Luke, ate out at restaurants around town, and hosted dinners for old friends who came to visit, including "Och"—Jim Ochowicz—the former Olympic cyclist who'd founded Motorola, and Dylan Casey, who had ridden with him on the U.S. Postal Service team. His mom came to visit for Anna's baby shower. Elenz checked the incision, removed the sterile bandages, and told him everything looked good.

Everything was not good. Bruyneel was getting panicked calls from those around Armstrong who believed the rider was about to announce his retirement again. Armstrong's responses to Bruyneel's text messages and phone calls were uncharacteristically laconic and sporadic. Finally, on April 5, Bruyneel was at the hospital for the birth of his second child, a son. When the new father called Armstrong, he told me, he suddenly knew what he had to do.

"We talked about everything that was going on," Bruyneel said. "And finally I told him he had to tell me what he was going to do. After a little bit he said outright, 'Well, you know, I could just quit.'"

Without any hesitation, Bruyneel told me, he said to Armstrong, "Actually, you can't. There's absolutely no way you can abandon. That's not who you are."

Armstrong took a breath. "Well," he said, "I guess we don't have many options, then."

Two weeks after this, the villagers of Antiguedad, Spain, would wheel a squeaky and decrepit blue bicycle out to the site of the most famous event ever to occur in their area and park it right there where Armstrong had sat in the ditch looking at the rock wall. A wooden plaque hung on the bike read LA CLAVICULA DE ARMSTRONG. It was a memorial only to an accident, not an ending, because Lance Armstrong was back on his bike and riding twice a day.

TOUR DE FRANCE, STAGE 4
Team Time Trial, Montpellier, 39 km
JULY 7, 2009

They hear the beep at the same instant they feel that sensation that is something like the weightless millisecond between sleeping and waking, the flicker of time between when the person holding on to the back of the bike lets go and when the force of the first pedal stroke explodes into its full power and flings them down the ramp.

Just as they practiced it, within a few feet of rolling off the nine-rider-wide start ramp they are slotted into a single-file line, the first rider's forward-thrust arms and head in its teardrop-shaped aerodynamic helmet cutting a passage through the air for all of them to slip through. Astana's team time trial has begun.

The 39-kilometer course is short and brutal. It starts into a headwind and climbs out of Montpellier on a series of five hills (the longest of which is about 3 kilometers), then circles back toward town on descending, twisting, bumpy narrow roads. Most TTTs, as team time trials are called, are longer (the Tour's last three were 65–69 kilometers) and have wide, smooth straightaways that stretch out for kilometers to let teams settle into a rhythm and maintain their top speed as long as they can. Instead of rewarding such steady horsepower, this course's forty corners and curves, plus eight roundabouts, demand that teams accelerate over and over, and slice through turns as fast they can without losing control—a feat not all of them have succeeded at.

The reigning world champion, Alessandro Ballan, crashed with his Lampre teammate David Loosli in the second corner. Beyond road rash, neither was injured, but Ballan would finish with a soiled and ripped rainbow jersey. Less than 15 kilometers later, Lampre crashed again when Angelo Furlan slipped and Marzio Bruseghin ran into him. Lampre would finish seventeenth out of the twenty teams.

Denis Menchov, the Giro d'Italia champion, wiped out in the first corner, forcing his entire Rabobank team to stop and wait for him. They would finish eleventh. A rider for Cofidis ran wide on a curve, braking to an emergency stop before he crashed, and his team would finish sixteenth. Three riders for Milram crashed, two early and one on the last turn of the course. They were fifteenth. Four Bbox riders rode straight through a corner and into a ditch; by the time they recovered, restarted, and overcame their jittery nerves they were reduced to second from last. Jurgen Van den Broeck touched the wheel of the Silence-Lotto teammate in front of him and wrecked: thirteenth place. And most embarrassing of all, Quick Step went down in a heap just trying to get to the start—and went on to finish twelfth.

Splits and separations caused by the frequent braking and reaccelerations were almost as bad as the crashes. Within 20 minutes of starting, one of the teams considered a favorite to win the TTT, Garmin, lost four riders. (A team's time is based on the fifth rider across the line. If you're the sixth rider or later but you're still in contact, which is defined as a gap of less than a bike length, you receive the team time, but those who become separated and straggle in on their own receive their actual finishing time.) Garmin was still technically capable of winning, but the five riders left had to work harder, with fewer chances to recover. The loss of just two riders takes a physical toll: based on a 45-minute finishing time (to make the math easy), if you led a full team of nine riders who each took a 30-second turn at the front before swinging to the side and fading back into the last place in the line, you would get 4 minutes of rest before you recirculated to the front and you would take ten turns up there in total. But with just seven riders, you would get only 3 minutes to rest each time and would also spend 50 percent more time battling the wind—fifteen turns at the front.

Even the last kilometer, which after a lazy shallow curve finished in a wide-open straightaway, proved hazardous. Frustrated from his team's earlier missteps, contender Cadel Evans drove so hard from the front as soon as he saw the finish that Silence-Lotto split into pieces. Evans and Johan Vansummeren crossed the line together, then waited to be credited with a final time until a fifth teammate rolled in.

Astana knew all of this had taken place because it had the coveted final starting position. The start order was determined by the team standings, which is a ranking of the total ride time of each team's top three riders on every stage. The Spanish team Caisse d'Epargne, with a total of 29 hours, 39 minutes, 11 seconds for the three previous stages, would begin the team time trial at 2:30 p.m. Every seven minutes after that another team would roll down the ramp. (The buffer changes with every time trial, factoring in the distance and course difficulty to come up with a separation that, barring a catastrophic crash or outright collapse, is just small enough to prevent each team from catching the one that left previously. Padding the buffer would extend the length of the event beyond the patience of the riders and the fans—and the event's allotment of live TV time. No team would catch another today, although in individual events, which commonly have a one-minute separation, it is not unheard of for the strongest time trialists to pass their "minute man," or sometimes even their "two-minute man.")

As Astana, with a combined time of 29:34:04, rolls away from the ramp seconds after their 4:43 p.m. start, they have the advantage of knowing the state of the thirteen teams that have already finished. Katusha, a high-budget team funded by a collective of Russian businesses (and named for a Russian rocket launcher), has the best finish at 47:52. Other teams will finish as Astana rides, and Bruyneel will radio the information to the riders as he hears it—in a few minutes, for instance, Liquigas will cross the line with a new top time of 47:27. But most observers believe there is only one team's fate that matters to Armstrong, and that is the team that left 14 minutes ahead of them, Saxo Bank. If Astana beats Saxo by 41 seconds, Armstrong will take over the yellow jersey from Cancellara.

Armstrong doesn't lose many TTTs. His teams won the last three they were in. But not even he is certain they can beat Saxo, which will be powered primarily by a racer who is the greatest time trialist alive and possesses the yellow jersey. The jersey, like all hallowed sporting grails, has its lore. One of the tenets is that its wearer rides with the strength of two men. That would give Cancellara the horsepower of four average time trialists. Armstrong himself, however, is a sort of sporting grail all his own. Like the yellow jersey, he sometimes seems capable of bending the race to his will. In the Tour's 2005 TTT, his Discovery team was behind the pace of CSC (the predecessor of Saxo) and its yellow-jersey-wearing Dave Zabriskie. In the last 2 kilometers, Zabriskie clipped a teammate's wheel and crashed into the metal barriers lining the course. He finished 1:26 behind his team, which lost to Discovery by 2 seconds. Armstrong had won the stage and the jersey. Zabriskie will still barely talk about the incident to this day. With more resignation than rage, at the line that day Bjarne Riis, CSC's director, called Armstrong "the lucky golden guy."

Zubeldia swings off after a 40-second pull at the front and Muravyev drops his head to the wind and maintains the pace, which is all he's supposed to do. Even the stronger riders won't make a big jump in speed in the TTT; instead, they'll gradually increase the pace or simply take longer turns at the front to give the weaker riders more time to recover. Behind Muravyev tuck in Rast, then

Kloden, Armstrong, Popovych, Contador, Leipheimer, and Paulinho. Zubeldia drifts back past the line of his teammates, tucking
in close enough to them that their elbows could touch. When he is
just a couple of riders from the end, he begins to accelerate so he
is still drifting backward without losing ground as quickly. He is
traveling almost the same speed they are, which is necessary to
latch onto the tail of the line. A rider who drifts back too lazily
won't be able to slide right into the last rider's draft and will be
forced to waste valuable energy closing the gap—or be left behind.

The sky is bright blue and the clouds are immaculate white, but
the gusting wind batters the riders, and remaining in formation
exactly behind each other is difficult. To stay aligned they are using
energy they would rather be pouring into their pedals. Contador
stands out in his yellow-and-red Spanish TT champion skinsuit. Armstrong stands out, too, with a yellow-and-black Livestrong helmet
instead of the team-issue blue-and-yellow one, though less obviously.

At the first time check, at kilometer 10, they equal the pace set by
Garmin, which despite being down to five riders looks as if it could
win the race. Saxo is well behind. Astana cycles through its rotation:
after Muravyev, Rast, then Kloden—who Armstrong will later say
was riding like an animal—then Armstrong, Popo, Contador, Leipheimer, and Paulinho, then again Zubeldia at the front. They take
short, 15-second pulls before some of the corners so a fresh rider can
accelerate out of a turn, and sometimes they settle in for 40-second
pulls when Kloden or Leipheimer gnash their teeth at the wind. Rast
comes off the back after 14 minutes and is lost. When Muravyev falls
victim to the pace and vanishes, too, the team starts to fray. Space
develops between their wheels, and the wind rushes into it and slams
at each of them. Bruyneel calms them on the radio, and they come
together with Armstrong at the front and piston on, the seven remaining members of Astana, and when Armstrong's pull is done he
drifts back and pops up out of the saddle, standing to accelerate into
the draft. They go through the second time check, at kilometer 19.5,
in first place.

A few minutes later, Garmin finishes with the new best time: 46:47. Saxo, meanwhile, is getting faster and faster, recovering from a slow start by increasingly resorting to the tactic of just hanging on to Cancellara for all they're worth as he burns a hole through the wind. The team time trial of 2009 is shaping up as another timeless duel between Armstrong and whichever unlucky man happens to be in yellow. What most people don't know is that Armstrong decided he doesn't want to fight only the racer in yellow. He wants to fight them all.

He'll take the yellow jersey if he gets it, but that's not what he wants most.

Before the start, Armstrong had gone to Contador and told him that, no matter what was going on between the two of them, "Let's ride perfect and make this race almost impossible to win for others."

Most expert analyses held that Armstrong had to have the jersey today. For one thing, he might not get another chance—he was closer to it than Contador only because he'd snuck into that split the day before and because Contador hadn't been able to unleash himself in the mountains yet. For another thing, if Armstrong took ownership of the jersey, he also would take control of the team. Given the unwritten rules of cycling and Bruyneel's strong leadership, if Armstrong was in yellow, the pressure on Contador to not mount a guerilla attack in the mountains would be overwhelming. In fact, there was a chance that even if Andy Schleck or some other contender could ride away from a yellow-clad Armstrong, Contador might be employed not to chase but to stay with Armstrong to help him cross or reduce the gap. There was, additionally, a good chance that the whole Tour de France would come down to the only stage in which Contador could ride directly against Armstrong without suffering the disgrace of disrespecting the jersey: the final individual time trial, Stage 18, on July 28. By then, if Armstrong had regained a little of his golden luck and not lost much time in the mountains to Wiggins, Schleck, Evans, and Sastre, he might have ridden himself into good enough shape to beat them in the

TT—and Contador, too, especially if Contador was tired from working for Armstrong day after day. All of this not only seemed logical from a strategic point of view but fit with everything I knew of Armstrong.

The only problem was that the Armstrong I knew was not this Armstrong. He'd been uncharacteristically loose before the time trial—blasting music in his hotel room and mock headbanging to Iron Maiden, then at the bus goofing around with Ben Stiller, who'd come to see Armstrong at the Tour and disrupted the usually intense atmosphere of the team's final warm-up by climbing onto Armstrong's bike (mounted like the others on a stationary trainer outside the bus). Popovych had reached over from atop his bike and, laughing, clicked Armstrong's bike into harder gears, bogging down Stiller's already jerky pedaling. Armstrong had come and kicked Stiller off, but the actor was so awkward on the setup that he damaged the chain as he wrenched the bike around while dismounting—just four minutes before the start.

It wasn't a disaster—the mechanics could replace a chain in about thirty seconds—but it was a distraction and an interruption of the schedule Armstrong usually had planned down to the second. But he just laughed the incident off. And he seemed just as unflappable when it came to getting another jersey, telling his team to think only about winning the stage and putting the Tour out of reach for as many racers as they could, then maybe they'd take a look at the General Classification to see who would be wearing yellow the next day.

And once again, whether through chance or destiny or with the immutable combination of the two that seems summonable by life's lucky golden ones, the Tour de France was about to bend to Armstrong's will and provide him with the circumstances that would prove genuine his lack of lust for the yellow jersey.

In winning the stage, Astana finishes 40 seconds ahead of Saxo Bank—the exact margin by which Armstrong trails Cancellara in the GC.

The judges scramble to review the photo finish images, the rules regarding ties, the electronic timekeeping records that can be teased apart to two decimal points.

Armstrong is thirty-seven years and ten months old. The oldest bicycle racer to wear a yellow jersey in the modern era was Alberto Elli, at thirty-six in the 2000 Tour. In 1922, Eugène Christophe wore one when he was thirty-seven years and five months old. When race officials announce that Cancellara has kept the jersey by 0.22 of a second, Armstrong doesn't flinch, doesn't curse, doesn't shake his head or squeeze shut his eyes. He congratulates his team for turning in a ride that won the stage and, more than likely, caused some of their rivals to lose the Tour.

"Today," he says later, "the Tour de France is finished for some riders. It's difficult—with no disrespect—to make up that time."

Menchov loses 2:20 today and is 3:52 in total behind Armstrong. Evans loses 2:35 and drops to 2:59 behind; Sastre adds 1:37 to his deficit on Armstrong to take it to a total of 2:44. Pereiro loses 1:29 and sits 3:03 in arrears. Still to be reckoned with are Wiggins, who was one of Garmin's first five finishers and sits just 38 seconds back overall, and Andy Schleck, who was lucky enough to sit in Cancellara's slipstream and, at 1:41 back, is still in striking distance given that he's a pure climber and the mountains are yet to come. But Armstrong is correct: Stage 4 slashed the list of possible winners to himself, Contador, Wiggins, and Schleck.

Afterward, in the car on his way to a hotel, Armstrong's cheeks and nose are burned red from the wind. He looks fatigued and strained, and indisputably happy. "That's the way it is," he says about not getting the jersey. "I have no regrets. I don't look at it and lose sleep."

So many times over so many years I had witnessed Armstrong bend the Tour de France to his will. Now for the first time I wondered if the race was, as it did with everyone else, bending him. Reshaping him. After the race, Armstrong had said he wanted to apologize to Sastre, Vande Velde, and "the guys who were a presence in last year's Tour" for assuming he could've beaten them, and for attributing some of his desire to return to the sport to their performance in 2008. "I realized," he said, "'Oh, shit, this is harder than I thought.' That's the truth. I'm not going to be last. But it won't be like 2004, 2005, 2001. It's going to be a lot harder than I expected. That's as honest as I can say it."

The Tour de France ennobles men, turns them into heroes. Then eventually it turns its heroes into men, by humbling them. This is nothing new. But now, the Tour seemed to be turning Armstrong into a man who was more noble than he'd ever been as a hero.

STAGE 4 RESULTS

1. Astana	0:46:29
2. Garmin	+0:00:18
3. Saxo Bank	+0:00:40
8. Cervélo	+0:01:38
11. Rabobank	+0:02:21
13. Silence-Lotto	+0:02:36

GENERAL CLASSIFICATION

1. Fabian Cancellara, Saxo Bank	10:38:07
2. Lance Armstrong, Astana	+0:00:00.22
3. Alberto Contador, Astana	+0:00:19
4. Andreas Kloden, Astana	+0:00:23
5. Levi Leipheimer, Astana	+0:00:31
6. Bradley Wiggins, Garmin	+0:00:38
12. Christian Vande Velde, Garmin	+0:01:16
20. Andy Schleck, Saxo Bank	+0:01:41
29. Carlos Sastre, Cervélo	+0:02:44
35. Cadel Evans, Silence-Lotto	+0:02:59
72. Denis Menchov, Rabobank	+0:03:52

TOUR OF THE GILA
Silver City, New Mexico, 505 miles
APRIL 29–MAY 3, 2009

It Only Makes Him Stronger

Lance needed something.

He was calling for Johan. That much could be heard over the static that roiled the airwaves of the borrowed radios. But just as Lance said his team director's name, the buzzes and pops swelled to a towering squeal and crashed down over the rest of the sentence. Bruyneel tapped the handheld mic against the dash of the rented Volvo wagon five or six times, and with his free hand used the steering wheel to pull himself forward and up, craning for a view that would somehow let him see past or through the three idling cars in front of him, the five or six revving motorcycles, and the 175 cyclists planted with one foot on the ground.

"Hey, Lance," he said into the mic. "Hey, we don't get that."

The radio spat back enormous amounts of fuzz. Bruyneel held the mic up and regarded it as if it were a tick or some sort of burr he'd just pulled off his body. "Aye," he said in a groan.

Chris, the mechanic, leaned forward from his seat in the back and said, "We are lucky to have them, man."

Stage 2 of the Tour of the Gila—pronounced like the lizard— was minutes away from starting. Though his star rider wanted something Bruyneel could not identify, let alone deliver, he nodded his assent, or maybe his acceptance, to Chris. They were lucky to have the radios, and even luckier to be at the race at all.

Armstrong's rehab from the broken collarbone had gone well. He'd set up at his house in Aspen, where the scarce air at high altitude would boost his blood's oxygen-carrying ability beyond levels he could achieve in Austin. Carmichael was there to drive a car that carried food and clothes for the changing weather. Armstrong pumped out seven-hour rides on some days, on other days did two separate rides, and sometimes would do a road ride then go goof around for hours with one of the mountain or cyclocross bikes Trek had given him. He sometimes climbed five mountains in a day, picking out the biggest, toughest, and longest peaks. He went so high he frequently ran into snowpacked roads. And he rode through rain, freezing rain, hail, and snowstorms. He took full rest days but, more often, for recovery he'd drive down to lower altitudes to find dry streets and ride for only three or four hours.

"He did huge, huge volumes of training," Carmichael said. "The kind of intensity and training hours only Lance can sustain. It would tear most people down. It makes him stronger."

Anna came out, and his kids, and Lance went sledding with them, and swimming at the local rec center. Bob Roll dropped by. There was a small group of hotshot locals who could keep up with him if he was going a little easier and not for too long, and they showed him their favorite routes. The whole scene that month of April was laid-back, and that lack of stress plus the big hours on the bike and the bonus training benefit bestowed by the altitude seemed to be just what Armstrong had needed. Kevin Livingston, a former teammate who was running a training center down in Austin, flew in so he and Lance could do some interval and threshold tests, and the numbers surprised them all.

"Let's just say," Carmichael told me, "no one else could have done what he did in terms of progression in that short of a time."

"But the numbers were not good enough yet to win the Tour," I said.

"No. But good enough to ride the Giro to get good enough to win the Tour," Carmichael said, inadvertently illuminating the problem with the stellar numbers: they were test data, not race results. Bruyneel, especially, was convinced that Armstrong needed racing more than he needed training. "You can't run into someone else's bike in a lab test," he said to me with an honesty that more than anything else conveyed his worry about Armstrong's unease in the pack. "You can't get run over. You can't get dropped to the back of a group or hung out in the wind. Numbers become meaningless in a race."

Another person on Armstrong's team told me that although it was plain that Armstrong had to ride the Giro to be anywhere near the fitness he'd need in order to be competitive at the Tour (let alone try to win it), there was also concern that if Armstrong rode in the Giro he might never make it to the Tour—people were worried he'd crash out again. Bruyneel had hoped that by doing the Vuelta Castilla and a few other races Armstrong would have his old pack ease back by the time he entered the Giro—so that instead of using the month of May to get reacclimated to being in the pro peloton, Armstrong would be able to focus on adapting to the sheer physical effort of a three-week stage race.

Rehabbing his collarbone not only had set Armstrong back in his training but, more crucially, had cost him any chance to race in Europe before the Giro. Signing up to compete in the Gila had seemed like an ideal way to get at least some kind of race time before heading to Italy. The five-stage race in New Mexico was close to the Aspen training base; it was small enough and remote enough to avoid turning into a circus the way the Tour of California had; it would be a challenging but not decimating level of competition—some of America's top domestic pros, sprinkled in with plenty of aspiring young racers and guys who were hanging on to their dreams or love of competition by fitting their racing around regular jobs. And, as a bonus, Armstrong's participation could be perceived as an altruistic gesture: he was helping to save one of America's most cherished stage races. Because of dwindling sponsorship money in the tough economy, Gila's director, Jack Brennan, had announced back in February that the twenty-three-year-old race was on the verge of cancellation. Brennan was about $50,000 short of the $170,000 it cost him to put on the race. In March, the component company SRAM announced it would buy the title sponsorship, saving the race from immediate extinction. Its long-term prospects seemed to be bolstered in April, when Armstrong began hinting that he might do the race. Media coverage doubled, then tripled, then went somewhere far beyond that, Brennan said, gaining Gila the kind of exposure and prestige that could lead sponsors to secure its future.

But as usual with Armstrong, his motivations were complex enough to allow both fans and critics to find something to fix on. He no doubt didn't mind helping to save a struggling race. His participation would also benefit the investment that SRAM, the company he was a part owner of, had made in the race. He also released a statement linking his decision to his philanthropic efforts, but it felt like an afterthought: "Our goal is to raise awareness of the challenges New Mexicans face when it comes to fighting cancer and to make progress against this disease."

Just two days before the race, things got really complicated. The UCI made official a rumor that had been bouncing around: Astana could not compete in Gila. The decision was based on a rule that prohibited teams at Astana's level from participating in national-caliber races (those sanctioned by a country's cycling organization rather than the UCI). In Europe, this rule made sense: it allowed hundreds of second-tier teams to exist by preventing the biggest squads from pillaging small races to snap up publicity and prize money. But in the United States, there was no chance that a top-level team such as Columbia (technically an American squad but one that operated primarily in Europe) would fly back to wipe out the fields at local criteriums whose prize money wouldn't even equal the team's travel expenses. The rule was routinely and benignly ignored in the United States—by riders and the UCI—not only because it had no practical application but because when a top American racer happened to be back in the country and made a rare appearance at a local or regional race, it actually benefited the sport: publicity and attendance would spike. Earlier in the year Leipheimer had competed with no interference at Sea Otter, a national-level race. And the well-funded domestic team BMC (which the following year would step up to European-level racing) openly competed almost exclusively in the United States, even though it was technically licensed by the UCI at too high a level to do so.

Bruyneel said he understood that the UCI decided to enforce the rule strictly because Lance was involved; after being harshly criticized for waiving the rule that would have kept Armstrong from competing in the Tour Down Under, the organization wanted to avoid any appearance of granting him favoritism. But even so, Bruyneel needed his racer to race. He searched for loopholes in the rule, and proposed compromises, and eventually, it was agreed that Armstrong could race if he restricted himself to two teammates and didn't represent Astana. The day before the race began, Armstrong, Leipheimer, and Chris Horner found out they would race as Mellow Johnny's, an ad hoc team sponsored by the bike shop Armstrong owned in Austin. They'd shown up without a team car, radios, a full set of race wheels, or uniforms. Bruyneel and Chris the mechanic had scrounged up the gear they needed, and the bike shop had sent its signature yellow-star-on-black jerseys and shorts.

"Lance," said Bruyneel into the mic again. He frowned. His BlackBerry rang. He hit the receive button and fiddled with the earbud stuck in his left ear, then smiled. "Hello, Victoria," he said.

It was his daughter, calling her dad at work. He listened, tapping the staticky mic against the dash again. The race radio—separate from the team radio—barked out commands about the start, and Bruyneel reached over, still holding the team mic, and turned the volume to an inaudible level. "No, no, no. Sí," he said and, speaking to his daughter in a mix of English and Spanish, told her he had a beautiful present for her but it had to be a surprise. Over the race radio came a series of noises that sounded like a language spoken on a planet made of static—it was saying something urgent, but none of us could interpret it. Bruyneel shook his head and tossed the mic onto the dash, then smiled as he listened to Victoria, who was wheedling hard to find out what her present was. "I can't tell you," he said. "I can't. No, I cannot. I can't. I cannot. You will see. No. No, I can't. Ah. Aha. Aha. No. No, I can't. Oh, I have to go. I love you."

The race was starting. Bruyneel punched the gas pedal and reached for the mic for another try at Lance, and as I put a hand on the dash to brace myself, I said, "I can't believe you held out and didn't tell her what you bought."

He laughed and said, "I couldn't tell her. I couldn't tell her what it was. I didn't buy it yet." From the backseat, Chris let out a one-syllable hoot and reached forward and punched Bruyneel on the shoulder.

I suppose Bruyneel is intimidating—that's how he's generally described—but I've gotten to know him well enough that, while being aware of that component of his personality, I no longer register it as predominant. I think of him mostly in terms of his enthusiasm, and how it hides behind the most alert and perceptive wariness I've ever encountered. The forty-four-year-old Belgian raced for a dozen years as a pro, making up for his relatively modest physical gifts with an intense study of the intricacies of racing. He would never be a champion, but he realized that if he attacked when the champions had weakened each other or were watching each other too intently, he sometimes could beat them. He won two stages of the Tour, one of them by somehow managing to be the only rider who mile after mile could hang on to the wheel of an enraged Miguel Indurain—a feat that, when he sprinted around Indurain at the line, also gave him the yellow jersey for a single day in 1995. In the next year's Tour, during a high-speed descent of the Cormet de Roselend he slid in a gravelly corner and plunged over the side of the mountain, falling a hundred feet into the treetops below. I asked him once if he could remember what he was thinking as he fell, and in his matter-of-fact way he told me he thought, "I just rode off a cliff." Plagued by injuries from that wreck, and spinal damage suffered when he was eighteen and rode at high speed into a ditch to avoid an oncoming car, Bruyneel retired in 1998. Armstrong, who that year had just returned to the sport after recovering from cancer, had been one of those riders who'd been unable to stay with Indurain back in 1995, and he remembered watching the less-talented Bruyneel ride away to a victory and a yellow jersey. He asked Bruyneel to be the director of the U.S. Postal Service team, which at the time was a low-budget team that even Armstrong described as "the Bad News Bears of cycling." Bruyneel found in Armstrong the factor he'd always lacked to achieve his dream of winning the Tour: unspeakable physical potential. Armstrong, for his part, found something he'd never encountered: someone who matched—perhaps even exceeded—his desire for winning. Bruyneel also possessed something Armstrong had never had: race savvy. Together they were the ideal Tour de France champion.

In the car at Gila, Bruyneel swung the steering wheel with the heel of one hand and with the other pushed the mic button and said, "Okay. Lance."

There was nothing but soft static again, so I said, "What's the plan today?"

The radio scratched and snapped and Lance Armstrong's voice said, "Johan."

Bruyneel flicked a look over at me. He has dark hair, a cleft in his chin, and piercing blue eyes much like Armstrong's, though Bruyneel's communicate more humor. Just before he pushed the button to reply to Lance, he answered my question. He said, "Don't crash."

You Could See Who He Was

The first stage, a 151-kilometer route ending with an 8-kilometer climb that gained 2,100 feet in elevation, laid bare Armstrong's state of race-worthiness. After a flurry of attacks early on, a fifteen-rider breakaway had escaped and built a lead that grew to about three minutes. Horner went to the front of the pack and more or less dragged the startled peloton behind him all the way to the foot of the climb. The break was just 16 seconds ahead when Armstrong hit the base, and he set a pace that shed everyone but Leipheimer and six others.

"I looked back," Lance said, "and there were just four or five guys with us. Levi asked me if I could go any faster and I said no. So—bam!—he swung around me and went hard and everyone tried to go with him. But no. They were with me, not him."

Leipheimer won the stage. Armstrong came in 1:40 later. The finish was an uninhabited, unglamorous intersection that a race organizer had accurately described to me the day before as "two dirt roads and a cattle guard." (She had also warned us, "The town of Glenwood will be closed tomorrow. So take food and drinks.") Armstrong was talking casually to a few reporters and ten or so fans. "You can't simulate that in training," he said.

I hitched a ride back down from the mountaintop with the SRAM neutral support car. At the base, we stopped so riders who'd borrowed one of the SRAM wheels could come by to return it and pick up their flat one in exchange. A racer named John Hunt, who rode for a team called California Giant Berry Farms, asked us if he could bum a ride back to Silver City. He was forty-four—seven years older than Lance—and after eighteen years in the sport still had to fit his training in around a coaching job, but despite these compromising factors he had finished just a little more than half a minute behind Armstrong. On the drive to Silver City, in the backseat with Hunt, I asked him what he'd thought of Lance, how he'd looked.

"For a long time, he sat farther back in the pack than I imagined someone of his stature would," Hunt said. "He didn't seem nervous. He just seemed . . . he just seemed like one of us. Until we got to the climb. Horner had been doing all the work, when there was work to be done. Then we got to the climb and Lance just tore us apart. That's when you could see who he was."

"You mean who he is," I said. "He might have torn you up as he is, but who he once was would have just leveled that mountain."

Hunt shot me a look. He said, "Maybe. But maybe for a few seconds he was who he was."

He Needs to Put His Own Race First

Lance said, "I'm going to drop my vest."

"Okay," said Bruyneel into the mic. "We are on the right side."

"Hot today."

We were driving out of town at 25 to 30 mph, sitting three cars behind the peloton. Directly behind them was the com, the car that carried the *commissaire*, or chief race official. Behind the com was the SRAM neutral support car, and behind that was the race doctor's car. We got to be the first team car because Leipheimer was in first place. The rest of the team cars lined up behind us according to the order of their highest-placed rider. Behind them came the media vehicles, the VIP vehicles, and various others. Ahead of the race ran a caravan of lead vehicles, including another com car and more media and VIPs, all escorted by police motorcycles. This was a standard formation; though the Tour of the Gila was a two-dirt-roads-and-a-cattle-grate affair, it was still a stage race and followed the peculiar rules of stage racing. What appears to uninformed observers to be anarchy on the road is in fact chaos contained within a highly regimented and formal structure.

For instance, under normal conditions all the cars had to drive on the right side. If a rider wanted to interact with his team car for some reason—to get water bottles or food or more clothes, or to have the mechanic lean out of the window and adjust a brake or shifter while they all rolled along—the rider would swing left out of the pack and raise his hand. The com would announce over the race radio that team X could come up. That car would swing to the left and accelerate until it had passed the other cars, then pull in front of them and perform whatever task its rider required. Then it would gradually make its way back to its designated spot by drifting down the right side as each car behind it moved left to let it pass.

A rider who had a flat or other problem would raise his hand as soon as he detected the problem, which helped the com identify the difference between a voluntary call for the team car, which was generally given from outside the pack, and a mechanical. Then the rider would drift out to either side, although the right shoulder was preferable. If the team car was close behind, it would stop and assist its rider. If not, the neutral support car would stop to help.

If you wanted to pass the pack—either to get to your team's riders in a breakaway, or if you were media or a VIP and wanted to drive ahead of the race—you had to drive up on the left behind the motorcycle referee who acted as a gatekeeper. He could hold you there until he thought the road was wide enough and the pack was calm enough to allow safe passage, or else he could send you back to your spot in the caravan. If given permission to pass, you couldn't drive beside the riders for long; you had to go directly through, although photographers on motorcycles were given some leeway.

It's a simple system. And it's easy to understand—until several cars are trying to feed their riders at once and two moto photographers want to drive through the pack as well as a media van and a wagonful of VIPs, and over on the right a rider is beside the road waiting to get a wheel change just as a breakaway opens up a big enough gap that the com thinks it's safe to allow all the team directors who have a rider represented in the break to drive through the pack so they can sit behind the lead group. In the bigger races, each team gets two cars and there are more coms and referees. There are often times when team cars are screaming down a twisty mountain descent three wide on a two-lane road while motos zip between them and a team car is trying to make its way backward through the caravan at the same time that a rider with a flat starts skittering all over the road trying to keep his bike up. And generally as this is happening Bruyneel will be talking on the team radio and his BlackBerry while also looking at the map of the stage cut out of the race bible and taped to the steering wheel.

"There it is," said Chris, his practiced eye spotting from the backseat the white vest lying in a pile on the right shoulder. Bruyneel slowed a little, and Chris opened the door, leaned out, and scooped up the vest as we drove past. Neither of them commented on this maneuver.

Chris was not sitting in the back because of me. The mechanic always rides back there surrounded by wheels, components, a cooler full of food and bottles filled with energy drinks, a spare map, and piles of clothes. One of his jobs is to find and hand items up to the director in the front seat, who passes them to riders. More dramatically, when a rider gets a flat, the mechanic flings open the door and leaps out before the car comes completely to a stop, changes the wheel, and returns to the backseat in about fifteen to twenty seconds. In urgent situations, the mechanic will hang out the rear window and fix a bike on the roll.

Bruyneel told Lance we had his vest. The com announced that a break had gotten away and gave the numbers of the riders. Bruyneel listened to this and repeated it over the race radio. In the back, Chris was writing the numbers down. Bruyneel waited almost exactly one minute, then repeated the numbers to the team again. He waited a minute, then did it again. Most people imagine that the team radio communication is filled with banter and inside information. There is some joking around, but for the most part, at least on Bruyneel's teams, the exchanges are banal and redundant: the expression of information in its plainest form. Over and over and over. "In terms of strategy," Bruyneel has told me, "bike racing isn't that hard. There are only three or four real tactics. What's hard is being able to think clearly during a bike race. What's hard is remembering what you were told two minutes ago or who is in a break or how far away the climb is."

When the com announced that the break had a one-minute gap,

Bruyneel clicked the button on the mic and said, "Just one minute to the break." He waited about thirty seconds, then said, "One minute to the break, so don't worry." He waited another thirty seconds, then said, "Just one minute, so no need to do anything. Other people are going to get excited and chase it." Then he called his wife on the BlackBerry. Chris handed up a sheet of paper, and Bruyneel read it while he talked to Eva and looked at the map on the steering wheel, and, of course, drove. He said goodbye to Eva and into the mic said, "Okay, boys: four riders in the break. Closest guy is three minutes twenty-two seconds behind Levi. Three twenty-two. So take it easy, boys. Take it easy." Each time he talked, Lance or Levi would confirm that they understood what he'd said.

Around halfway through the stage, Chris leaned forward and said, "Here comes Taylor." Taylor Phinney, who rode for Armstrong's Livestrong developmental team, had been dropped on the second climb of the day and on the flats and rollers was making his way back to the pack. "Let's give him bottles," Chris said. If Taylor would take water to the front, it would save Horner a trip back through the pack.

Bruyneel rolled down his window and when Taylor drew even said, "Are you going to the front?"

"I'm fine," said Taylor.

Bruyneel smiled. This was what he'd been talking about—the difficulty of merely thinking during a race. He pointed ahead and said, "Are you going to ride all the way up to the front?"

"Do you want me to?" Taylor asked.

"No, no. But if you are, can you take bottles?"

"I'm going to the front," Taylor said.

Bruyneel nodded and cocked his right hand over the seat back. Chris put a bottle in it, and Bruyneel handed the bottle out to Taylor, who took it and stuck it in one of the jersey pockets on his back. Bruyneel did this three times, and each time he counted the bottle out for Taylor. "One." Then: "Two." On the third bottle, he held on to it for five seconds or so, and so did Phinney. Bruyneel gunned the gas and swung left so we could creep up past the car in front of us, then he let go of the bottle, slinging Taylor ahead. Technically, that was an illegal tactic.

Bruyneel watched Phinney leave to perform the favor, then said, "He needs to put his own race first, you know?"

Around 25 miles from the finish, the com announced that the gap had grown to 2:55 and that another group had gotten away from the pack and was closing in on the break. Bruyneel clicked the mic and said, "Okay, guys. All kinds of information. Break has two fifty-five. Two minutes fifty-five seconds. Two fifty-five. There are three riders going to join. That will make seven. BMC should work with us. Talk to them, Levi. If they won't work, tell Chris to say fuck it and sit up."

But the radio, which had been working fine, suddenly rumbled out nothing but static. Bruyneel repeated his instructions. More static and hisses. He dropped the mic, swung left, accelerated, and pulled even with the com car, hitting the switch to roll my window down as he did. He leaned over me and shouted, "I need to go up front and say something to my riders."

"Old school," said Chris, soft and with appreciation. This was how directors talked to their riders before radios: you drove up into the pack. The coms in the car looked at each other, got on their radio, and flipped through some booklets, and Bruyneel revved our car as they did so, nosing it up ahead of the com car, then back, up, then back.

"Sorry," said the driver. "Com one says no."

Bruyneel took both hands off the wheel in a gesture of exasperation. "No," he said. "No, you are kidding." He punched the window button and rolled it up. We dropped back into our place, and he picked up the mic and said, "I can't hear you. I don't know if you can hear me. It is now seventeen miles to the finish. We'll see. As I told you this morning, it doesn't matter to me. We can give the jersey up for this stage."

We hit the base of the final climb, and as we labored up the slope it was as if someone had loaded a bunch of racers into a shot-gun, pointed it at us, and fired. At times Bruyneel had to nearly come to a standstill to pick his way through the carnage. Horner was at the front destroying the race.

I said, "I wonder if, instead of hearing you say 'fuck it and sit up,' the static made them think you said 'fuck it up.'"

Chris laughed. Bruyneel kind of grunted. "Horner is flying," he said, nodding.

With 5 miles to go, Horner had brought the pack to within 1:30 of the break. From there, everyone knew the sprinters' teams would make sure the gap was erased. The pack was going about 40 mph. Bruyneel picked up the mic and said, "Boys, it's going to be danger-ous. Very dangerous. Dangerous, boys. Stay out of the sprint. No risks."

The radio worked.

Lance said, "No risks."

Not Having a Good Day

"What's the plan today?" I asked when I got in the car.

It was the last stage, and the most fearsome—a 170-kilometer race known as the Gila Monster, with 9,131 feet of elevation gain over six climbs. The route started in Silver City, went over the Continental Divide, then plunged down straight to the base of an 11-kilometer ascent to the Clinton Anderson Vista (at 7,493 feet the highest point of the five-day event). The riders descended that, then dashed along a short, flat road to a turnaround and rode smack back into the climb—which was steeper from its backside. Once they came down off that, a 17-kilometer climb still stood between them and the finish. The map in the race bible carried descriptions such as "dangerous descent," "use caution," and "blind corners." The roads were narrow, with sheer drop-offs and no shoulders in many places.

Leipheimer had the victory locked up. He'd won the Stage 3 time trial with a new course record. And despite damaging his bike when he got caught behind a crash with two laps to go in the Stage 4 downtown criterium, he'd finished with the same time as the winners—thanks to Horner, who'd been following Levi and quickly dismounted and gave his bike to his captain, then limped in on the crashed bike. Armstrong had finished third in the time trial, 1:23 slower than his teammate, and stayed safely in the bunch during the crit.

If ever there was a time for Armstrong to play it safe this season, it was on the last day of the last race before the Giro d'Italia, on a stage the bible made sound about as venomous as the race's namesake.

Bruyneel said, "Did you bring gummies?"

This was my pass into the car: Haribo gummy candies. For years the company had sponsored races and teams in Europe, most famously the Haribo Classic in France from 1994 to 2006, and it still maintained a major presence in the Tour de France caravan—throwing samples to spectators during the commercial parade that preceded the race along the entire route every day. They were the favorite bon-bon (Euro-speak for candy) of many racers and ex-racers. I pulled a fresh bag out of the backpack that sat in the floor at my feet, tore it open, and passed it to Bruyneel.

He took a few, tossed them in his mouth, and chewed, and when he was done, he said, "Today, Lance goes for the win."

I pulled a shark out of the bag of candy and studied it. Why had I called it a shark in my mind? It was a candy. But it *was* also a shark. I held it by the tail as if it were a miniature trophy fish and waggled it between me and Bruyneel.

"Hey, Chris," I said. "What is this?"

"I don't want any," he said. He was looking down at the course map.

"Chris," I said. "Hey—is this a shark or a candy?"

"No," he said. He looked up, folding the paper in his hand and stuffing it into a pile of papers and energy bars beside him. "None for me."

Sixteen riders attacked on the descent coming out of Silver City, and the pack seemed content to let them go. The gap grew to about 3 minutes, but Bruyneel was unflustered. "The day doesn't start until we turn around and come back up that big hill," he said. The mood in the car today seemed more tense, more serious. There was something at stake besides training miles.

When the team, along with the main pack, started the first climb to Clinton Anderson Vista, Bruyneel said into the mic, "So, boys, remember the downhill of this climb is very, very dangerous. Crashes every year. Very, very dangerous."

I knew better than to ask why the strategy for Armstrong had changed from "don't crash" to "win the stage." Bruyneel had done the psychological math in his head and figured out that the value of a victory was greater by an order of magnitude than the risk of a Giro-ending crash. Later in the season, he would admit to me that he thought a win on this day was almost necessary.

"Pay attention on this downhill," Bruyneel said to the team. "Pay attention. Watch the downhill. Pay attention on this downhill."

The climb had stretched the pack out, then broken it into several groups, as if each string of riders were a section of a rope that gravity had pulled on until it snapped. The car caravan was stuck behind the slowest group, which meant that our riders at the front were getting out of the range in which we could quickly reach them and offer assistance if anything went wrong. Bruyneel swung out of line and drove up next to the com car. He leaned down and looked right, into their car, and pointed forward, signaling his intention to move past the stragglers. In Europe this is routine. But the com driver shook her head.

"Aghh!" growled Bruyneel. He honked his horn and pointed forward, and again a no came from the com car. He picked up the

ABOVE After the Stage 4 team time trial was over, Armstrong (second in line) had missed taking the yellow jersey by twenty-two hundredths of a second—but he seemed happy that Astana had distanced most of its rivals.

RIGHT After 21 days and 3,459.5 kilometers of racing, the man Armstrong calls "maybe the greatest ever" can finally raise his hands in victory as he crosses the finish line in Paris.

TOP With the Arc de Triomphe in the background (and Frank Schleck still shadowing him), Contador rode the final laps of the Champs-Élysées knowing he was the first Tour champion to bring down Armstrong since 1999.

ABOVE RIGHT When he won atop Verbier, Contador made a pistol of his hand and fired off an imaginary shot—and the victory salute became his trademark.

ABOVE LEFT On the mountains of Stage 16, "Lance did a lot of work," Contador (in his first day in the yellow jersey) said. "But I didn't need his help."

At rest, Contador is quiet and almost shy—a personality completely at odds with his persona during the race.

RIGHT By winning the Stage 18 time trial, Contador would prove he was fresher and stronger than all of his rivals—including Armstrong, who finished 16th, 1:29 behind his teammate.

BELOW In the Tour's third week, Contador felt so isolated from his teammates that after the time trial he could joke about his earpiece falling out: "It's okay. I'm used to it."

The first comeback: Armstrong was diagnosed with cancer on October 2, 1996, underwent surgery almost immediately, and endured chemotherapy through mid December. He began training seriously in January 1998 but wouldn't become a Tour champion until he hooked up with Johan Bruyneel for the 1999 season.

ABOVE After Contador destroyed the race on the final climb of Stage 15, Armstrong (leading here on Stage 16) said, "I'm a *domestique*," and vowed to work for his teammate and rival.

RIGHT "Armstrong—why not?" asks a French spectator who seems, like many in France, to have become a Lance fan as the champion struggled and showed a more human side.

Armstrong was so mobbed at the Tour and other races that he often couldn't even move through the crowd without a phalanx of bodyguards.

Instead of routinely speaking to journalists at press conferences, during the Tour Armstrong taped his remarks, and Astana's press director, Philippe Maertens (seated), would play them to a crushing mob of reporters.

A specially designed "Chalkbot," conceived and created by Armstrong sponsor Nike, drove along roads of the Tour spraying personal messages from his fans onto the pavement.

Bruyneel (left) talked Armstrong out of abandoning the comeback after his crash in Spain; then, from the team car, he directed him to an increasingly improved performance in the Giro d'Italia that, by the end of the race, surprised many skeptics with its power.

LEFT In the moments before the opening time trial, Armstrong enjoyed a sensation he'd missed dearly during his retirement—the sensation of butterflies in his stomach.

BELOW Armstrong might have been older, but he showed up leaner than he'd been for any of the Tours he'd won when he was younger—so much so that his custom-fitted jerseys hung loose around his arms.

TOP A former track-racing specialist, Bradley Wiggins showed up spectrally thin and haunted Armstrong and Contador all the way to Mont Ventoux.

ABOVE When it came to anything having to do with the Tour, Bruyneel (left) and Contador (center) never saw eye to eye.

When Armstrong passed me on this climb in Stage 17, sweating and blowing spit from his mouth, I ran a few steps beside him and screamed wild encouragements into his ear—I'd become an unapologetic fan.

LEFT Ryszard Kielpinski—Richard—hands Armstrong a drink at the end of the Stage 18 time trial.

BELOW Andy Schleck, Contador, and Armstrong on the final podium in Paris.

race radio, pushed the button, and said to the officials, "How much time do we need? How much gap before we can drive up?"

"I'm getting told by com one not to let anyone through," the com replied. The window of the car came down and she stuck her arm out.

"The donut!" screamed Chris.

Her hand was holding a round red sign on a stick handle. It meant no one could pass. The other side was green, and when she flipped the sign around we'd be able to drive by. They'd been seeing this all week, apparently.

"I hope she gets tendonitis," Chris shouted.

"The red donut!" Bruyneel spat out. He pounded the steering wheel. Chris gargled some deep-throated, mucus-tinged words that I assumed were Flemish obscenities. Then Bruyneel picked up the team radio. In a voice so calm that the donut might never have existed, he said "Okay, guys, we are not behind the peloton. We are not behind the peloton. We cannot get through. So careful down. And study: what we go down now we come back up after the turn-around. Pay attention."

The road topped out and we came over the crest onto a precipitous, narrow, shaded strip of asphalt. Chris whistled, and Bruyneel drove two wide alongside the com. A small pack of riders, three or four, were knotted in the center of the road in front of us. Just ahead of them was another small bunch.

To see a group of top cyclists descend a mountain is to watch a thing with the feel of inevitability, as if the riders sweeping line to line on the road in their plummet embody the flow of time as sure as the arcing from side to side of a pendulum. There is also the kind of awe you get at witnessing nature's plain graces, when you happen to spot a hawk diving or see a porpoise streaming beside a boat. The guys in front of us, however, were fighting the descent, braking too hard, cutting lines too tight on corners or drifting too far, shying from each other instead of slipstreaming.

"*Cascadeurs,*" said Chris. I turned and looked at him with my eyebrows raised. Pantomiming a plunge with his curved hand, he said, "Off a cliff. Like a waterfall."

If we had to follow these guys, we might still be descending this road as the leaders had already turned around and started back up—hopelessly beyond contact with the team. The com must have realized this, because the donut flipped to green. Without a word, Bruyneel pinned the gas pedal to the floor, and the car jumped. We swept past the com, the medical car, and the moto referee and in a hairpin corner passed the terrified riders. Chris was chortling in the back. Bruyneel steered with one hand and with the other clicked the mic and said, "Here we come, boys."

We caught them on the flat after the turnaround, just before they started back up the climb. "Chris," Bruyneel said to Horner over the team radio. "You start to drive it, eh?"

The race at last came fully undone, the final intractable knot sliced apart by Horner's pace. We drove through blown riders as if they were a fog in front of us, and soon just a small group labored behind Horner. There were Lance and Levi; Phil Zajicek, a five-foot-nine, 139-pound American riding for the Canadian team Fly V Australia; Burke Swindlehurst, a tall and sinewy climber—five foot eleven, 145 pounds—riding for Bissell Pro Cycling and who'd won Gila the previous year and in 2005; his teammate Tom Zirbel, a big powerful all-rounder who'd won two stages at Gila the previous year; Chris Baldwin, who'd won the Gila overall in 2006; Peter Stetina, a twenty-two-year-old prodigy who was riding for Garmin's developmental squad and had finished second behind Levi on the Stage 1 climb that Lance had broken up; and two BMC riders.

"Horner has exploded it!" Bruyneel said to the team. "Horner has exploded it. Good job, boys. Good job. Don't let up, Chris. You are killing them. You are killing them, Chris."

To Chris the mechanic, Bruyneel said, "Stetina will probably fall off. I heard he is sick, and anyway is young. Zirbel is too big and won't help Swindlehurst much longer. Swindlehurst is tough, but I think we can distance him with Levi and Horner punching on the final climb. Baldwin, too. But I don't know about Zajicek. He's in fifth, but I don't know if he's fast at a finish."

Chris shook his head. He looked at the copy of the overall standings he had with him and said, "Yeah, he's in fifth. Thirty-three seconds behind Lance. I don't know."

Horner dragged the riders up through the remnants of the early breakaway and past them, and we drove through them, too.

We were just behind the tiny pack now, a com car and one support car in front of us, but with the small pack and open road we were free to drive far to the left so we could see Horner working and the guys behind him bobbing. Chris the mechanic said, "Horner, man," and, thinking about endurance, he told a story about a twenty-something woman who'd come to stand in front of the team bus that day at 7 a.m. She was holding up a bike frame for Lance to sign, up high above her head to make sure she'd get his attention whenever he happened to show up. "She held it for thirty-five minutes," Chris said. "Straight. So I went over to talk to her, and she told me, 'It's for my boyfriend in Iraq.' I told her you never know if Lance will sign, but she should keep holding it because she'd already been there so long that what was a little more time?"

Bruyneel clicked the mic and said, "Hold that pace, Chris. Don't back off. You are hurting them all."

"He signed the frame," said Chris from the backseat.

Horner stayed at the front over the top, and down the descent, and on to the last big climb of the day. Stetina and Baldwin, who were in second and third overall, dropped back from the pack and faded, and we drove past them. Bruyneel turned to watch them as we passed. He lifted a hand to Stetina. "Good kid," he said. Then he clicked the mic and said, "Levi, tell Zajicek that second and third just dropped and he can get third if he works with us. Two and three are dropped. Zajicek should work. Chris, let Zajicek work."

But Horner kept pulling, hammering away at his pedals. Lance stayed tucked in behind Levi. Bruyneel seemed to be studying the riders for ten or fifteen seconds, silent, then he said to me and Chris, "If Horner hits them, the only guy who will follow is Zajicek. The others look like toast. It will be Horner, Levi, Lance, and Zajicek then. But I don't know if we want to try on this climb or wait for the little one to the finish."

Levi's voice crackled over the radio, asking for a bottle. He raised his hand, came off the group, and drifted back to us. Bruyneel drove forward around the com, and rolled his window down and pulled even with Levi and said, "Do you need any gels?"

"No, thank you," said Levi. Chris handed two bottles one by one to Bruyneel, who handed them one by one to Levi through the window, counting, "One. Two," as he did so. Always the same routine. After Levi rode away and we drifted back past the com car, Bruyneel said, "Fucking Levi. A walk in the park."

Lance raised his hand. Bruyneel honked and we drove past the com and pulled alongside Lance. His skin was shiny with sweat; his jersey and shorts were sopped. He looked into the car and said, "What do you want to do?" and took a breath.

"Let's wait for the last little climb at the end," Bruyneel said. "How are your legs?"

"Okay."

He rode beside us for a few seconds, then said, "I'm here." He shook his head.

"The other guys are fucked," said Bruyneel.

"Okay," said Lance.

"Wait for the last climb and go. You can win it."

"Yeah."

"First victory of the comeback."

Armstrong appeared to be, as Bruyneel might have described it, a little fucked. But he also looked old. It was something about the way the skin hung at his cheeks, a softness under the chin, a retreat around the eyes and the wrinkling erosion of his face. When young riders become worn away by the sport they look gaunt, and take on the appearance of greyhounds; for the first time I realized that

Lance was like the other veterans of the road, inhabiting a spooky grizzledness, as if they'd all been on a long journey to the same place, had seen where time was taking all of us.

He took a bottle from Bruyneel—"One"—and hung on a few seconds for the slingshot, and Bruyneel rolled up the window and we dropped back behind the com. Nobody said anything for a bit. After a while Bruyneel finally picked up the mic and said, "Okay, boys. Okay."

We were still climbing. One of the BMC riders attacked in a hairpin and Bruyneel shouted, "Woop woop woop!" into the mic, and Lance and Levi jumped across the gap and slotted in behind the rider. Horner fell away from the group, seeming to falter for the first time all day, then visibly sat up with his hands on the top of the handlebar and floated back down the hill, past the com car and past us. Bruyneel had already rolled down the window, and he slowed the car to keep pace with Horner for a few seconds and said, "Good job. But keep going. Keep riding. You never know."

"I will," Horner said. His eyes looked furry—not glazed or watery but dense with fatigue. We pulled forward, and Horner vanished behind us. Levi took over the pacemaking and dropped Swindlehurst. Lance attacked, and Zajicek followed him immediately. Bruyneel clicked the mic and said, "Zajicek is there, Lance. Zajicek is there." The riders regrouped, and Swindlehurst rode back up to them.

"He's not . . ." Bruyneel shook his head. "He's not having a good day."

Lance raised his hand. We honked through the com, and Lance drifted back. He leaned into the window and said, "Is there another hill?" He was having trouble thinking.

"There is one more hill after this," Bruyneel said. "The finishing one. Look." He pulled the profile map of the stage off the steering wheel and held it out so Lance could see it.

"Okay," said Lance. "There's one more hill."

He rode back to the group.

Swindlehurst got dropped again, and the BMC rider attacked and we rode up over the crest and started downhill. Lance threw his water bottle off to the side of the road. A full water bottle weighed a pound, and that was one less pound he'd have to carry up the last climb.

Horner rode alongside us just before the climb to the finish. Bruyneel jumped a little when Horner appeared in the window and nodded to us without really looking in at us. Everything in him was focused on clawing his way back to the group. Bruyneel rolled down the window and screamed, "Come on, Chris! Come on!" He grabbed the mic and said, "Levi, slow it down a little. Horner is back. Horner is coming to you. Chris is here! Chris is here!" When he reached the tiny, four-person group, Horner rode right to the front and began pulling.

"Motherfucker," said Chris the mechanic.

"Okay," said Bruyneel into the mic. "Chris, keep the speed high high high, and when you are done, Levi, you go. Lance, you wait. Wait. Wait. Wait and win it in a sprint. Just stay on the wheel here, Lance. Wait. Wait. Wait . . . wait . . . wait . . ."

We were in the final mile. A sign told us there was 800 meters to the finish. There were starting to be spectators scattered in pairs, threes, fours, then full lines of people running the length of the road. Bruyneel took a deep breath, then clicked the mic and shouted, "Levi, blow it up! Lance! Go!"

Armstrong sprinted out of the saddle, bashing his bike from side to side under him, but Zajicek followed, then sprinted around and crossed the line for the win.

"Shit!" Bruyneel screamed, banging his fist against the steering wheel. "Fuck." Then a single, guttural Flemish roar of an obscenity.

A course marshal waved us off into the deviation marked for the team cars, and Bruyneel parked and shut the car off and sat for a moment with his head down. "He didn't have the legs," he said.

We opened the doors and got out and walked into the mob scene

that is every finish of every pro bike race ever held. There was Zajicek, his arms high, his girlfriend with her arms thrown around his
shoulders. He appeared to be just done crying. Armstrong was pushing through the crowd to get to the team car. Bruyneel put a shoulder into the journalists and fans surrounding Zajicek, stuck out his
hand and said, "Great race," and talked a few seconds, then walked
away.

"That was the biggest win of my life," Zajicek said to everyone.

I walked around a little, watching some of the others finish,
shell-shocked, dirty, reeking, some of them shivering. I saw Bruyneel and walked over to him. He was being interviewed by Billy
Witz of the *New York Times*. As I came over, I heard Bruyneel saying, "We could have won if we'd decided to win for the team, but
we thought it was worth the risk to try to win with Lance." Witz or
someone else asked Bruyneel if he was disappointed, and if Lance
was disappointed. "Ah, it's bike racing," Bruyneel said. "He's a bike
racer for a long time, he's lost a lot of races. You lose a lot more
bike races than you win. Racers know that."

Witz kept doing his job, which was essentially asking the same
question in a lot of different ways, trying to get the answer everyone sensed was true: this was a disappointment. And Bruyneel kept
doing his job, which was to give the media an answer that was true
enough without betraying anything about the team.

Once when Witz paused, another voice brayed, "Do you really
feel confident going into the Giro now?"

Bruyneel looked around the crowd. All of his attention had
been on the *New York Times*, the biggest paper here, the one that
everyone around the world would read, and the most important
interview to get right.

The man who had spoken leaned in from where he'd been
standing behind Witz, stuck his chin past the reporter's shoulder,
then stepped up in front of Bruyneel. It was an older man wearing
Lucky jeans held up by a brown snakeskin-patterned belt, green
Pumas, a blue T-shirt that said LEVI IN '08 in a mock election slogan,

and an Ouch hat signed by several riders. He had his hands at his waist, with his fingers sticking out, and he repeated his question.

Bruyneel regarded him. The questioner was not a reporter, just a fan. The other reporters looked at the man. Bruyneel smiled. He said, "Yes, I feel confident going into the Giro. All I have to do is push on the gas pedal. For me it is easy." Trying for a joke.

The man, Jim Levi, an orthopedic surgeon who lived in Tucson and had gotten up at five-thirty that morning and driven 220 miles to be there at the top of the hill, said, "I mean the team." Pressing for an answer.

Goddamn, Bruyneel thought. *Everyone pushing.* He sighed and gave Jim Levi a version of the same answers he'd been giving the reporters.

Nobody could know how much they wanted to win.

TOUR DE FRANCE, STAGE 5
Le Cap d'Agde–Perpignan, 196.5 km
JULY 8, 2009

Everyone knows the early breakaway is going to be allowed to run for a while when behind the six escaped riders much of the peloton pulls to the side of the road for a mass *arrêt pipi*—a pee stop. Though the course heads inland from the coast just briefly before turning south to parallel the Mediterranean, the winds today are not blowing in from the water but southward from the Pyrenees mountains. The pack will have a tailwind most of the day. About 30 kilometers from the end, where the route makes a U-turn toward the finish town of Perpignan, the wind suddenly will be in their faces. Most of the riders think Cancellara is going to ask Saxo to try to split the peloton there the way Columbia did in Stage 3. But that's about four hours away, and the 80-degree sun feels good on their muscles, and many of them are tired or banged up from the team time trial the day before, so the pack is happy enough to allow the breakaway some open road.

Besides, one of the six in the break is Thomas Voeckler, a Frenchman riding for Bbox. He's popular with the pack, and Bbox was one of the previous day's bad-luck teams, so there's a general though unvoiced feeling that Voeckler is worthy of some time out front, some publicity for his sponsor, some heroics in front of his countrymen. Five years ago to the day, a largely unknown, twenty-five-year-old Voeckler snuck into an unlikely break that ended up finishing 12 minutes ahead of the pack, and he took the yellow jersey with a huge 9:35 lead over Armstrong. The gap was larger than Bruyneel and Armstrong had hoped to grant, but their strategy was intact: the responsibility of protecting the jersey across the next several flat stages would fall on Voeckler's team, allowing U.S. Postal Service to conserve its energy until the race reached the crucial stages in the Pyrenees mountains, where Armstrong figured to get into yellow for good. But Voeckler mounted one of the most improbable jersey defenses of the modern age, holding on to his lead for ten days. With his face contorted and his body shivering, Voeckler rode in a way nobody—not even himself—ever would have guessed he could, and on the first day in the Pyrenees, on the massive Col de Tourmalet, he preserved half of his lead over Armstrong. On the second day, he saved the jersey by 22 seconds, repeatedly climbing back into contention after getting dropped on Plateau de Beille. "I did it on guts alone," Voeckler said. He kept the jersey through the flat stages that followed as a transition to the Alps, then lost it to Armstrong on the first day of that round of climbing. Possessing the yellow jersey and riding like two men was one thing, but riding like Armstrong in the third week of a Tour was another. But even the legend had been impressed by the suffering Voeckler was able to endure. "When you have a rider like Voeckler who gets dropped and then comes back, gets dropped and comes back and fights all the way to the end, and he keeps the yellow jersey, he absolutely earned it, he deserves it," Armstrong told Cyclingnews.com after the finish on Plateau de Beille. "He absolutely deserves to have that jersey for another day or however long until he loses it."

Today, though, there is no thought of the yellow jersey for Voeckler or anyone else in the break, or for Armstrong or anyone else in the pack besides Cancellara. The race will be hard when they turn into the wind, but until then they are sailing and the course is easy, with just two small climbs. They even stop at a railroad crossing, forced to wait for a train to pass. It is as if the Tour de France itself is taking a breath.

As they mill along the road in the pack, they are chatting and bumping shoulders the way people at a party jog each other in greeting, and sometimes one of them squirts a stream of water onto the back of a friend who left for another team, or in passing reaches into the other's jersey pocket and lifts out an energy bar or gel, making sure to get caught in the act so thief and victim have a chance to laugh.

In all of this, Carlos Sastre finds himself for a moment riding beside Armstrong.

Sastre's Tour win in 2008 was not much appreciated by the general public but was applauded by many who deeply love the Tour. After years of turmoil and scandal, the race had rewarded Sastre, a quiet, classy winner who made one big move at the perfect time. And he deserved the win: in the 2002 Tour he was tenth, the next year ninth, the year after that eighth, then fourth and third in two of the next three years before his victory. His name had never been connected to any doping scandal, not even by hints, and he won the Tour with a brave sustained solo attack on one of its most beloved climbs, Alpe d'Huez. Sastre is one of those racers who is either the personification of his riding style, or else his riding style is the manifestation of who he is. He is so slight as to be wispy, at five foot eight and 130 pounds not so much a diminutive person as the distillation of one. He has sad-looking eyes, straight eyebrows, and upward-curving wrinkles on his forehead under tightly curled black hair. He carries himself with dignity more than pride.

Armstrong's dismissal of Sastre's Tour win was true to his character and even in a way justifiable—those guys weren't riding with the aggression and force Armstrong had brought to the race. But because the insult landed upon Sastre, it felt less like sporting trash talk than petulance. And it only amplified Sastre's class. He and his win—and the Tour itself—had been denigrated by the greatest rider of his generation; he acknowledged that he'd been wounded by the remark and that was all.

Riding there beside Armstrong today, Sastre is without hope of winning the Tour de France. Yesterday his team finished 1:37 behind Astana (with Armstrong and Contador), 1:10 behind Garmin (with Vande Velde and Wiggins), and 57 seconds behind Saxo (with Andy Schleck). Combining that with getting stuck on the slow side of the Stage 3 split and the time lost in the opening time trial, even Sastre knows he is no longer in contention. Still, this morning before the stage he had ridden around to the teams that had done well and congratulated them.

Now as he rides beside Armstrong, he offers his personal congratulations.

Maybe Voeckler being out in the break reminds Armstrong of how he once admired a brave performance. Maybe as they pedal along he looks at Sastre and realizes the resilient, willowy man beside him is riding his fourth Grand Tour in just a little over a year's time. More than likely there are many reasons Armstrong does what comes next. Even though he made a general apology to Sastre in public yesterday, he apologizes in person, right to his face, as they ride with a tailwind at their backs and a split sure to come.

"It was a dickhead thing to say," Armstrong will tell me after the Tour is over. "I was right—based on the numbers and the performances from 2008, I would have won that Tour with my 2009 performance. I was spot-on but nonetheless still a dickhead. I shouldn't have said it. I should have just thought it to myself and talked about it internally and kept it out of the press."

It is a day of surprises. When Cancellara forces a split it comes not at the U-turn but 30 kilometers sooner, on a bridge between a lake and the sea. Forty riders make the split, including all of the favorites, so Cancellara eases the pace and the main pack regroups. Ahead of them, the breakaway with Voeckler makes it to the U-turn with a 41-second lead, and during the run-in to Perpignan they begin attacking one another. This is the moment a breakaway fails, when its riders stop working together to maintain speed and turn on one another while the single-minded pack relentlessly chews up the gap between them. But today Voeckler reaches back to 2004 and retrieves some of that magic. He slips away from the break and crosses the line in exhaustion just 7 seconds in front of the all-out-sprinting pack.

Sastre tells everyone he has regained respect for Armstrong. When I see him afterward, I ask him about it.

"You said it was important for you to hear his apology personally," I say.

"Yes," Sastre says. "That is true. And it is true I have regained my respect that day." He rubs his nose with his hand. He has fine fingers, a delicate nose. Small teeth. Thin lips. Yet somehow he projects the heart of a giant. He says, "But it was also as important I believe for him."

"What do you mean?" I ask.

"For him himself," Sastre says. Then he puts a hand on my shoulder and says he's sorry but he has to go.

Back in February, Armstrong had said something at the end of the Tour of California that I wrote in my notebook and circled, then wrote on the inside front cover of the notebook I took to the Tour de France. At the big press conference at the end of the Tour of California, Armstrong was once more being asked what it had been like to work as a *domestique* for Levi, and if he would or could do the same for Contador or even Kloden. His usual answers to this question explained that everyone on a team of Bruyneel's knew they would work for the strongest rider no matter who that was, and he usually reminded people that he had said from the beginning that the comeback was not primarily about winning the Tour but battling cancer. But maybe because it had been a fast, aggressive race in abysmal conditions and he was fatigued—he admitted so twice during the press conference—in the midst of the stock patter he said something I'd never heard him say before: "You know, I think it might be good for me personally to do things that . . . I spent fifteen years sitting on people's wheel and waiting for the final moment to attack and take all the glory. It's kind of cool to be the one up front pulling."

He said, "That might be good for my life."

I'd been close to something important on that corner in Hanford, California, and when I stood looking at a child's chalked plea for Papa Rick's life. But after that, I'd gotten so caught up in Armstrong's struggles in Europe and in the little races in the United States, and even here at the Tour, that I'd started thinking too much like him, of winners and losers. I needed to get back to whatever it was about the comeback that was important enough to compel me to spend a year of my life chasing a man who seemed to understand even less about what he was doing than I did.

After talking to Sastre, I look at Armstrong's quote again. When I see Ekimov by the team bus later I ask him about the direct apology to Sastre, what he thinks it might mean.

"I cannot speak for him," Eki says.

"I know. But neither can he."

Eki doesn't say anything, doesn't even smile, so I say, "I'm just asking if you think he's different. More mature or something, I guess."

"He has so much pressure I try never to bother him or be a bother," Eki says. "I never want to add to his burdens."

"I think it's important somehow that he apologized to Sastre's face. I don't think he would have before."

"I can't say that," Eki says. He looks away, out at the crowd, at some people holding up flags, at the circus-colored hats, giant green foam hands and babies waving overhead. Ekimov says, "We just had a baby girl, you know. The week before coming. She is changing so much. She opens her eyes. She looks at you." He turns back to me and says, "Lance is more serious now. Serious as a man. As a cyclist, he's always been serious. As a person, maybe no."

"Do you think that's what the comeback is really about?" I say.

"Do you think, I don't know, do you think he's trying to grow up? Not on the bike. As a man?"

"I think he's trying," says Eki, "to wear the yellow jersey."

STAGE 5 RESULTS

1. Thomas Voeckler, Bbox	4:29:35
17. Andreas Kloden, Astana	0:00:07
24. Fabian Cancellara, Saxo Bank	
33. Cadel Evans, Silence-Lotto	
34. Christian Vande Velde, Garmin	
36. Andy Schleck, Saxo Bank	
39. Alberto Contador, Astana	
41. Lance Armstrong, Astana	
48. Bradley Wiggins, Garmin	
56. Carlos Sastre, Cervélo	
59. Levi Leipheimer, Astana	
62. Denis Menchov, Rabobank	

GENERAL CLASSIFICATION

1. Fabian Cancellara, Saxo Bank	10:38:07
2. Lance Armstrong, Astana	+0:00:00.22
3. Alberto Contador, Astana	+0:00:19
4. Andreas Kloden, Astana	+0:00:23
5. Levi Leipheimer, Astana	+0:00:31
6. Bradley Wiggins, Garmin	+0:00:38
12. Christian Vande Velde, Garmin	+0:01:16
20. Andy Schleck, Saxo Bank	+0:01:41
29. Carlos Sastre, Cervélo	+0:02:44
35. Cadel Evans, Silence-Lotto	+0:02:59
71. Denis Menchov, Rabobank	+0:03:52

GIRO D'ITALIA
Venice–Rome, Italy, 3,457 km
MAY 9–31, 2009

So Sudden to Come and Disappear

Lance Armstrong smiled.

You missed it if you were watching the Tour of Italy on TV. Even if you were at the finish of Stage 10 in the little town of Pinerola, right there hanging your arms over the metal riot fencing under the pink *arrivo* arch in the Piazza Vittorio Veneto, screaming not only for the men riding past but also to become part of the screaming, with sirens whetting the hubbub and cars honking multitone tunes out from under their stickered hoods, and whistles shrieking and, even through all that, the sound of cassettes clicking as the racers coasted for the pure pleasure of being done with 262 kilometers of racing—even able to take all of that in, you would have missed the smile of Lance Armstrong if, at the wrong instant, you blinked.

The smile would not be mentioned in any of the news reports about that day. It would not be commented on in the video blog Armstrong posted to his website that night. There seemed no need for anyone to remark on it. It was not the toothsome, long-playing grin Armstrong uses when he finds something funny or feels sated by triumph, nor was it the rehearsed beam of a superstar he has learned to flash at celebrity events, nor the giddy snarl that emerges at the conclusion of a slaughter, and not at all the intractable smirk—is he making fun of you or asking you to join in the bemusement?—that sometimes washes back and forth across his face during conversations. This smile was a flutter of a thing that curled up the right side of his mouth and exposed a single canine tooth as Armstrong rode under the finish banner, so sudden to come and disappear it seemed more reflex than expression. To any-one careful enough to watch Armstrong so closely, such a smile on such a day revealed more than whatever he might have said had he been asked to explain it.

Stage 10 not only was the longest of the Giro but went up and over a *prima categoria* climb (the highest rating of toughness, based on grade and length) as well as another that ranked as the Cima Coppi, or the highest point the racers would ride to in the whole three weeks. Additionally, as part of a celebration of the Giro's cen-tennial, the stage included the key sections of the route that the re-vered Italian champion and five-time Giro winner Fausto Coppi had ridden when, exactly sixty years ago, he'd pulled off what many ex-perts consider one of the greatest cycling exploits ever—breaking away from the pack early and riding solo for 192 kilometers over five mountains to gain an advantage of 11:52 over his archrival, Gino Bartali. So, aside from the sheer geographical challenge of the day, the difficulty of Stage 10 would be intensified because the top Ital-ian racers in this year's Giro—collectively an impulsive, passionate group under normal circumstances—had let it be known that they were committed to decimating the pack to ensure that one of them took the cherished victory honoring Coppi (and, not immaterially, generating valuable exposure for their sponsors).

The stage was the most potent form of the madness that is the Giro d'Italia. It was not at all the kind of day that anyone ever would have guessed would incite a smile from the embattled, bat-tered, struggling Lance Armstrong.

Yet So Powerful

The Giro is a lot like the Tour de France logistically while being nothing like it at all in personality. Both races last three weeks, cover around 2,100 miles over about twenty stages of racing, take place mostly in the countries they are named for but make excursions into neighboring nations, are covered live on TV in their countries and rivet the native populace, and have an iconic jersey (pink for the Giro). But while the Tour de France has come to be considered the greatest bike race in the world, the Giro outright defies that kind of categorization. Calling it a runner-up to the Tour's top billing isn't accurate because that implies that they can be compared point by point and ranked. Nor does thinking of it as the second-biggest stage race (which it is) quite capture its prestige, allure, and oddity.

The Tour de France follows a logical rhythm, almost always opening softly with a prologue or individual time trial, then giving sprinters a week to prance before the overall race contenders get down to business in the mountains and long time trials. The 2009 Giro, just to look at one year, started with a team time trial, threw two mountain stages into the first week, and willy-nilly mixed in courses for sprinters, escape artists, and hometown boys from little teams who intimately knew the roads from their childhood. The Giro pounded the pure climbers with multiple mountaintop finishes with no real break between—forcing them to choose whether to give it all for a stage win or ride with reserves to try to finish high each day. It confounded the time trialists: Stage 12, at 60 kilometers, not only was one of the longest individual time trials of the modern era (there hadn't been one this length in seventeen years) but also went up two climbs separated by a descent so technically demanding that almost all the racers opted to use their regular—and more nimble— road bikes instead of their TT-specific straight-ahead-speed machines. To understand what a weird time trial it was, consider that the wispy climber Stefano Garzelli (who won the Giro in 2000 and would go on this year to capture the mountain jersey) finished third, while two-time world TT champion Michael Rogers finished fourteenth, more than a minute behind Garzelli—and after taking a look at the course, in outrage TT god Fabian Cancellara abandoned the race rather than ride that day.

This erratic nature is one reason that, while every professional bike racer longs to do the Tour—and many judge the success of their year based on making their team's nine-man squad each July—lots of racers contentedly skip the Giro year after year. Armstrong had never competed in even one before his comeback. Contador, who won last year, said he decided to skip this season's to concentrate on training for the Tour, as did Cadel Evans. Some riders say that riding the Tour in top form is impossible after doing the Giro, and some say the Giro is ideal preparation for the Tour. Sometimes the same rider voices one sentiment then, the next year, the other. The Giro is not a fixed point.

The race also has an intimacy the Tour lacks. At the start, more riders mingle with fans, kissing children and young women, signing autographs, sipping water or espresso in the start village with a nonchalance that is merely a memory at this point of the Tour de France's evolution. As one of the Italian *tifosi*—superfans—told me one day, panting after returning from his back-slapping run up the mountain alongside the Italian racer Danilo DiLuca, who was battling Denis Menchov for the pink jersey, "If I approach him so at the Tour de France, the gendarme beat me." He reached up and adjusted his pink fright wig, then offered me a slug from an open bottle of red wine.

At the end of one stage, I walked back down the final, 2.1-kilometer climb to the monument of the Santuario della Madonna di San Luca on an arched, elevated walkway that paralleled the road. The grass on the steep slopes that angled down to meet the pavement was barely visible under the tens of thousands of Italian cycling fans who'd turned the entire climb into a party. During the race, at each straight stretch the fans had spilled over the barriers and were sitting, dancing, drinking, and singing out on the pavement itself. (They knew enough to stay behind the barriers in the corners, where the riders pass by so tight they brush your shoulders and hands as they go.) Now that the race was over, the street was clogged with spectators and, as I stood on the walkway, I watched the racers descend back to their team buses through the fans. The *tifosi* weren't accosting the racers, weren't slapping them on the back or getting in their way; even the most raucous and drunk fans became sober and almost timid at the approach of a racer. But for the riders the descent was still the equivalent of shouldering through a wall-to-wall house party. Columbia's Michael Barry told me it took him longer to ride down the hill than up it. I could imagine no postgame mingling like this in any major sporting event anywhere.

But not even that conveys the essential otherness of the Giro. Maybe the best explanation is this: though it will drive the French nuts to hear this, the stature of the Tour de France can be grasped when filtered through the steely, heroic vision of Lance Armstrong, whereas the Giro can only be appreciated through the elegant, tragic view of Fausto Coppi.

In 1938, Coppi was nineteen years old. He'd been racing for four years, the first three without a license and as an amateur while working in a butcher shop in Novi Ligure. In his first year as a pro he was still working there to supplement his meager earnings, which included small amounts of money and prizes such as an alarm clock and a salami sandwich. He was a gangly, frail boy who was often sick and cried easily at the various disappointments teenage life metes out, and he was awkward off the bike, his arms and legs forever finding funny angles that seemed to turn simple actions, such as walking down steps or sitting, into complicated processes that could be achieved only through much deliberation and revision. But he was fast on a bike. He won race after race against the other amateurs. He was also something more than fast: he was beautiful. When he rode, everything sad and silly and sickly about him turned into an unexpected and odd but unmistakable elegance.

One of the regular customers at the butcher shop was Biagio Cavanna, a 250-pound blind masseur who'd worked the bodies of Italy's great cyclists, such as Alfredo Binda—a five-time winner of the Giro who'd been so dominant that in 1930 the race's organizers paid him not to enter just so other riders could have a chance. You can imagine Cavanna hearing talk of Coppi's races in the butcher shop. You can picture him tilting his chin upward, sniffing the air to find amid the meat smells the scent of this boy so full of contrasts. Finally, one day Cavanna asked for Coppi to be brought to him.

Several sources give various versions of what happened next. Instead of limiting myself to the choice of one from the books, newspaper accounts, films, and opera—yes, opera—dedicated to Coppi, I've woven my own myth based on multiple sources and the story as told to me by an old man tending the bar in a café in Treviso a few years ago.

The room Coppi walked into was dim and spare, with no decorations and for furniture only a single massage table. As Fausto walked through the door, pushed in and onward by his friends, Cavanna boomed, "I have heard much of Fausto Coppi," and motioned for the boy to lie on the table.

After a few minutes, Cavanna stopped, rubbed his hands together perhaps, took a step backward, and looked at nothing, at the wall, at a view no one but he could see. "You must listen to me," he said. "My hands see better than any person's eyes. Within you is a great champion. Maybe the greatest champion. But you must do as I say: you must not race for three months."

"But," Fausto said, "I shall not be paid. I must race."

"Then that is too bad for the world," said Cavanna. "You shall win your money this year, but we shall lose our champion." Coppi took the rest of the 1938 racing season off.

In 1939, Coppi began winning races by margins approaching 10 minutes. A year later, he won the Giro d'Italia in his first entry. He set the hour record in 1942. He went on to win the Giro five times, the Tour de France twice (the first one coming, like the Giro win, in his first attempt), Milan–San Remo three times, the Tour of Lombardy five times, Paris-Roubaix and the world championship once. In 1949 he became the first rider to win the Giro and Tour in the same year. In his home country, he was something like a combination of Michael Jordan and John F. Kennedy. Throughout cycling, he was proclaimed *Il Campionissimo,* The Champion of Champions. Though we sometimes call today's top racers *campionissimo,* there is to this day only one who is referred to as "*The* Champion of Champions." In an astonishing period from 1946 to 1954, according to some reports, Coppi was never caught after he broke away from the pack. (Eddy Merckx himself cited this fact when he told me he believes Coppi is the greatest cyclist of all time.)

But in various wrecks, Coppi fractured two collarbones, his pelvis, a shoulder blade, his kneecaps, his skull twice, and several vertebrae. His brother Serse died in a bike crash. His father was crushed by two oxen. On his way home from World War II (which cost him three years of riding), a truck he was riding in flipped into a ravine, killing everyone aboard but him. He left his wife and daughter in 1954 for Giulia Occhini, a married woman who came to be known as "The Lady in White," causing a scandal of such depth that spectators spat on their former hero, the police arrested him for adultery, and Pope Pius XII personally asked Coppi to return to his family. By 1959, he could barely hang on to the back of the pack, and there were reports that sympathetic race organizers sometimes spontaneously shortened the course so as to not embarrass him. He abandoned the last three races of his career. In December 1959, he contracted malaria on a hunting trip to Africa, then was misdiagnosed when he returned home and treated for a bronchial infection; he died on January 2, 1960, at the age of forty.

That's the Giro d'Italia—frail, tragic, awkward, full of scandal and regret, yet so powerful for all of it that you can scarcely believe it is real.

I Don't Know What He Was Thinking

Armstrong seemed out of place at the Giro from the start.

"I don't have the condition to win," he admitted the day before the race. "I'd like to win a stage, but I don't know if I can and if I'm fit enough."

He and Bruyneel were still searching for that elusive first win. Both of them knew that a win at the Tour of the Gila or one here at the Giro wouldn't make a difference in how the Tour came out two months from now; once they were 95 miles into the mountains and the July sun was hammering at their backs and only three or four riders out of 190 remained together on the road, Armstrong's rivals would neither care nor remember that he'd won a stage in May. And Armstrong's psyche had never been so weak or impressionable that he would receive a boost from such a rote psychological trick— unless he willed it to, in which case the will was already more important than the win. I'd been around long enough by this time to understand that they didn't so much need the victory as they needed to defeat the fact that they couldn't get a victory.

His best chance was probably the opening stage's team time trial, a specialty of Armstrong's squads going all the way back from Astana through Discovery to U.S. Postal Service. Bruyneel had instructed the team to let Armstrong cross the line first, so that in case they won, he would be awarded the leader's pink jersey. They had the firepower. Besides Armstrong, the picks for the Giro team included Leipheimer, Horner (who told me he was in the best condition of his life), Popovych, Chechu Rubiera, Jani Brajkovic (who in 2004 was the under-twenty-three world TT champ and in 2009 would win the Slovenian national TT title), a big Swiss diesel named Steve Morabito, the climbing *domestique* Daniel Navarro, and a Kazakh no one knew much about, Andrey Zeits. But Astana could do no better than third, 13 seconds behind the winner, Columbia, and 7 behind Garmin.

The race left Venice and began making its way north, toward the mountains of Austria and Switzerland. The next two stages were flat, allowing the overall contenders to sit in the pack while the sprinters fought for primacy. But for Armstrong even this was little respite from uncertainty.

His past brushes with doping resurfaced when his contentious relationship with the Italian racer Filippo Simeoni became news again.

Simeoni had been a client of Michele Ferrari, an Italian doctor and trainer who became one of the sport's most controversial figures in relation to doping. By the mid-1980s, Ferrari had become one of cycling's most successful trainers. Riders working with him had won the hour record, swept the podium in Classics races, and taken the top five spots at the Giro, and he developed and honed revolutionary innovations in training. For instance, with Dr. Francesco Conconi in the early 1980s, he helped create what became known as the Conconi Test, a workout on a stationary trainer that let riders determine their anaerobic threshold without the expense or hassle of submitting to complex laboratory tests. (The reason modern amateur athletes can so easily and successfully follow workout plans tailored just for them is because the Conconi Test made heart rate, endurance, power, and recovery comprehensible and usable to the general public.) Ferrari also developed the concept of VAM, an abbreviation for the Italian phrase *velocità ascensionale media*, which doesn't directly translate well into English but is essentially a measurement of how many meters a cyclist could ascend in an hour. It is the most objective way possible to calculate and compare climbing performances when speed and slope are accounted for.

But in addition to his unquestionably legitimate training methods, Ferrari was also linked to doping. In a 1994 interview with *L'Equipe*, Ferrari said that he didn't prescribe EPO to riders he was training, but noted that they could buy it in some countries without a prescription. "And if a rider does, that doesn't scandalize me. EPO doesn't fundamentally change the performance of a racer," he said. When the reporter asked him if the use of EPO was dangerous, Ferrari gave what has become his most infamous quote: "EPO is not dangerous, it's the abuse that is. It's also dangerous to drink ten liters of orange juice." In 1999, the cyclist Francesco Moser revealed that when he'd trained with Ferrari to break the hour record in 1984 he had resorted to blood doping—withdrawing his own blood, then later reinjecting it to boost the number of oxygen-carrying red blood cells in his body. (This was not illegal in 1984 and, in fact, some of the members of that year's medal-winning U.S. Olympic cycling team blood-doped.) In 2001, after seizing medical documents and training diaries from Ferrari's home, the Italian courts put him on trial for sporting fraud in relation to doping.

One of the racers whose records were found in Ferrari's home was Simeoni. In the trial, he testified that Ferrari had led him to use EPO and human growth hormone. (In 2001 and 2002, Simeoni was suspended from cycling for six months for admitting to doping.) In 2004, Ferrari was convicted on two charges related to doping, a verdict that was overturned on appeal in 2006.

In the meantime, newspaper reports and the French-published book *L.A. Confidentiel: Les Secrets de Lance Armstrong* revealed that Armstrong had quietly worked with Ferrari since as far back as 1995. (Though training documents related to Armstrong were seized from Ferrari for the trial, no records linking the rider to doping were among them.) Until the conviction was rendered, Armstrong defended Ferrari, citing the doctor's well-known legitimate training methods. And as part of that defense, in 2003 Armstrong ended up calling Simeoni a "liar," according to a report in the French newspaper *Le Monde*. Simeoni launched a defamation lawsuit against Armstrong, who countersued, and both agreed to drop their cases in 2006. The strangest twist in the whole tale came during the 2004 Tour de France, when Simeoni bridged across to a breakaway in Stage 18 and Armstrong—in the yellow jersey—followed. The presence of the jersey in the break would doom it; Armstrong's rivals would never let him gain more time and would chase until they caught him. Simeoni claimed that, as revenge for their differences, Armstrong refused to leave the break unless Simeoni did, too. Reluctantly, Simeoni said, he eased up and returned to the pack, giving up his chance for a stage win. One day while I was on a ride with Armstrong, I asked him what had happened.

"I just attacked on impulse," he told me. "Sometimes the yellow jersey has to be aggressive, surprise people, never let them settle in. Indurain used to do it, Hinault used to do it. It's not like I made it up. Once I got to the break and saw that no one had chased me, I decided to go back on my own."

"You never told Simeoni he had to go back with you?" I asked.

"Simeoni's a baby," he said. "I don't know what he was thinking."

Now, all these years later, Simeoni had not been invited to the Giro even though he was the reigning Italian national champion. The director of the Giro, Angelo Zomegnan, had given an interview to the Italian sports television network RAI Sport that seemed to hint that Simeoni's relationship with Armstrong was one reason (along with his lack of recent results) for his exclusion: "At Milan–San Remo he had seven hours to meet Armstrong and clarify the 2004 incident," Zomegnan said of Simeoni. In response, Simeoni returned his champion's jersey to the Italian cycling federation, the only time in a hundred years such a thing had happened.

Armstrong's troubles didn't end with unearthed history. He was having difficulty with the present and future as well. The coalition of Astana's Kazakh sponsors had stopped paying out the money required to run the team. Citing financial difficulties, since January 2009 five of the companies had defaulted to various degrees on their agreements to fund the team. To pay salaries and operating costs, the team had been forced to clean out a $2 million escrow fund that every Pro Tour team is required to maintain. As the Giro started, the UCI issued a warning that unless the $2 million was restored and payments to riders and staff made current by May 31, it would withdraw Astana's license, disbanding the team. Armstrong might never make it to the Tour.

Bruyneel was scrambling to reopen Astana's cash flow and simultaneously to secure a new sponsor in case the team fell apart. "But," he told, me, "we are going to corporations in the middle of the fiscal year—in this economy—and saying we need twenty million dollars in two weeks. How do you think that's going?"

Then the Giro hit the first of its mountains, and things got really bad.

The Closer You Get

Stage 4 was a 162-kilometer race that finished with two big climbs. The first was the Croce d'Aune, an 8.5-kilometer uphill with an average grade of 7.9 percent. After descending this, the race would gradually rise for about another 12 kilometers just to get to the base of the final ascent of San Martino di Castrozza. This 13.75-kilometer climb wasn't steep—the average grade was only 5.5 percent—but the pre-race buzz was that Danilo DiLuca was going to light up the stage by making that last climb at leg-cracking speed.

DiLuca, a sharp-dressing Italian with fine features and long brown hair who happily goes by the nickname "The Killer," won the Giro in 2007. At the end of that season he'd been suspended for three months upon the conclusion of an investigation into his involvement in a 2004 doping scandal centered on the Italian doctor Carlo Santuccione. Narcotics investigators had taped a phone call in which Santuccione told DiLuca to use EPO, and had video of DiLuca waiting outside Santuccione's office while the doctor prepared syringes. He returned to the sport in 2008 with a small team, LPR Brakes, which hadn't earned invites to any major races until it was selected as a wild-card entry into the 2009 Giro. The Killer was out for revenge.

A six-man break got away early in the race and built a lead that extended as far as seven minutes. But only three riders were able to stay together over Croce d'Aune, two Italians on small teams and Saxo Bank's escape artist, Jens Voigt. DiLuca sent his LPR teammates to the front to reel in the remnants of the break, and by the time the pack got to the base of San Martino di Castrozza, the breakaway trio had a lead of just 3 minutes. Voigt eventually shed his two companions and hung on until, with just 3 kilometers to go to the mountain-top finish, a group of about forty riders overwhelmed him. DiLuca was there, with Leipheimer, Horner, and Armstrong, as well as Sastre, Basso, and most of the other favorites. The riders began attacking one another, and DiLuca leaped away for the win, just ahead of an elite group that included overall hopefuls Leipheimer, Menchov, Sastre, Basso, and Garzelli, as well as strong lieutenants such as Horner and Popo. Armstrong couldn't hang on and finished 15 seconds back.

He said his bike wasn't shifting right.

Menchov, who would go on to snatch the lead for good in the Stage 12 time trial, meant it as praise when he said that Armstrong was "showing strength that is impressive for a rider who took years off and had an accident just weeks ago." But a comeback with qualifiers hardly rated as a comeback, at least in terms of the expectation attached to Armstrong. He was coming unglued on a 5 percent slope on the first day of climbing. Maybe the shifting on his bike was balky, but he'd once won a stage of the Tour de France on a bike with a broken frame. The Giro that had embraced Armstrong—with a special place in the opening ceremony, with what organizers were calling record roadside crowds, with the unprecedented presence of more than a thousand journalists—seemed suddenly soured by disappointment. The Italian newspaper *Il Giornal* said he was riding like "an old-age pensioner."

Publicly, Armstrong presented a light, unconcerned attitude. About the team's financial crisis, he joked, "All I know about Kazakhstan is Astana and Borat." He posted to Twitter a snapshot of the team's cook playing air guitar and advised, "Stay in the kitchen Duffy."

And maybe he was okay with the idea that all he was really doing out here was training. By the time I got in the team car the morning of Stage 5, it was more or less understood that Lance was going to get dropped again today in the mountains. Eki—Viatcheslav Ekimov—told me that Lance was figuring on losing 2 minutes. I was going to be in car 2 with Eki driving and Craig Geater, the gnome-loving mechanic, in the backseat. Bruyneel and Chris the mechanic were in car 1. They'd follow the lead group, and we would trail behind to support anyone who got dropped.

Hearing Eki and Bruyneel talk so straightforwardly about Lance planning to lose time reminded me how different this all was for fans and the team. For Astana, this was just another training exercise. For me, because Armstrong was riding the race of Fausto Coppi for the first time in his career, I wanted to see him ride at least a little bit like Fausto. I knew he wasn't in top form, but I'd seen him pull off so many miracles that I held on to a hope that didn't exist for the team. What spectators perceived as miracles were just results that had been under construction for months, years, lifetimes.

Today's stage departed from San Martino di Castrozza, the ski village we'd climbed to the day before. It started by going straight up over the Passo Rolle, 8.2 kilometers of riding uphill from the gun. No warm-up, no flat rollout through a beautiful town.

"They'll probably take it easy, though, right?" I said. "To start?"

"You are kidding, man," Eki said. "This is the Italian world championship every day. A mountain cannot interrupt it." He looked sideways at me and gave a kind of goofy sneer. Eki had turned pro in 1990, thought he wanted to retire at the end of the 2001 season, but missed the sport so much he came back the next year and rode until 2005. In his sixteen-year career he finished every Tour de France he started—fifteen—and had helped Lance in five of the seven victories. While riding for WordPerfect in 1994, he'd beat a young Armstrong at the Tour DuPont. He earned Olympic gold in track cycling in 1988 and another in the individual time trial in

2000, won two world championships on the track plus stages in the Tour and the Vuelta, and had stood on the podium at Paris-Roubaix. When he announced in 2005 that the Tour he was riding would be his last, the peloton paid its respects by letting him ride ahead alone into the Champs-Élysées for the first of the eight finishing circuits there. Mostly when people say cyclists are tough, the reference pertains to their bearing on the bike, the ability to suffer, to climb the steepest pitches at speeds that make them go blind, to ignore the smelting of their bodies. Eki was tough in a bar-fight way. He walked with a swagger that also communicated humor. Coming out of the Eastern Bloc, he'd been pugnacious and worn a mullet, but now had a cool haircut and designer jeans, and favored either flip-flops or expensive leather shoes. He was, as Chris the mechanic said, "the coolest guy on the team."

There was fog over the peaks, but the sun was visible behind the thinning white layer of it. Instead of waiting with the other secondary cars far back in the caravan parking lot, Eki was driving ahead of the race to find a spot to pull over and wait. The car was beeping as we took off—he didn't have his seat belt on.

"There's kilometer zero," he said, nodding at a placard that designated the official start of the day's route. He wheeled in just ahead of the sign, put the car in neutral, and lifting and straightening his body above the seat, he dug a hand into his front pants pocket. He pulled out a little metal rectangle and held it up to show me. "My little friend," he said. It was the metal tongue of a seat belt clip, and he stuck it in the empty clasp and the beeping stopped. None of the directors ever wore their seat belts.

The pack came by, flying up the hill just as Eki had predicted, and he punched the gas and we pulled in right behind them. When Bruyneel caught up and got into the right spot—it always took some time for the caravan to sort itself out—we'd drop back.

"Guys," Eki said into the team mic, "we are right behind you. Let's do a radio check. Lance, do you copy? Chris? Levi?" Each in turn said yes. "Chechu, you copy us? Okay, we start the race now. It's nine k for the first climb. Good luck."

In less than five minutes Bruyneel came barreling up the left side of the road and drove up beside us. We were inches apart. The two directors nodded at each other. Eki drifted right so our wheels were off that side of the road, and we began to fall back through the caravan. You could be fined if you didn't take your assigned spot. Over our radio, Bruyneel said, "What is the plan today, Bill?"

I looked at the radio as if I hadn't known it could emit voices.

Eki punched my shoulder and said, "Ya, you should talk."

I picked up the mouthpiece from where it lay on the center console between us, holding it just like I'd seen Bruyneel and Eki do, and I tapped my index finger against the talk button without depressing it. I was in a team car at a Grand Tour for Lance Armstrong's comeback and I was getting ready to speak over the team radio.

Eki bounced my shoulder again and said, "You got to respond, man. The boss asked you."

The plan was for Lance to lose time. The plan was for Lance to ride like just another racer in the pack. The plan was for Lance to disappoint his fans and feed his critics. The plan was for Lance to just survive the Giro so he could win the Tour. Eki hit my shoulder.

"I was hoping to find out some secrets," I said, "about Trevor." Craig's gnome. There might have been some cracking up on the other side of the radios or there might have been just static.

Bruyneel said, "You are lucky. No other journalist gets this chance. Every journalist will be so fucking jealous." He paused, and said, "There's not one journalist in the world who gets to ride with an Olympic double gold medalist."

Eki was making a jack-off motion with his hand, from seat to ceiling.

We drove for a little bit listening to Bruyneel talk to the team, his patter soothing them less with its words than its rhythm. There wasn't much to see back where we were. Each of the twenty-two teams had a lead car ahead of us, plus all the coms, medical vehicles, media, and VIPs. Astana's highest-placed rider, Popo, was fourth, so even back here in the second rank there were three car 2s ahead of us. It was a little bit like driving to work on some strange sort of commute, except every once in a while we could look up when the road switchbacked and see the caravan on the road above us and on the road above them the riders. The mountainside was deep green dotted the color of snow-bleached stones. Only a few people were scattered along the road this high and this remote. Eki looked out the window awhile, then said, "You get along, you know. Why don't you travel with the team for what you're doing?"

I thought that Eki was one guy on the team who would understand if I told him that I thought Lance, or at least his comeback, might be better understood from the outside, and that also the more inside you got the more bound you were to tell the approved story. I thought I could probably even tell Eki I wasn't sure the comeback was such a good idea, that it looked like it wasn't working out. I thought of admitting that I didn't want Lance to lose 2 minutes today, that I wanted him to turn himself inside out and spill his guts on the road, and that, instead of listening to him complain about bad shifting, I wanted to watch him ride a broken bike all the way to victory like he'd done on Luz Ardiden in 2003.

I said, "I don't want you guys to get sick of me."

"Hm," Eki said. He nodded. He tapped the wheel and we listened to Bruyneel talk a little. Eki said, "It's a good tactic, I think. With Lance, maybe, the farther you are the closer you get." He nodded and smiled at me.

Over the radio, Bruyneel said, "There's the first attack, boys. First attack. Move up a bit."

"Look at this mountain," said Eki. The switchbacks were piled so tight that the road seemed to coil like a dropped rope. He flipped on the satellite TV, a Kenwood the size of a paperback book that was mounted on the dash, directly above the team radio under the dash. (The race radio was stuffed in the glove box.)

The TV flickered and jumpy color images came on. The reception was spotty. A racer named Marco Pinotti had attacked, an Italian—"What did I tell you?" Eki said—and six or seven others were riding with him. We were about 2 or 3 kilometers from the crest, and I could still see five switchbacks stacked up outside my window. Now, snow crusted the sides of the road and lay in big heaps around the fields. A helicopter hovered over the valley to our right, just about even with our car.

"Boys," said Bruyneel, "for the downhill stay a little bit in front. You can see it's a little wet because of snow. Stay a little bit in front for the downhill." After a few seconds, when the riders must have done what he instructed, Bruyneel said, "Good job, boys. So we get to the top here, boys, and it's twenty kilometers downhill. Twenty k downhill."

As we rose over the peak, Eki said to me, "You have problems with car sickness?"

"Nah," I said, and I was lucky I was not lying. We plummeted down the wet road, and in the corners you could feel the tires just start to break loose before hooking up and dragging us out of the turn and into the next one. Around us, tires squealed and engines cried. Later in the year, Lance would say that the fastest he'd ever descended on a bike was at this Giro—75 mph.

When we were most of the way down the hill, Lance came on the radio. "I'm again having trouble with my drivetrain," he said. His voice sounded far away and diminished, as if he had been submerged in wind.

"What is it doing?" Bruyneel asked over the radio.

"It's skipping around. The chain seems loose."

"We're almost at the end of the downhill. End of the downhill," Bruyneel said. "In the valley, Lance, if it's a problem, come back to the car. If it's a problem, we'll do a bike change. To the one you had at Gila."

To Craig, Eki said, "What could it be?"

"We don't know," Craig said. "The chain is only two days old. It might be a bad batch of cassettes. We don't know."

Eki shook his head and looked back at Craig in the rearview mirror, and Craig looked at him and shook his head. They stared at each other for a few seconds like that.

A few minutes later Bruyneel said, "Eki. So we have done the bike change. You have his other spare, so just in case, we need to put that bike on car one so we have a good spare for the final."

We could see Bruyneel's car stopped ahead of us, off to the right of the road, and Eki swung in behind them. Chris was already standing outside of car 1, and he ran to our car, pulled the bike off the rack, ran it back to car 1, racked it, and jumped in. I timed the whole thing: it took nine seconds.

"A bit slow," said Craig.

The race continued, climbing here and there, descending, winding through vineyards but generally on a course that dropped toward the valley floor from which the final, 24.9-kilometer climb up Alpe di Siusi would begin. The gap to the breakaway got as high as 25 minutes before Basso ordered his Liquigas team to the front to reel back some time.

Eki's phone rang, and he lifted it and began speaking Russian. On the radio, Bruyneel said, "Eki, so listen: I get picked up in Plato at kilometer one hundred. So at kilometer ninety we switch." Eki kept talking in Russian to his phone, dropped it a few inches away from his mouth, and said into the radio mic, "I have Eurosport Russia live now," then continued his radio interview. Craig leaned forward and explained to me that Bruyneel had to leave midrace to catch a flight to Belgium to work on the sponsorship problems. Eki was going to take over car 1 and Craig was going to drive car 2.

"Eki." It was Bruyneel. "If they ask about the sponsorship, you don't have mercy. Tell the truth: we have done our part and delivered results. You are the fucking Olympic champion, man. Never forget that." Eki rolled his eyes. Bruyneel was kidding in a way, but because he'd never achieved many big victories as a rider, he also held immense respect for those who had.

Lance said, "Johan, I'm going to come back. I'm having a little problem with my bars. They're slipping."

"Okay," said Johan. "We're ready. We are ready."

"I need an Allen key," said Lance.

"Okay. Do a double-click when you're in coast." Coasting, he meant—slowing by the side of the road so they could stop and do the repair. "Chechu has the tool. Chechu will bring the tool for you."

Eki punched my shoulder again and said, "I need my stopwatch," and motioned down to the center console. I saw a little blue zippered case there, and I opened it and pulled out a stopwatch. Eki took it and put the strap around his neck.

"A stopwatch?" I said. "A satellite TV and two different radios and GPS and you use a stopwatch?"

He gestured out the window, up at the hulking outline of Alpe di Siusi. "When I see the leaders go by a point I click, and when I see our boys at the same point I click, and I know the difference before anyone, huh?" He was driving somewhere over 85 mph while he was talking, blazing up the left side of the race. We entered a roundabout with the car feeling as if it were jacking up on its front wheels as Eki braked. Just beyond, we could see Bruyneel's car pulled over and waiting for us.

"Okay, amigo," said Eki as he stopped and opened the door at once. He pointed at me and said, "Stay far to get close." He was gone. Craig clambered into the driver's seat and Bruyneel came in through the open back door and as we pulled out onto the road Bruyneel leaned forward into the front and said, "You know the plan."

Craig nodded. "We move up past dropped riders until . . ."

He cut his eyes toward Bruyneel in the rearview mirror. "We keep moving up," Craig said, then trailed off again. He looked over at me, and Bruyneel said, "It's good, man."

"We move up until Lance gets dropped," Craig said. "Then we stay with him."

I had the feeling that Craig's hesitation was not so much worry about spilling a team secret in front of me but a personal reluctance to commit public heresy, to admit for the first time outside the tight bonds of the team that Lance not only could get dropped but went into the race knowing he would.

Craig pulled the car off the road at the base of the climb, and Bruyneel got out, then leaned in my window and said, "Okay. I go get money now." On the radio, Eki was running the team, which was already on the slopes: "Guys, you can see Liquigas taking initiative on this climb, so that means Basso is ready to take some action. Levi, that should be a good wheel for you. In about four k we have a flat spot. This is a good warm-up for Liquigas. For sure they're going to make a big move in the second part after the flat."

Almost immediately we passed the first dropped riders, a group of three from Silence-Lotto, Xacobeo Galicia, and Cervélo, and from that point on we would never be on a clear road. Liquigas and Basso were burning the pack down from the front, and the men who came off the back were charred. We passed a Bbox rider and another Xacobeo, then a group of fifteen or so. An AG2R rider grabbed on to the seat of a moto as it passed by, lost his grip, and grabbed at the side mirror of the car that drove past behind the moto. Other riders were doing the same, latching their hands onto the hinge of the rear door of the ambulance, pushing each other, searching for and giving whatever few seconds of relief they could manage. It was only illegal if a com saw. The riders were glistening with their own sweat, hollow in the eye sockets, sunken in the cheeks. As we passed, they peered into the car as if watching a king go by on a litter. On the radio, Eki told the team the real climb would start soon.

We drove up beside Morabito, the Swiss Astana rider. "We have to keep going," Craig said. We had to drive until we saw Lance.

The gap to the break was down to 1:18. The pack seemed to be like a sack open on its downhill side and spilling out its contents as it got dragged upward. We passed great groups of riders, whose stench floated behind them and ahead, and we also passed riders on their own, such as the American Tom Danielson, who once had been the next Lance Armstrong, and the great Classics racer Philippe Gilbert.

"In about three kilometers we start to really, really climb now," Eki said.

We passed a Liquigas rider spent from his work at the front, getting a push from a fan. There were thick crowds now lining the road, leaning toward the car as we passed, screaming, sometimes their hands or even heads plonking off our windshield. They were dressed in pink, in Liquigas green, in Bbox blue. They had their shirts off. They were painted pink on their chests, their faces, their arms, in war stripes across their cheeks. They threw beers at us and draped flags over the windshield. All this time we passed riders. We drove by number 71, for Fuji. I didn't know who it was, but I knew it was particularly bad that he was here: the first number of every set of tens is the team leader, 1 and 11 and so on.

Armstrong was 21. We were supposed to pass through this madness until we saw number 21. Below us, the ski lifts looked tiny, the size of Chiclets.

"Guys," said Eki, "you are looking very good on TV. Very good."

I looked at the TV as we drove through two Columbia riders, a Fuji, a Serramenti. On the screen Basso, DiLuca, Sastre, Menchov, Horner, Leipheimer, and one or two other riders bobbed lightly in time with the fluttering of their legs.

"Lance, you are looking good. Looking good, man," said Eki. "Come on, come on, come on. You are looking good."

But he wasn't. I could see that on the TV. He was coming out of the back of the group, standing, jerking with every stroke as if he were being shot each time he pedaled. The race radio said, "Armstrong en difficile."

Craig looked away from the TV, passed riders from Acqua

& Sapone, Barloworld, LPR, Milram. "I don't know what people expect," he said. "He's come back and pissed all over people, being this far up after so long away. I don't know what people expect."

I was one of those people he was talking about. Except worse: the team had let me know enough to know better than to expect a miracle, but I couldn't prevent myself from wanting one anyway.

Choppers were above us, driving all the noise of the race plus their own back down upon us, and this crazed the crowd even more. Racers seemed to fly back toward us and past as we drove around them, but every one of them was suffering in such slow motion I could see the sweaty slumped shoulders and the sinews twanging hard against the skin layered with single-digit percentages of body fat, could watch the muscles wriggle the spandex uniforms in convulsive spasms, their bearing pleading for this to stop somehow but their minds refusing to let them stop because, after all, they loved the sport and even now couldn't wait for their chance to do this all again tomorrow.

Garzelli, the number 1 for the whole Giro, appeared in front of us, lingered centered in our windshield, wobbled to the right, and slid backward past my window. On the TV Basso began to labor, his mouth open simply because it took less energy to hang that way, his body sagging down into his bike.

"Dropped!" Eki said. "Dropped. Dropped from the group!" And there he was in our windshield, number 21.

He was out of the saddle, ticking the bike from side to side, and now the TV showed me what I was seeing through the windshield except for the TV cameraman on the moto riding beside Armstrong. Less than a car length in front of us was the famous Lance Armstrong I could see on the TV in front of me. The suffering of the tiny digital image was apparent in its motion, and the suffering of the real man on the road was apparent in some bigger way, some dread and noble aspect to his quavering. There was in him all the riders we'd driven through, and Craig's hesitancy to speak of the moment that now lay before us, and also Eki's matter-of-fact tone.

On the team radio Eki was coaching Horner not to pull the group, and on the race radio Sastre was attacking and on the TV Menchov and DiLuca were chasing Sastre and in the windshield Lance Armstrong had settled in and was slumped down, hanging his head.

Craig picked up the mic and said, "You're in the last k, Lance."

Eki said, "It will be more than two minutes, then."

Armstrong ground away at the kilometer. Basso passed us going down the hill, done with his race and wearing a sock cap and jacket, on his way to the team bus. Armstrong got out of the saddle and jerked his bike up the last bit of the mountain. Though I was no longer watching the TV, was no longer watching anything, really, Armstrong must have been shown on the screen, because Eki obviously saw him riding and said, "Good job, Lance," as he came in 2:58 behind.

No One Could Say What He Expected

One day I was hanging around the team bus, which was hidden pretty far back in a tree-lined parking lot behind the hotel Astana was staying in. The mechanics, Chris and Craig and an Englishman named Alan Buttler who liked to work with no shirt under his tool apron, had their truck open and had set up stands and were sprucing up the bikes, checking that the glue was still good on the tubular wheels, sorting through their tools. Bruyneel had been out and had a water fight with Chef Duffy, with the water hoses the mechanics had run out from the hotel spigots. A few of the riders had come out now and then. Lance had walked out earlier and signed an autograph for an Italian man who'd survived cancer and was waiting there with his daughter. After Armstrong had gone back inside the hotel, the man had left and, about half an hour later, returned with eleven beers for the mechanics.

They thanked him. Speaking a little English, the man asked if he could show his daughter Lance's bike. The mechanics shrugged, and with a cone wrench Alan pointed over to Lance's yellow bike clamped in one of the stands. The man and his daughter, who was maybe around ten, walked over and stood two or three steps from the bike and the man pointed at parts of the bike and spoke to her in a soft voice, hushed as if not wanting to offend, as if in a church. I had the sense this moment was important to the man, and he was trying to make it important to his daughter.

I had just gotten off the team bus. It was more than just transportation for the team. Before and after a race it was a sanctuary for the riders, an inviolable space free from fans and journalists. They could pull gray shades down over windows tinted so dark no one could see in anyway, and they pulled blue curtains across the windshield and similarly cloaked the entrance to the front door. Thus, the bus was a mystery and yet one more source of longing for fans who ached to be in there, to take part in the team's rituals and listen in on their meetings, to snack on their food and drink the espressos the team drew in the little kitchen and strip down in the shower room built into the back and afterward dry off with an Astana team towel before sinking into one of the deep-seated, deeply cushioned seats that slanted downward from front to back so that your butt dropped lower than your thighs. I wanted to do all that, too. Instead I mostly just walked through the bus, taking notes on what was in there—though I did open the dope-free, blood-bag-free refrigerated cabinets, just to take a peek and make sure they were that way. When I'd asked Bruyneel if I could go in alone and take a look around, he kind of frowned and lifted an eyebrow, and said, "Sure. It's a bus, you know. There's not much to interest you."

"No one's ever allowed in it," I said. "That makes it interesting."

"I guess. Okay. You will see there is nothing to fascinate."

But he was wrong.

A lot about the bus was what I'd expected. There were sports balms on the shelves and in the bathroom, warm-up lotions scattered around, and blue plastic trash cans that were so clean they must be scrubbed by someone. There was a big can of Smith & Nephew Moisture Vaporpermeable spray dressing for wounds, and there were lots of scissors lying around, in the cup holders, on a couple of seats, on the shelves, and around the sink. There was a control panel for the sound system and television. And across the back of the bus there was a partitioned room with a door, a private sleeper.

Over the door was the fascinating thing.

There were two stickers above the entrance, the kind that are put on the racer's bikes for easy identification, with each racer's name and nationality printed on a transparent adhesive strip. Contador's sticker had been put above the door. Just above it was a fresher sticker: Armstrong's.

"You have a beer," Chris said when I was back out by the mechanics' truck. I looked at the man still talking about Lance's bike with his daughter, then I took the opened bottle from Chris, Birra Moretti. I swallowed down a swig, then said, "What's up with those stickers over the private compartment in the bus?"

"Oh, man," said Chris. "That's where the leader sleeps, you know."

"Yeah." I took another drink. "I get that. But who will get the room at the Tour, when they're both on the bus?"

Chris laughed, and giving a sort of cockeyed nod he does with his head, he said, "We will see, huh? The best, okay?"

"Yeah."

"Oh, shit," said Chris. "It's Skippy." He tilted his chin up behind me, and I turned. Riding toward us was a man in blue bike clothes on an all-pink bike. He had a white beard, bright blue sunglasses, and a protruding, uneven smile. Chris walked away.

Craig said, "Oh, come on now, Chris. He's your friend."

"Like hell."

Up in the truck, Alan guffawed.

Skippy coasted in toward us, braked, and got off his bike. He was tall and skinny. He propped the bike lengthwise in front of his body and leaned over it. One hand held the handlebar and the other, supported by an elbow propped on the saddle, cupped his cheek. He'd settled in. Chris was looking through a toolbox, and Craig was working at some of the sugary gel that had dripped onto one of the frames and could not be removed by the degreaser they liked to use for everything. Alan stood in the open bay of the truck. No one said hello, and Skippy didn't seem to expect them to. He watched us, his front teeth nibbling at his bottom lip.

He said, "How's Levi?"

"I don't know," said Craig.

"Oh," said Skippy. "How's Pops?"

"Who?"

"Pops. Popovych."

"Popo," said Chris. "His nickname is Popo."

"I don't know," said Craig. "Good, I guess."

Skippy said, "Lance looks pretty good." No one answered him.

The man who'd brought the beer was kneeling in front of the yellow bike now. His daughter had kind of sat her rump against his thigh and had one skinny, bare arm thrown around his neck.

Skippy watched us all. I was the only one not engaged in something that would allow me to not look back at him. I took about six sips of that beer.

"Chris," said Skippy. "Do you mind if I wash my bike?"

Chris ignored him, rattled some metal things around in the toolbox.

Craig looked at Chris, looked at Skippy and back at Chris, and said, "Oh, go on." He motioned with the rag he was holding in one hand. "Back around the truck there."

Skippy walked off, his shoes clicking on the asphalt.

"Who was that?" I said.

"He follows us everywhere," Craig said. "Chris can't stand him, but I suppose I feel a bit for him. He says he raises money for the disabled, and I suppose he does. He goes through our rubbish sometimes, and everyone's, and when he finds old parts and pieces we've thrown away he takes them. He says he gives them to charities."

"Oh." I watched the man with the daughter get to his feet, rub his knees. He turned and dipped his head to Craig, a little bow. Craig nodded and said thanks, and I held up the half-empty beer. The man smiled, then he took his daughter's hand and they walked off.

Chris was uncharacteristically silent, and for a few minutes more Alan and Craig bantered about handlebar tape and tire glue and whatever little job it was they turned to, but gradually they, too, fell silent. I finished my beer and sat on the tailgate of the truck, and listened to the scrape of tools fitting into bolts and sliding back into their little holsters in the tool kits. I could hear the hose running, too.

It was the quietest moment for me of the whole Giro d'Italia. Skippy washed and washed and washed his bike back there in private, as if wanting for as long as he possibly could to cleanse his bike with Lance Armstrong's water.

No one could say what he expected out of such a thing. Nor if the cancer survivor's daughter ever could have guessed when the day began that she would watch her father kneel before a bicycle. Skippy and the kneeling man and me, I figured, we were not so different. We all expected something from Lance, and we all had to make the best out of whatever it was we got. I sat and watched the mechanics and listened to the water in the hose and looked at the yellow bike from time to time and, finally, I realized that was true for Lance, too.

What No One Understands

Stefano Garzelli had attacked on the first real ascent of Stage 10, the 14.6-kilometer Moncenisio, which climbed almost 1,000 meters and had one horrible stretch of a 14 percent grade. He gradually opened a Coppi-worthy lead of 6:30 and, when he crested the mountain all alone just about halfway through the 262-kilometer day, the nation of Italy went a little apeshit.

Behind him, the pack had begun shedding its sprinters and those who'd worked to pull the peloton to the start of the ascending, as well as the sick, the injured, those who hadn't been able to recover from the first week of racing, the undertrained, and the unlucky. Armstrong had gone to the front.

And, as a surprised DiLuca would later say, "He set the pace for a good way." (DiLuca would be surprised about this Giro in other ways: after the race was over, test results from two stages would show him positive for CERA, a new generation of EPO. He was hit with a two-year suspension and a $400,000 fine, but still denies doping.)

The course plunged down Moncenisio. Then, in one of the routine awful realities of bike racing, the road rose upward for another 34 kilometers that were counted not as a climb but merely as the approach to the climb: Sestriere. This mountaintop was the Cima Coppi—the highest point of the whole Giro—and Armstrong seemed destined to crack here.

After giving away nearly a minute more than he'd already planned on losing in Stage 5, Armstrong had lost another 39 seconds the next day when, after making it over the stage's two climbs with the pack, he'd gotten inattentive or fatigued or both, and slipped back out of a huge group of more than sixty riders screaming together toward the finish. He lost 18 more seconds the next day, and by Stage 8 was more than 4½ minutes behind the pink jersey of DiLuca. Stage 9 was supposed to be one of the premier events of the centenary celebration, a ten-lap race around Milan that started from the Piazza Duomo, but after previewing the course some of the racers thought it was too dangerous to ride—there were train tracks running lengthwise in some roads, cobblestones, tight corners, high curbs, and other hazards. Some of the team leaders met and decided the pack would ride at a neutralized, processional speed—around 15–18 mph—until the last lap. The confused crowd jeered the riders, lost interest, dispersed until attendance dropped to tens of thousands from hundreds of thousands. During one lap the entire peloton stopped at the finish and DiLuca took the announcer's microphone and apologized to the fans. Armstrong was just one of the riders who made the decision to shut down the racing, but he took the most criticism. The Giro's director, Zomegnan, had, without naming names—or, really, needing to—said, "This circuit was explosive, full of bursts, and required you to get your ass off the seat. But it seems like certain riders who aren't so young anymore didn't want to do that. Today, the riders' legs were shorter and their tongues grew."

Armstrong's critics and doubters were especially eager to see his tongue drag on Sestriere. Ten years earlier, the mountain had coronated him as the champion of his era. In the 1999 Tour de France, the twenty-six-year-old cancer survivor had taken the yellow jersey in an earlier time trial, but his rivals expected to crack him into pieces as soon as the race got to what had been his traditional weakness—the mountains. Using the descent before Sestriere as a launching pad, two of that year's contenders, Fernando Escartin and Ivan Gotti, attacked and got away; they pedaled onto the slope of Sestriere with a 30-second lead. Armstrong rode them down and won the stage by a little more than half a minute, a span of seconds that stretched into a seven-year reign. But that was so long ago that, during one of his video blogs at the Giro, Armstrong admitted he couldn't really recall much of the day. "I remember the finish," he said. "I remember seeing the buildings . . . but don't remember the climb." Prompted by Leipheimer that it had rained that day, Armstrong searched his memory, then said, "I didn't get rained on, but everybody else got rained on. That was lucky."

Garzelli crossed over the Sestriere clutching a desperate 6-minute lead over the main pack, and fellow Italian Ivan Basso ordered his Liquigas team to the front and began a ferocious chase. The pack shredded.

Armstrong hung on. It wasn't pretty. He stood and muscled his bike from side to side, twisting his shoulders and his ass, horsing his way up the climbs with power, and the beautifully blurry spinning cadence he'd been so well known for seemed to be as faint a memory as a rainstorm he'd managed to avoid a decade ago. It looked oddly familiar to me, and I watched him a long time before I remembered sitting on a motorcycle in 1994 and pulling alongside him to watch him ride just this way.

By the time the race was onto the last climb and had chiseled itself down to the leaders—DiLuca, Leipheimer, Menchov, Basso, Franco Pellizotti, Sastre, and a few others—Armstrong was still there. DiLuca dove into a nervy, edge-of-disaster attack on the twisty descent and held on for the win—and the honor of honoring Coppi. A lot of riders got crushed that day. Twenty-eight-year-old Damiano Cunego, for instance, who won the Giro in 2004, was 1:34 behind. Twenty-five-year-old Thomas Löfkvist, who'd worn pink for a day after taking the jersey on the climb to San Martino di Castrozza, finished 1:39 back. Armstrong finished with the scattered remains of the lead pack.

And he smiled.

Eight months after he'd officially announced it, his comeback finally seemed to be going forward. He'd gotten, at last, what he'd expected. And he'd given me, at least, a little of what I'd been hoping for without ever being fully able to admit to it.

He would go on to ride better and better from here, growing stronger as the Giro made its way south toward Rome. By Stage 16 he would actually be fresher than Leipheimer, and paced his cracking race leader up Monte Petrano. On Stage 17 he felt good enough to attack the pack on the final climb.

One day I was hanging out with Chris before a stage and I said, "I guess you fixed his shifting."

"No problem," Chris said.

"What was it?" I asked.

"I mean, there was no problem. Not here." He pointed to the

bike. "There was a problem here." He pointed to his head. "You see, man?"

I saw Chechu at the team hotel one night and I said, "He's back, isn't he?"

"What no one understands," Chechu said, "except us who ride with him, is that improvements that take us two weeks, three weeks of training, he does in nine days. It has always been this way." He might not have believed in miracles, but he believed in Armstrong.

TOUR DE FRANCE, STAGE 6
Girona–Barcelona, 181.5 km
JULY 9, 2009

The racers know Stage 7 is going to hurt. It's the longest of the Tour, it's the first mountain stage, and it ends with a 10.6-kilometer climb to the top of 2,240-meter-high Andorre Arcalis, the road on which Contador, who has been unable to hide his desire to wear yellow, is almost certain to finally lash out at those who stand between him and the jersey. So today, Stage 6, is supposed to more or less play the role of a decent warm-up.

From Girona, the pack is expected to meander over to the coast, then cruise south to Barcelona, where for the entertainment of a metropolis full of spectators they will race like hell for the final 13 kilometers.

The weather doesn't follow this plan. Neither does David Millar.

For 50 kilometers, everything is great. The sun is shining and there are no serious attacks to chase, none of the relentless testing of the pack's resolve in the opening kilometers that is by now as routine as it is dreaded. Dave Zabriskie attacks on the first little climb of the day but is back in the group before they crest. Zabriskie, who rode for Armstrong's U.S. Postal Service team from 2001 to 2004, is supremely talented. He's a five-time national time trial champion, and the only American to win a stage in all three Grand Tours. But since he crashed while wearing the yellow jersey in the team time trial of the 2005 Tour, he's been hesitant to ride as close to other cyclists as he should. He often spends much of a race on the outer sides of the pack, pedaling mile after mile unsheltered with the wind in his face, a strategy that keeps him safe but wastes an unspeakable amount of energy. Many of his teammates think he would win a lot more races if he'd simply ride in the pack like all the other pros. This isn't the only characteristic that sets him apart. He has a sense of humor so dry he appears to not even be aware he's funny, and as Bruyneel once said about him, "He's just kind of weird, man. If you ask him a question he might start howling like a wolf or sing a song." In 2009, while he was racing the Tour of California, thieves broke into his Utah home and stole, among other things, $11,000 worth of comic-book figurines, including Hellboy and Lara Croft.

Fifty kilometers into the stage, David Millar gets away. Millar is most famous for being a reformed doper. After his apartment was raided and he was convicted in 2004 of using EPO and banned for two years, he confessed and promised to come back clean to show it could be done. (And it could: he's since won three British national championships, the prologue time trial of Paris-Nice, and a stage of the Vuelta a España.) I don't know what he was like before the ban, but since I got to know him in 2007 he's been nothing but incorrigibly honest. I met him at a winter training camp where part of his job was to shill for the team's sponsors—tell everyone that everything was the greatest equipment he'd ever ridden. When he walked in the bar we were meeting at, he gamely had a go at explaining the bike's technology for a few minutes, then gave up and admitted, "When you look down at the wheels, it just looks fast. And that makes you feel faster."

Millar is joined by two riders, and as they speed toward Barcelona with a gap that hovers around 2 minutes, they run into a drizzling rain. In Spain that's the worst kind. It floats leaked diesel and oil up out of the pavement without washing it away, and makes the streets slicker than wet metal. The first raindrops fall at 2:45 p.m., and at 2:46 in the pack a racer named Eduardo Gonzalo crashes. When he gets up, he puts on a rain cape that he's given from his team car and rides back into the group. At 3:05 David Le Lay and Rubén Pérez crash. Laurens ten Dam goes down. Bbox wrecks in a big pile of blue jerseys again. Michael Rogers of Columbia crashes. Sastre and two teammates tangle up. George Hincapie falls over a fallen rider. Simon Spilak crashes twice. Every turn, every irregularity in the road, every slight bank is treacherous. There are bloody jerseys, ripped shorts, hobbled bikes, wincing riders everywhere.

The rain also ruins what should have been a welcoming party for Contador. With the Tour ending in his home country, he was expected to ride through a daylong corridor of cheers. The streets of inner Barcelona are as packed as most Tour finishes, but much of the length of the course is sparsely attended. And, anyway, the riders are too intent on staying intact to pay much attention to the crowd.

Near the end, Astana goes to the front to keep Armstrong and Contador safe, and this raises the pace. Millar attacks his breakaway companions with 29 kilometers to go, but by then the sprinters' teams sense they're close enough to deliver their men to the line, and they run Millar down with exquisite timing, catching him only in the last kilometer of the race. The Norwegian Thor Hushovd, who rides for Sastre's Cervélo team, wins a slippery sprint that is probably best summed up by Alessandro Ballan, who is the reigning world champion but opts out of the final rush because, he says afterward, "I had never seen so many crashes." Hincapie says he'd never been that scared on a bicycle. A twenty-six-year-old Dutchman riding in his rookie Tour de France, Kenny van Hummel, wobbles in nearly 16 minutes behind, and plummets to dead last in the standings.

And every one of them, from Hushovd to van Hummel, knows that tomorrow is going to be harder.

STAGE 6 RESULTS

1. Thor Hushovd, Cervélo	4:21:33
9. Cadel Evans, Silence-Lotto	Same time
10. Fabian Cancellara, Saxo Bank	
11. Andreas Kloden, Astana	
13. Andy Schleck, Saxo Bank	
20. Levi Leipheimer, Astana	
23. Alberto Contador, Astana	
24. Bradley Wiggins, Garmin	
27. Lance Armstrong, Astana	
30. Carlos Sastre, Cervélo	
36. Christian Vande Velde, Garmin	
75. Denis Menchov, Rabobank	+0:01:02

GENERAL CLASSIFICATION

1. Fabian Cancellara, Saxo Bank	19:29:22
2. Lance Armstrong, Astana	+0:00:00.22
3. Alberto Contador, Astana	+0:00:19
4. Andreas Kloden, Astana	+0:00:23
5. Levi Leipheimer, Astana	+0:00:31
6. Bradley Wiggins, Garmin	+0:00:38
8. Christian Vande Velde, Garmin	+0:01:16
14. Andy Schleck, Saxo Bank	+0:01:41
23. Carlos Sastre, Cervélo	+0:02:44
26. Cadel Evans, Silence-Lotto	+0:02:59
64. Denis Menchov, Rabobank	+0:04:54

NEVADA CITY CLASSIC
Nevada City, California, 44 miles
JUNE 21, 2009

The Craziest Thing

At the site of Lance Armstrong's final chance to hone his legs and secure the elusive victory that would erase the psychological smudge of going winless into what was arguably the biggest race of his life, the media pit was not crammed in some remote off-course corner like so many were, or exiled so far from the start/finish line that the only real chance to see the racers was on a TV feed. Here on Broad Street in the gold rush tourist town of Nevada City, the media could stand right out on the pavement with not even a single strip of yellow caution tape separating them from the course. As the racers lined up for their early evening start, they brushed their arms and knees and handlebars against some of the reporters. The odors of the liniments that glossed the racers' legs and the acidic tang of the sweat produced by their warm-ups wafted into the media pit. Nervous pre-race chitchat was easily overheard, along with nose-clearing sniffs, coughs caused by no malady other than jitters, and big, lung-clearing sighs of dread or disbelief or desperate hope or sometimes relief.

I'd ensured myself access to these riches of sensory detail by introducing myself to the race promoter, Duane Strawser, and, after explaining who I was and summarizing my credentials, requesting a prestigious front-row spot for the start.

"Sure, go on," said Strawser.

I recognized a few of the racers filling the street in front of me. There was Justin England, who rode for California Giant Berry Farms and had won here last year and in 2004. And there was big, strong Ben Jacques-Maynes, who rode for Bissell and for a while had hung on past the point of common sense in that climbing group with Armstrong in Stage 5 of the Gila. These guys were no doubt thinking about what a win against Armstrong might do for their careers. But there were a lot of elite-level amateurs, too, and some developmental racers, and even some who, I could tell by their jerseys, were what in cycling is called "unattached," privateers who belonged to no team. These guys were wondering things like if it would be too embarrassing to ask Armstrong to autograph their race numbers with the permanent markers they happened to have in their jersey pockets. (And the answer for at least one of them, I would see after Armstrong rode up to the line in a few minutes, was no.)

To my right in the exclusive front row of the media pit was a young woman holding a white, fuzzy headband decorated with black panda ears. She noticed me looking at the ears and waved them and a camera at me and said, "Do you think Lance will wear these for me?"

"No," I said.

"Oh." She seemed genuinely disappointed. "I have this web project, Panda of the Week, where I show pictures of famous cyclists wearing panda ears."

"Of course," I said.

"Levi wore them for me. And Tyler Hamilton."

I said, "Lance is not going to put those on his head."

But then I thought I shouldn't have been so sure. Wearing panda ears wouldn't be the craziest thing that had happened to him that month.

Toughness Is Being Redefined

On June 1, the two men who'd been arrested in connection with the theft of Armstrong's bike during the Tour of California back in February both pled no contest to their charges. According to reports from the Sacramento Police Department, the two had been arrested on April 7 after an investigation that began when Dung Hoang Le turned the $10,000 bike in to the police station on February 18, three days after the theft, saying he'd bought it for $1,500 (presumably from a person he didn't know and without knowing it was stolen). Realizing it was Armstrong's, he said, he now wanted to return it. After questioning him, police obtained a search warrant for his mobile phone and computer, and discovered four conversations between Le and Lee Monroe Crider, who was on parole for bike theft. Crider told police he'd stolen the bike and sold it to Le for $200. Le received three years of probation and ninety days in jail. Crider was sentenced to three years in prison.

On June 4, Armstrong's son, Maxwell Edward Armstrong, was born. He weighed 7 pounds 5 ounces, just a little more than the amount his father would lose in the month between the end of the Giro and the start of the Tour. (Armstrong had tipped off the impending birth to careful followers of his life by alluding to Anna's labor in a Twitter post that said, "Toughness is being redefined today.")

On June 5, Armstrong was insulted by Bernard Hinault, one of the four riders who won the Tour five times and whose riding style most people sum up by referencing his nickname, "the Badger," but which I prefer to characterize by citing one of his great statements of his race strategy: "As long as I breathe, I attack." The newspaper *Le Parisien* reported that, speaking at a presentation for one of the towns on the Tour route, Hinault said of Armstrong: "I hope he will not be there. . . . He cannot win the Tour. I hope that Contador gives him a beating."

On June 6, Armstrong referenced the news reports about Hinault on his Twitter site and said, "What a wanker. Five TdF wins doesn't buy you any common sense."

On June 9, speaking about performance-enhancing drugs at a conference at Coventry University in the United Kingdom, Greg LeMond again accused Armstrong of doping. The two champions had been feuding since 2001, when, in an interview published in London's *Sunday Times,* LeMond criticized Armstrong for maintaining a relationship with Michele Ferrari. The next month he released a statement apologizing for his criticism. He would later claim he was forced to issue the apology by Trek, the company that builds Armstrong's Trek bikes and had licensed the LeMond name for a separate line. (In April of 2008, Trek severed its relationship with LeMond, prompting a LeMond lawsuit and Trek countersuit that were both settled out of court for mostly undisclosed terms in early 2010.) After years of accusations and rebuttals, at the bike industry's annual trade show in September of 2008, LeMond sat in the front row of a press conference about Armstrong's return and, called upon by Armstrong to pose the first question, grilled him and Don Catlin about the accuracy and integrity of the independent anti-doping program they were planning. Then in the June 2009 speech, which also lambasted Ferrari, LeMond recounted details of a phone call he says occurred between him and Armstrong after he criticized the relationship with Ferrari: "In this conversation he said, 'Come on, Greg. You're telling me you haven't used EPO. Everybody's used EPO. Your win in 1989 was like mine. It was a miracle.'" While taking questions from the audience, when asked if he thought Armstrong would ever admit to doping, LeMond said, "Him? No way. Absolutely not. He has no conscience."

On a June 10 Twitter post, Armstrong linked to a video of LeMond's talk and commented, "Uh oh . . . someone drank too much Hate-orade and ate too many Hater-tots." That same day, Astana stopped using the faded jerseys they'd been wearing since Stage 7 of the Giro to protest their financial crisis. Bruyneel had commissioned jerseys that kept the team's three paying sponsors (Nike, Trek, and KazMunaiGaz, a Kazakh petroleum company) at full visibility while fading the five others and the team name on the chest to a ghostly outline. Astana had avoided losing its license outright—and being disbanded—when the main sponsor replenished the team's $2 million escrow fund as required by the UCI. So the jerseys had gone back to full color. But now the UCI was demanding that to prove solvency Astana come up with an additional deposit of up to $9 million to cover estimated expenses for the rest of the year—an amount not many people thought Astana could deliver. Bruyneel and Armstrong were trying to put together a sponsorship to start a new team that would be branded Livestrong. Contador, meanwhile, had assured Bruyneel he'd ride with Livestrong but was quietly negotiating with other teams as well.

On June 14, in an interview with *Gazzetta dello Sport*, Contador characterized Armstrong as one of his Tour rivals: "I will have to deal with Menchov, Evans, the Schleck brothers, Sastre, and my teammates Armstrong and Leipheimer."

On June 17, the UCI announced that Astana had met the financial guarantees and would retain its license. Bruyneel and Armstrong abandoned the plans to form a new team. Contador's own extracurricular negotiation was awkwardly exposed. He had assumed Astana would default and, according to a source inside the team, had already set up a new deal with Garmin. The agreement was solid enough that an announcement date of June 20 had been established, and Garmin team bikes were already on the way to Contador in Spain. (Tour winners don't come cheap, and Contador had demanded that Garmin also sign his personal mechanic, soigneur, and Astana teammates Benjamín Noval and Paulinho. To cover the approximately $2 million this would cost just for the rest of 2009, Garmin had reportedly agreed to bring on Herbalife as a new co-sponsor.)

On June 18, the UCI announced that it had approved an experimental ban on the use of radio earpieces during Stages 10 and 13 of the Tour de France. (Some experts believed radios reduced the excitement of racing by eliminating the need for riders to make their own split-second decisions or formulate their own strategies in response to attacks and breakaways, and by allowing so much communication there was never any uncertainty about time gaps or which riders were where. Armstrong—like Bruyneel—was not a mere proponent of radios but among the biggest beneficiaries of the technology. It was Bruyneel who introduced to the sport the idea that every rider on a team should have a two way radio, and who has inarguably made the best use of it.) On the same day, Armstrong announced that as final preparation for the Tour de France he, Leipheimer, and Horner, who were all training together in Aspen, would race at a well-regarded but little-known circuit race in Nevada City in three days.

On June 21, Armstrong loaded up his family and teammates into his private plane and flew from Aspen to Nevada City, where he was about to wrap up the month by getting asked to wear panda ears.

100 Percent Sure

Armstrong appeared from somewhere and rode to the start on a wave of noise.

Nevada City's population hovers around 3,000. By a quick estimate I'd made earlier while walking the course, I figured there were at least 5,000 people on the length of Broad Street alone. The entirety of the 1.1-mile circuit wasn't entirely packed with fans, but there were long stretches that were lined with lawn chairs and picnic benches with a row or two of people standing behind. And a long, steep climb on the backside and a series of twisting streets that began with a treacherous downhill corner were too thick with people to even make a decent guess. Strawser said that by comparing the size of this crowd to the years when he could make an accurate count, he figured there might be 20,000 in attendance. If Armstrong were to draw that sort of ratio in Manhattan, the borough's temporary population would jump to 11.4 million people—or more than ten times the size of the estimated crowd that fills Times Square on New Year's Eve. All of which is to say that there had never been such a noise on Broad Street in Nevada City as there was on June 21, 2009.

Armstrong, wearing Livestrong kit and riding a black bike with no decals, cruised over to the announcer and, like a rock star fluffing a venue, began telling the crowd—about 10 percent of whom might have lived there—how much he liked their town. Horner had coasted up right in front of me, in Astana kit. I liked Horner. When he was riding hard, his face took on a grimace that manifested as a smile, so he projected the perverse expression of a man thrilled by suffering. He and Armstrong had started racing at about the same time. Just about a month younger, Horner had taken a stage of the 1996 Tour DuPont that Armstrong had won outright. But instead of becoming a superstar, Horner had embarked upon a circuitous route to becoming one of the best *domestiques* in the peloton. He'd signed with the European team Française des Jeux in 1997, but as a sacrificial worker rather than protected royalty, he couldn't adapt to the harsh life and unfamiliar culture, and returned home to race in 2000. Retreating from Europe is typically the death of the dream for U.S. cyclists— and a not uncommon fate. But after five years stateside Horner had made a name as a savvy, tough, skilled racer, and after a top-ten finish in the 2004 world championships he was signed by the European powerhouse Saunier Duval, then later worked for Cadel Evans at Silence-Lotto before being recruited by Bruyneel in 2008. Bruyneel, who had relied on similar gifts during his racing career, had told me that he admired Horner's tactical sense and grittiness—and the ultimate proof of this was that Horner was one of the few cyclists who'd spoken negatively of Armstrong in public and been able to remain a close teammate. In a 2007 interview with Cyclingnews.com, after the Discovery team folded upon Armstrong's retirement, Horner had characterized Armstrong as someone who rode "because he was a businessman more than for the love of the sport." In 2009, when asked by Cyclingnews if Armstrong's return inspired him, Horner had laughed and said, "I don't need him to inspire me!" Despite this, Armstrong trusted Horner, seemed to like him—he'd given the pickup-driving Oregonian the nickname "Redneck"—and counted on him, teammates told me, with an intensity somewhat like a minor version of the bond he felt with Chechu. Horner horrified nutritionists and amused teammates by eating Little Debbie snack cakes on rides, and hamburgers during stage races; at the Tour of the Gila we'd compared notes on the country's burger joints and I'd impressed him with my just-gained knowledge of the local chain Lotaburger. "Thanks for talking meat," he'd said as he clicked his foot into the pedal to follow the pack out of the start area one morning.

When I saw him in Nevada City, I said, "You guys are crazy for doing this." I was referring to riding, just a few days before the start of the Tour de France, among amateur and semipro riders on a course known for spectacular crashes in a tight corner at the bottom of the 40- to-50-mph descent down Broad Street.

Horner laughed, shook his head, and said, "We had breakfast in Aspen, flew here with Lance's whole family, and are going back right after this so we can finish our altitude training for the Tour."

But Horner wasn't going to make the Tour. He didn't know it yet.

Bruyneel was in the biggest strategical dilemma of the year. "My heart wanted Lance to win," he had told me. "My head said Alberto was going to. My worst fear was that neither would—that the conflict between them would tear the team up and we'd lose the Tour to Evans or Schleck. I'd be the guy who went into the Tour with four racers who'd been on its podium—and two racers who between them had eight Tour wins—and couldn't get the job done." He'd come up with a brilliant but cruel strategy: he would put neither Contador's favorite *domestique* (Noval) nor Armstrong's favorite (Horner) on the Tour roster. He believed this would prevent the formation of divisive camps during the race, and also might force his star rivals to cooperate out of sheer necessity: with the climbers Noval and Horner replaced by the bigger workhorses Muravyev and Rast, Contador and Armstrong might end up having to depend on each other for support in the mountains.

"I knew Horner deserved to go," Bruyneel had told me after he'd made the decision but before it was announced. "But I also knew he couldn't go."

Lance was in front of us again, and the panda woman was asking him to wear her ears. I saw him shaking his head. I heard booming like a bass riff at a concert the announcer shouting exhortations: Nevada City had never seen a crowd like this! How about Armstrong, who'd finished third last time he'd raced here, as an amateur nineteen years ago! The winner of the first lap would win a luxury houseboat vacation on Bullards Bar Reservoir! I heard under all that the voice of Armstrong telling the panda lady, "I am 100 percent sure that I don't want to do it." I watched Horner smiling, which was the same expression he made when he was suffering.

Open Hearts, Open Minds

It is always stunning how fast pro cyclists go. I've been attending bike races for more than a quarter century and I am never not shocked at the speed. What they do on a bicycle is as different from the way most people pedal as a Formula 1 car is from a go-cart. It is barely the same sport, as separate as golf and mini-golf.

There had been races going on all day in Nevada City, beginning with a kids' event at 12:45 (everyone was a winner), then various amateur categories split by age (all the way up to masters' 45+ races), and the pro women. The race that finished just before Armstrong's was Cat 3 men, which is the level about as high as a physiologically ordinary cyclist with a normal job and happy family can reach, and the crowd had become acclimated to that speed.

When the pro pack screamed into the first corner I saw people actually flinch, step backward, gasp in surprise. "Blazing fast!" a guy yelled into his wife's face. Another said, "Good god!" Then the pack passed and the trailing wind blew by, riffling hair and fluttering race programs, and in the street sucking straw wrappers and leaves and small twigs after it, and everyone was smiling. Watching was an adrenaline rush.

The fans weren't the only ones surprised by the speed. By the time the race hit the first climb on the backside of the course, the head of the pack already seemed to be about half a minute in front of the tail, which was bleeding riders all over the road. Of the 104 who started, only 51 would finish.

A racer named Graham Howard won the houseboat vacation, then Leipheimer attacked on the third lap and got a gap. Armstrong bridged to him on the fourth lap, dragging a tail of racers with him, but the only one who could stay was Ben Jacques-Maynes. "Those are two guys who are leaving in a few days to race the Tour de France," Jacques-Maynes told me afterward. "I knew better than to try to go toe to toe with them. I was just trying to sit on their wheels and not make myself look ridiculous."

Horner played the good teammate and sat in the front of the pack until the pair had a minute or so lead, then began working harder and wove through dropped and lapped riders. There was going to be forty laps of this. I decided to walk the course.

On an open stretch of Cottage Street I stopped by a family, a dad in khakis and a blue button-down, a mom in a pink tank top and blue shorts, and their son in a soccer jersey and riding a training-wheel bike.

"Is that Lance?" the boy asked as the remnants of the pack went by.

"No," said the dad.

"Is that Lance?"

"No."

"Is that Lance?"

"No."

"Is that Lance?"

"No."

"Is Lance tall?"

A pause. "I think he's tall. Yeah, he's tall."

Farther back on the course, at the Nevada City United Methodist Church, a letterboard sign out front announced upcoming events and boasted the church's policy of "open hearts, open minds, open door." Strung across the entrance to the front stairs, which led up to a landing and a wide patio, there was a thin rope, and braided onto that was a hand-lettered cardboard sign that said RESERVED N.C.U.M.C.

And as I continued to walk, I found that, as it is everywhere Armstrong goes, he had his detractors. On York Street, I saw the work of someone who must have heard that in the big-time races in Europe the fans spray-painted the roads, and had decided to use the format to aggravate Armstrong. The street graffiti proclaimed that its creator hearted Sheryl Crow, one of Armstrong's ex-girlfriends. And in a shop window, some owner had displayed an enormous scrapbook-style posterboard celebrating the Nevada City Classic's most famous winner, three-time victor Greg LeMond.

A Matter More of Faith

I've always found it intriguing that it was Armstrong's most bitter public enemy, LeMond, who came up with the only proposition regarding dope and Armstrong that everyone can agree with. "If Lance is clean," he told reporter David Walsh in that 2001 *Sunday Times* interview, "it is the greatest comeback in the history of sports. If he isn't, it would be the greatest fraud."

Everything else—and people on both sides of the dispute disdain me for this stance—is a matter more of faith than fact.

The purported evidence that argues for Armstrong's innocence or guilt when it comes to doping is open to interpretation, and always has been.

In 1999, in the first stage of the Tour, a urine sample taken from Armstrong showed traces of synthetic corticoids. This is a type of steroid that is banned by the UCI unless the rider has a medical prescription that authorizes its use to treat such ailments as skin infections or asthma. According to several journalists who saw the document that year and afterward, the standard form Armstrong filled out in conjunction with his test that day indicated that he was taking no exempted medicines. But eighteen days later, after news of the test leaked to the press, the UCI stated that it had, in fact, received a medical prescription authorizing Armstrong to use such an ointment to treat a skin allergy. Armstrong's critics, who include a member of the 1999 team's staff, cite the late-surfacing prescription not as exoneration but as a cover-up that is nothing more than further proof of his culpability. What's more confounding is that technically Armstrong didn't even need the exemption: though his detractors still characterize the result as a positive for doping, the trace amounts detected in the sample were below the limit that was legally considered a positive.

In 2005, a month after Armstrong's retirement, *L'Equipe* reported that six urine samples, which had been taken from him during the 1999 Tour and stored at a French lab, had shown traces of EPO during what was supposed to be a series of anonymous retests as part of a program to create a better method of detecting the drug. (No test for EPO existed in 1999.) Identity numbers on the samples reportedly matched the numbers on Armstrong's doping control forms. (Numbers are the only way samples are tracked in the labs, so that the technicians conducting the tests don't know which riders the results are for.) Armstrong's critics hailed this as the incontrovertible proof they'd been looking for. Armstrong and his supporters argued that the tests could hardly be considered valid because a laboratory that was violating its own policies on anonymity could not be trusted to have securely stored the samples, to have ensured the chain of custody of the samples had never been breached, or to have prevented someone from tampering with either the samples or the identity numbers. In addition, the pro-Armstrong camp contended, the findings couldn't be considered positive even theoretically because no second confirmation test had been performed in the presence of the athlete, as required under cycling's regulations. The UCI hired a Dutch lawyer who'd headed up his country's anti-doping program for ten years, Emile Vrigman, to investigate the matter. In May 2006 Vrigman issued a 130-page report that "exonerates Lance Armstrong completely," concluded that the samples were mishandled to the point that invalidated the results, accused the lab of behaving "in ways that are completely inconsistent with the rules and regulations of international anti-doping control testing," and recommended that another investigation be conducted to determine if the World Anti-Doping Agency, the lab, and others involved in the leak had committed ethical or legal violations. "It doesn't even qualify as a finding," Vrigman told the news agency Reuters. "It may suffice for research purposes but for a valid doping result—no way."

And that's how it was for all the years between those two incidents: every claim had a counterclaim, which itself often spurred a counter-counterclaim. Personal testimonies conflicted, had gaping holes, or could not be corroborated. Relentless research by journalists such as David Walsh, Pierre Ballester, and Paul Kimmage eventually piled up into a mountain of circumstantial evidence, but they found not one person who would go on the record as actually witnessing an act of doping by Armstrong, not one solid piece of evidence such as his DNA on a syringe or from a blood bag, not a single receipt for drug products or treatment such as has been found for many other convicted cyclists. By the time I was watching him race in Nevada City, Armstrong said he'd undergone thirty-two drug tests since his comeback began. During the Tour de France later that year, Bruyneel would tell me that he counted eighty-one drug tests for Astana; the next closest team was Saxo Bank with fifty-nine. Through all of that, and since turning pro in 1992, Armstrong had never tested positive.

The worst that could be factually said of him was that he was the greatest Tour de France rider in a time of great Tour de France doping. A survey of the eight riders who occupied the twenty-one available podium steps with him from 1999 through 2005 clearly shows this.

In 2005, the second- and third-place racers were Ivan Basso and Jan Ullrich. Basso was suspended in 2007 for two years after admitting to "attempted doping" in relation to his involvement in Operación Puerto, a wide-ranging investigation into blood doping that centered on Spanish doctor Eufemiano Fuentes. (In the most prevalent form of modern blood doping, cyclists remove their own blood and harvest the red blood cells, which are frozen for storage then reinjected shortly before competition. This increases the number of oxygen-carrying cells in the cyclist's body, which boosts their endurance, speed, and recovery.) Two months after Ullrich retired in February 2007, the German sports news service SID reported that DNA samples confirmed that his blood was in nine bags taken as evidence in Operación Puerto. A year later, in return for German prosecutors agreeing to close their investigation into his alleged blood doping, Ullrich made a payment to the public treasury that was disclosed only as "six digits" but was widely reported to be 250,000 euros. It was not considered a legal admission of guilt, and on his website, JanUllrich.de, Ullrich wrote, "There can be no confession because I have never cheated anyone."

In 2004, Basso was third and Andreas Kloden was second. Though in May of 2009 Kloden's name was mentioned in a report summarizing an investigation of blood doping at a German university, he has never been convicted of doping by a legal or sporting authority or failed a drug test. Two racers accused in the report of receiving illegal blood transfusions in 2006 with Kloden were Matthias Kessler and Patrik Sinkewitz. Kessler was first suspended and then fired by his team in 2007 after failing a drug test for testosterone. Sinkewitz was suspended then fired by his team in 2007 after testing positive for testosterone, and later that year admitted doping with his own blood and EPO.

In 2003, Ullrich was second and Alexandre Vinokourov was third. Vinokourov tested positive for blood doping in the 2007 Tour de France, resulting in the withdrawal of his team and his eventual two-year suspension from the sport.

In 2002, Joseba Beloki was second and Raimondas Rumšas was third. Beloki was initially implicated in Operación Puerto and banned by his team from the 2006 Tour de France, but later cleared by Spanish courts. Rumšas was banned from the sport for one year after testing positive for EPO at the 2003 Giro d'Italia. In 2006, he and his wife were given four-month suspended sentences by a French court for importing prohibited drugs, stemming from charges brought when she was caught after the 2002 Tour with growth hormone and EPO in her car.

In 2000 and 2001, Ullrich was second and Beloki was third.

In 1999, Alex Zülle was second and Fernando Escartin was third. As part of what became known as the Festina Affair, in which the Festina team was banned from the Tour and five of its riders admitted to doping, Zülle served an eight-month suspension after confessing to four years of EPO use. Escartin has never been linked to doping. Two years after he retired, his former team, Kelme, had its invitation to the Tour withdrawn after an ex-racer, Jesús Manzano, claimed to have been part of the squad's organized doping program under Eufemiano Fuentes, a claim that led to Operación Puerto. But Escartin's name never was associated with the investigation or Manzano's allegations.

To sum it up: of the eight riders who shared a Tour podium with Armstrong during his win streak, five (Basso, Ullrich, Rumšas, Vinokourov, Zülle) admitted doping, were suspended for it, were convicted of it in court, or paid a fine to have charges settled; two others (Beloki and Kloden) were linked to doping investigations, then

cleared or never charged; just one (Escartin) had no direct association with doping allegations. Even the staunchest proponents of
Armstrong's purity can't deny that the years of his domination were
filthy were dope.

None of this meant Armstrong cheated. Or that he didn't.

I thought that people first decided what they believed about Armstrong, then constructed a canon from the same set of incidents cited
by those who just as passionately swore the opposite. What I ended
up believing was that I couldn't know if he'd ever doped. After wad-
ing through the evidence as objectively as I could for a decade, I'd
become an agnostic. And it was with an admittedly indefensible act
of faith that in 2009 I ended up believing without reservation that,
however unknowable the past might be, Armstrong was clean for
his comeback.

If I wanted, I could try to credit my conversion to what some
people might marshal as reasons: the number of tests Armstrong
underwent; the fact that Horner, universally considered a clean rider,
rode so compatibly with Armstrong; and maybe most persuasively
of all the willingness of Garmin, a team founded on the premise of
being openly and staunchly anti-dope, to hire Contador, a rider who
won under Bruyneel's direction the same as Armstrong had. (Bruyneel and Armstrong are sometimes theorized to have together mas-
terminded a doping program that cannot be detected, or replicated
at any other team, and Contador had fallen under this same suspicion.) But these new contentions are as easy to refute as any of the
old ones. Just to take the first one, for instance, throughout 2009
Armstrong and Astana were accused of delaying anti-doping officials who showed up to conduct tests. (The most publicized instance
was Showergate, when a representative from the French anti-doping
agency showed up for a surprise, out-of-competition test without a
credential; Armstrong took a shower while Bruyneel validated the
official's standing, resulting in a 20-minute delay that Armstrong
could have been sanctioned for.)

When it comes to trying to construct proofs from the known

facts about Armstrong and dope, any rigorously objective conclusion always adds up to zero. The only way to shift to plus or minus, though no one who is passionate about either position will admit so, is through faith. Maybe I'd been moved by appreciating the way Chechu, Popo, Horner, and the other riders closest to Armstrong accepted his physical and mental superiority. Maybe it was being there at the Giro to personally witness from up close the transformation of his body. More likely, it was simply that the inexplicable and unpredictable human need to believe had for some reason washed over me. Like a true person of faith, I was content that, even though I had no proof, I had the only answer I needed.

The Last Sort of Celebration

With six laps to go, Armstrong, Leipheimer, and Jacques-Maynes had lapped everyone else in the race at least once, including Horner and last year's winner, England, who didn't seem to care much. After the race, England said that it had been an honor just to start next to Armstrong. "That's kind of a once-in-a-career chance for a rider like me," he said. "That was a lot of fun."

Armstrong attacked on the hill with six to go and rode the rest of the race out front by himself. On the last lap, people were running into the road as he streaked by. He lifted both arms high in the air as he crossed the line, his knees locked against the top tube of his bike to stabilize it, and his face said that this mattered, the Nevada City Classic, the first win of the comeback of Lance Armstrong.

Despite the one motorcycle and fifty racers still coming down the road somewhere behind him, the crowd crashed over the curbs and filled the street. The announcer jabbed the microphone at Armstrong and, panting, Lance elicited a roar from the crowd by saying, "From the smell of barbecues, from the smell of beer—in turn two I thought I smelled something I won't go into—anyways, the atmosphere, just the last sort of celebration lap, people running the streets . . . I'll put this crowd up against anything we race in Europe."

Jacques-Maynes came in second just ahead of Levi, 21 seconds behind Armstrong. "I couldn't take a single pull," he told me. "If I'd gone to the front once, I'd have been dropped. It was that fast."

Armstrong waved to Anna and his kids, who'd watched the race from a balcony above the finish line. It was Father's Day. He signed autographs and congratulated the kids who'd won their races. He had a jet waiting, and a Tour. He had his victory, finally, too. The only thing he didn't have when he left Nevada City was the trophy he'd won. He forgot it.

TOUR DE FRANCE, STAGES 7–21

Barcelona, Spain–Paris, France, 2,643.5 km

JULY 10–26, 2009

Not Even a Dream of the Yellow Jersey

The breakaway is perfect, Bruyneel thinks. Just 34 kilometers after leaving Barcelona for the start of Stage 7, a group of nine riders had coalesced out front after numerous opening attacks and chases. Now, 60 kilometers into the day, Bruyneel is happy to see the gap at slightly more than 12 minutes.

Fabian Cancellara is going to lose the jersey today on the climb to Andorre Arcalis. Even he knows it.

The identity of the yellow jersey's new owner is a great concern to Bruyneel. The best outcome for Astana is that one of the contenders from another team is foolish enough to take the lead. No one can ever predict what the first mountain will do to the riders—there is always the risk, with even the fittest and most determined, that their bodies will go into a kind of shock upon slamming into the first extended, steep grade. But even if both Contador and Armstrong have a bad day, Bruyneel is almost certain none of their serious rivals will ride into the yellow jersey. Saxo Bank's team director, Bjarne Riis, is too smart to let Andy Schleck into yellow. Riis is thinking the same thing Bruyneel is: no sense in wasting the team trying to protect the jersey from here all the way to the Alps, which don't start until Stage 15 and are where the Tour will most likely be decided. The two Garmin riders, Wiggins and Vande Velde, are both close enough to take the jersey by a few seconds with an all-out attack on today's final climb. And Garmin could use a victory. Vande Velde had won a stage of Paris-Nice, their sprinter Farrar had won one at Tirreno-Adriatico, and Tom Peterson had taken a stage in California, but that was it in terms of big results. But though Garmin's team director, Matt White, can be a bit erratic, as inexperienced directors sometimes are, he rode for Bruyneel from 2001 to 2003 and knows the conventional wisdom is to not take on the burden of the jersey this early.

If none of the overall hopefuls will impose the jersey upon their teams, the next best scenario for Bruyneel is what is happening. The highest-placed rider in the break is an Italian who rides for AG2R, Rinaldo Nocentini, a thirty-two-year-old who is more of a one-day specialist than a stage racer. He's strong enough and savvy enough to hold on to the jersey for a while if he gets it—he won a stage of the Tour of California this year, and was second at Paris-Nice last year. But his team isn't so deep that Astana will encounter significant resistance taking it from him when the right time comes. Nocentini is 3:13 behind Armstrong (and 2:54 behind Contador), so a win of even five minutes would give him a lead Bruyneel feels confident managing.

The worst outcome is that either Armstrong or Contador decides to fight for the jersey, and Astana gets rent into opposing camps. Bruyneel is sure Armstrong will understand the harm of having the jersey; they've been through this seven times together and have won, in part, because they were willing to give the jersey to other teams when it made sense. Armstrong says he'll work for the team. Bruyneel believes him.

Contador, he can't be sure about. Bruyneel has to admit that he just doesn't understand the kid. Even Armstrong would always listen to Bruyneel when it came to strategy—no matter how famous the rider got, no matter how successful. But from the beginning, Bruyneel says, Contador had to be talked into almost every decision in every race—and gave the impression that he was going along with a plan he knew wasn't as good as his own. Bruyneel had guided riders to twelve Grand Tour victories in ten years—the best directorship in cycling ever. But Contador seemed to convey that he could have won more and by bigger margins and with more spectacular rides if he'd been able to do it his own way.

The tension between them was nothing new. It had just been kept private before. They'd almost parted in June of 2008—not only before Armstrong had returned, but in an incident that ended up contributing to Armstrong's return. It was just after Contador had won the Giro, and Bruyneel was visiting him in Spain to talk about their goals for 2009. According to both Bruyneel and a confidential source who often rode with Contador, at that meeting the racer revealed that another sponsor had offered to build a team around him, letting him make all the management and hiring decisions and paying him significantly more than he made at Astana. "I have to take this," Contador said. He wanted to leave Astana right then. And he'd asked Bruyneel to be the toothless director of the new team.

"You have a contract until 2010," Bruyneel had said. "You can't do it. I won't do it." Contador had then demanded more money to stay with Astana, and, in anger, Bruyneel had left. He'd called Armstrong right after that.

"I'll never forget it," Lance told me one day. "I was dating Kate [Hudson] at the time, so I was driving back to her house and I was sitting at the light at PCH and Sunset and he called me and he was telling me this, and I said, 'Tell him: fuck him.' If he wants to go, I thought, let him figure out how to buy his way out of his contract and go. Then I called Johan the next day or later that day and I said, 'By the way, if you let him go, I'll come back and race again.' I was kind of half serious, but serious enough that I was ready to do it."

Contador decided to stay, but whether it was because the other deal fell apart, or he'd decided, however reluctantly, that he had a better chance of winning with Bruyneel, or for some other reason entirely, Bruyneel never found out. But he can't worry about that now, here in the team car headed toward Andorre Arcalis. He picks up the radio mic and says, "Okay, guys, remember when we reach the base, we talk. We don't know what happens there, so most of all we talk to each other." This was what he'd said at the team meeting that morning, too: *Get to the mountain with the other rivals, set a hard pace, wait for them to attack, follow them, don't lose significant time. If you feel good and want to try to distance some rivals, before you do anything talk to me and to each other.*

"I've said all along my obligation is to the team," Armstrong had said. "The others will attack before we do. Expect Carlos [Sastre] to make some accelerations. We can wait and watch the others."

Contador was more enigmatic. "The mountains are my territory," he'd said. "I'm feeling good, but you always like to confirm that."

"I don't need a team meeting to know that he's ready to go," Armstrong told Bruyneel.

At the base of the mountain, the breakaway of nine riders has a 6:33 lead. Bruyneel tells the team to be at the front but to wait for attacks, to be patient, and he reminds them that the first kilometer, at a grade of 8.7 percent, is the steepest, then there are three at 7.7 percent, and from then on the climb gets shallower as it rises. The break toils away, the riders making feints here and there but staying together.

Perfect, thinks Bruyneel. "Chill out," he says to the team. "Slow it down a little if you can."

Paulinho, Popo, and Zubeldia set a high but reasonable pace when they hit the slope, and within a kilometer there are only forty or so riders left in the main group. Armstrong is grinning.

Up ahead, the break passes under the banner that announces 5 kilometers to go, and Brice Feillu of Agritubel attacks. He opens a gap and puts his head down and spins his pedals and opens the gap more. Nocentini lets him go; he's thinking only of the yellow jersey and doesn't want to risk blowing himself up by chasing.

Cancellara, who'd managed to stay among the forty dragged uphill by Astana, finally runs out of yellow jersey magic and gets shot out the back of the group. Popo does a long pull, and Bruyneel calms the team.

Cadel Evans attacks. Armstrong covers the move, riding right up to Evans. Contador follows, and Kloden, too, and the Schlecks and Wiggins and Vande Velde. Half of the forty can't, and fall away. Kloden takes the front and pushes the pace, hoping to prevent any more attacks.

Feillu is a kilometer from a stage win. Nocentini and the rest of the break are about 25 seconds behind him, and behind them Kloden is coming up the mountain like a motorcycle. Astana is in complete control.

And that's when Contador leaps. He bounds away with one of his vicious, slashing assaults. Though it had appeared that Kloden was about to leave scorch marks on the road, when Contador goes, the riders in the pack suddenly seem as if they're out on a Sunday ride. He is going so fast that when he slices into a left turn he has to lean his bike over for traction the way riders do on downhills.

Whatever Bruyneel is saying to him, Contador will never hear. Somehow, his earpiece has come out and swings from the tape above his jawline as he skitters up the hill.

Wiggins, who is riding near Armstrong, takes a look around and thinks, he says later, that all the riders still there look as if they have the fear of god in them. He also notes that Armstrong appears to be blocking for Contador—riding at the front at a pace that might be high enough to discourage attacks but that is almost certainly slower than his teammate's speed.

Feillu is in. He's won. Nocentini and the break are in. Contador inhales the mountain. He's 20 seconds in front of Armstrong and the others. And he's closing so fast on the finish that he might end up in yellow.

When he crosses the line, no one seems sure of who the new leader of the Tour de France is. Evans comes in 21 seconds later with Schleck on his wheel, then Wiggins and Frank Schleck and

Levi and Lance and Menchov and Sastre and Vande Velde. Just past the finish banner, a panting Armstrong spits out, "That was not the plan. But I didn't expect him to go by the plan."

"Today is the most beautiful day of my life," Nocentini says. "When I awoke I had not even a dream of the yellow jersey." He kept it from Contador by six seconds.

STAGE 7 RESULTS

1. Brice Feillu, Agritubel	6:11:31
4. Rinaldo Nocentini, AG2R	+0:00:26
9. Alberto Contador, Astana	+0:03:26
10. Cadel Evans, Silence-Lotto	+0:03:47
11. Andy Schleck, Saxo Bank	
12. Bradley Wiggins, Garmin	
14. Levi Leipheimer, Astana	
15. Lance Armstrong, Astana	
17. Denis Menchov, Rabobank	
18. Carlos Sastre, Cervélo	
20. Christian Vande Velde, Garmin	
24. Andreas Kloden, Astana	+0:04:10
67. Fabian Cancellara, Saxo Bank	+0:09:16

GENERAL CLASSIFICATION

1. Rinaldo Nocentini, AG2R	25:44:32
2. Alberto Contador, Astana	+0:00:06
3. Lance Armstrong, Astana	+0:00:08
4. Levi Leipheimer, Astana	+0:00:39
5. Bradley Wiggins, Garmin	+0:00:46
6. Andreas Kloden, Astana	+0:00:54
8. Christian Vande Velde, Garmin	+0:01:24
9. Andy Schleck, Saxo Bank	+0:01:49

15. Carlos Sastre, Cervélo   +0:02:52
18. Cadel Evans, Silence-Lotto   +0:03:07
34. Denis Menchov, Rabobank   +0:05:02

The Easy Week

The 2009 Tour de France route had been unveiled to the public, like always, in a grand presentation ceremony in October of the previous year, and since then everyone had been calling these next seven stages "the easy week."

Stage 8 would climb out of the principality of Andorra, then drop to the French side of the Pyrenees and, avoiding the worst of the mountains, finish with about 25 kilometers of downhill. The next day's 160.5-kilometer route from Saint-Gaudens to Tarbes could have been a monster. It crosses the Category 1 Col d'Aspin and the *Hors Catégorie* (so hard it is considered "beyond categorization") Col du Tourmalet, which climbs from 837 meters to 2,115 in 17 kilometers and is typically one of the most feared mountains on any Tour. But both ascents fell in the middle of the route, which would give dropped riders plenty of time to regroup and cooperate to catch back up. There would be none of the dramatic, race-changing mountaintop finishes that leave the peloton shattered all along the slopes. From there the riders would leave the Pyrenees, flying by plane into central France for a rest day in Limoges before beginning to head north and east toward the Alps on five flat and slightly rolling stages. At the end of Stage 14 they would be in Besançon, staring at the Alps. In seven stages over eight days they'd pedal 1,334 kilometers and go over five climbs rated Category 1 or *HC*. But in the Tour de France, such a stretch of riding is considered nothing more than a transition from the blank slate of the opening days to the bloodbath of the final week, which this year held the race's four toughest mountain stages and a time trial.

This was the easy week. That's how the story is usually told.

At the bus the morning after Stage 7, Armstrong is smiling, joking around, bumping shoulders with Levi.

"He's pissed," says Chris the mechanic, coming over to stand beside me. We're inside the velvet rope—the caution tape and portable metal fencing that abuts the bus and keeps the mass of fans, the photographers, the TV crews, and the daily media away from the riders. Three separate knots of people are singing the Contador song. Contador is wearing Sidi podium shoes—special footwear made for looking sharp at post-race appearances—that are the luminescent white of a baby's teeth. He is not quite prancing, not preening, but perhaps showing off his buoyancy and his boyishness at once.

Chris says, "Lance is pissed. Off."

"I can see that," I say, and I mean it. Armstrong is happy to be furious. Throughout his career, he's used resentment and anger to fuel some of his greatest performances, a personality trait he sometimes publicly disavows but is aware of and welcomes as motivation.

In a few minutes all the riders are going into the team bus for a meeting, and Bruyneel will make what he later tells me is his biggest mistake of the Tour. In the meeting, he reviews in objective terms what happened on Andorre Arcalis and how it deviated from the team plan, and explains why that could have cost them the Tour if it forced them into a defense of the yellow jersey that weakened the team. He says it's his opinion that yesterday they made an error but got lucky by not ending up with the jersey, and so today they can get back to their original plan: wait for the Alps.

Then he makes the mistake. He asks if anyone has anything to add.

"Of course," Armstrong will tell me months later, of the moment so private no one on the team would speak of it to me then, "I had to take that opportunity to say to Contador, 'Look, are you going to follow team orders? I mean, obviously you're the favorite here, you're in the top position, but are you going to listen to the director or not? You have to have respect for team orders.' Then Contador said,

'You don't have any respect for orders.' I think he was talking about the split at Grande-Motte. It got ugly. This guy is getting in my face telling me I don't have any respect for the team? It was nearly fisticuffs after that—oh yeah, oh yeah."

That morning, although nobody on the team will tell me what has just occurred, one of them does say to me, "All the guys in their hearts now are with Lance, except Paulinho, who is Alberto's roommate, and Dimi Muravyev, who doesn't really know what's going on."

"What do you mean?" I ask. I want to hear it.

"They want Lance to win."

They're professionals, and they're not going to ride against Contador—they would, in fact, support whichever rider on the team seems most likely to bring them a victory and a bigger paycheck. (Not doing so would be a terrible career move: no team would hire a guy who helped throw the world's most important race because he didn't like the leader.) But they hope their leader is Lance. And if Contador stumbles even once, Armstrong will exploit that hope and take over the leadership.

"He knows how to mind-fuck better than anybody," says a close member of his personal staff. "He knows every nook and cranny of the Tour de France, and over the years he's done so many mind-fucks there you can't even count them. Ullrich, Beloki, Basso: mind-fucked. Every one of them."

And already that day I talk to an Astana team member who tells me he thinks Lance will beat Contador by 15 minutes.

Evans attacks on the first of the day's three climbs and Schleck on the last, but Astana brings both back and, behind a four-man break that will stay away for the win without changing the top GC positions, they slow the pack on the final climb when Nocentini gets dropped. He stays in yellow another day. Contador and Armstrong are tested for drugs at the end of the stage—their third test in three days. The two of them, plus Leipheimer and Kloden, also had been tested in the hotel that morning by anti-doping officials. Anne Gripper, head of the UCI's anti-doping program, said that in addition to the typical drug controls, fifty riders had been targeted for what she called a "focused" testing program during the Tour and in the five weeks before it. The names weren't revealed, but the frequency of tests seemed to indicate that the four Astana riders were probably among those selected. In addition to the focused testing, there were unannounced tests on randomly chosen riders in the mornings, plus eight urine tests at the end of each race, and for every rider on every Thursday morning there was a biological passport test (which compares specific markers in the blood to previous levels taken from the same rider over a period of time). After the Tour ended, the French anti-doping agency, AFLD, would complain that some riders, including those on Astana, were granted favors that invalidated the testing. This morning, for instance, the AFLD said that the UCI officials let the riders delay the tests by forty-five minutes instead of administering them immediately. No sanctions were handed out to riders or testers.

The next day I remember something. "Hey," I ask Chris. "Who got the private room?"

"The small one."

"Yeah," I say, "the little room in the back. The private sleeper."

"No, no," he says. "That's what Lance calls Contador: The Small One. Lance told him to take it. He wants to be out with the guys." Chris turns and points to a middle window on the bus and says, "Lance sits right there. With everyone else, you see, while The Small One is alone in the back."

The nickname is classic Armstrong. It diminishes Contador yet will be defensible when Alberto happens to hear about it: he *is* smaller and wispier than Armstrong, and in cycling such characteristics are typically considered advantageous.

Nocentini makes it over the Tourmalet and hangs on to the jersey. He again says it's a dream. The next day is supposed to be the first of the two radio-free days, and that night after the stage there is a lot of talk about a team protest led by Bruyneel and Armstrong. For the record, Bruyneel admits he's talked about the issue with other directors but says he isn't leading any sort of organized protest; in reality the teams have agreed to try to put on the brakes in a slightly less ostentatious way than they did during the Giro in Milan.

The morning of the radio-free slow day, Stage 10, I'm standing outside the bus talking to Bruyneel when Armstrong comes out.

"Do we have any spare tubulars?" he says. "Someone should wear one." He's referencing the earliest, low-tech days of the sport, when the riders had no support and had to carry their own spare tires wrapped in an X around their shoulders and across their backs. He sees me and says, "How are you doing?" and comes over and shakes my hand.

Bruyneel says, "Hey, Bill has an idea."

I'd been telling Bruyneel about an old Italian journalist who still writes his story in the pressroom each evening on a typewriter, then posts it by reading the text over the telephone. "Give him an exclusive interview," I say. "He's the best guy in the world to interview you about racing without a radio."

Chris says, "I'm finding your tubular, man."

"Forget it," says Armstrong. "I can't wear it. It'd get blown up into too big of a deal."

It's Bastille Day—the holiday of French independence—so three French riders get in a publicity-generating break ahead of a pack so docile the Tour cancels the next radio-free stage. For much of the intermittently drizzly stage the break spins along out in front at about 23 mph. At the end the pack closes so there can be a sprint, and Mark Cavendish takes the third of the six stage wins he'll get this Tour. Armstrong calls it "one of the more relaxed days I have experienced in ten-plus Tours."

But this is what must never be forgotten about the Tour de France: there are no easy days. Kurt Asle Arvesen of Saxo Bank was cruising along today and got brought down in a crash that put at least six riders on the road. He got up—he was the last one to do so—got back on his bike, and started riding off after the peloton. He was holding the handlebar with one hand. His left arm was tucked up against his stomach, and he held his shoulders aslant, the right pointed high and the left drooping.

Determined to get back in the pack, Arvesen pedaled by the race doctor's car without slowing. About ten minutes later, he dropped back to the medical car and talked a bit. The doctor reached out through the open window and stuck a pill in Arvesen's mouth.

At the feed zone, Arvesen realized he couldn't lift his left arm to get his lunch out of the *musette*. Cancellara, who'd been able to stay in yellow seven days partly because of Arvesen's work for him, now took Arvesen's bag and, riding beside him, piece by piece fed his lunch to him.

Arvesen, a thirty-four-year-old Norwegian, has maintained the slender build of a twentysomething neo-pro. He stands about six feet tall and weighs around 150. As you'd guess, he's a brilliant climber. But he's no finicky angel of the mountains. He's tough and tenacious: in 2006, he crashed into a car during a training ride, injured his knee, got horrendously cut up, and raced anyway the next week. In the 2008 Tour de France, he got into a thirteen-man break, got dropped on the final climb, then came back to win the stage by two centimeters.

Now there he was on Stage 10 of this year's Tour, left arm dangling, able to eat only if a teammate fed him by hand. He never did quite catch onto the lollygagging field. At the finish, feet unclipped, he needed more than a full minute to coax his body into doing what it needed to do to get off the bike.

In the Tour de France there is no moment of racing placid enough that even a minor mistake or an ordinary spot of bad luck can't erupt into disaster, no stage so short that a split-second grazing of wheels can't ruin a year's worth of sacrifice.

Within half an hour of the start of Stage 11, the next easy stage, Angelo Furlan, an Italian rider for Lampre, would go down. He'd appear to suffer nothing besides some bruises, but he'd have to abandon the Tour the next day because he was simply too stiff and sore to pedal. Then Quick Step's Sébastien Rosseler and Garmin's

Christian Vande Velde and Ryder Hesjedal would get tangled up with some spectators, causing such a discombobulation that the race had to be neutralized until the road cleared. Just a few kilometers later, sixteen more riders would hit the deck, ending up with injuries that the official *Communiqué Medical,* in its daily rider-by-rider list, would catalogue as *"contusions multiples, importante contusion, importante traumatisme."* One of those fallen riders would be Nocentini, but he'd manage to get back up and finish in the pack, preserving his 6-second lead. Hesjedal would go down again about 50 kilometers from the end of the race. Arvesen, his left collarbone broken in two places, wouldn't even make it to the start of Stage 11.

I'm ambling around the start area that morning when I see Wim Vansevenant, one of my favorite riders of all time: He retired after the 2008 season as the greatest *lanterne rouge* ever.

This French phrase for "red lantern" refers to the racer who is dead last in the GC. (It's derived from the historical practice of hanging a scarlet light on the caboose of trains, which let station operators know that none of the cars had come uncoupled.) The title is no insult, especially once the race reaches Paris. The guy who sticks out the suffering and indignities of the Tour despite being a good three hours off the podium elevates losing to a triumph. He's outlasted the approximately 20–25 percent who each year are driven out of the race by illness, injury, or pure exhaustion, and those who were eliminated for failing to finish within each day's time limit. In the Tour de France, you can't coast into last place; you have to tear yourself apart for the honor.

The stubborn refusal to fail mixed with the inability to win can turn *lanterne rouge* riders into cult favorites—a fact that grates on the organizers, who since 1980 have refused to acknowledge the honor. That year, an Austrian named Gerhard Schönbacher—who had won the title the previous season and was on his way to a second—annoyed race officials by getting too much attention. "I got daily interviews," Schönbacher told journalist Rupert Guinness.

"I was very popular with the crowd and I continued to tell everyone that I liked being last. [The organizers] said I made a mockery of the Tour."

The officials were so incensed that midrace they instituted a temporary rule: the last-place racer would be eliminated each day. Schönbacher showed the stuff of a champion loser, riding with calculation and guts so that he just managed to finish in second-to-last place every day until the last, when he swooped down to claim the *lanterne rouge.* Along with Belgian Daniel Masson (1922 and 1923), the Dutchman Mathieu Hermans (1987 and 1989), and Frenchman Jimmy Casper (2001 and 2004), Schönbacher is one of five racers in history who twice won the last spot.

Wim did it three years in a row.

He hadn't won a race in more than ten years when he retired, but he'd been a consummate *domestique* for champions such as Paris-Roubaix winner Peter Van Petegem and Tour hopeful Cadel Evans, carrying extra bottles from the car up to teammates, grinding out kilometer after kilometer to keep a race in check, dragging his leader across vast gaps, giving up his wheels when needed, whatever it took. Up until 2006, he gloried in the routine anti-glory of sacrificing his body, bike, and, ultimately, any chance he ever had for fame. That year, in the normal course of obliterating himself for the good of his team, he unwittingly found himself fighting two-timer Casper for the *lanterne rouge*—and he also found his destiny. Before Wim won three last-places, the greatest *lanterne rouge* was probably not one of the two-time winners but Jacky Durand, a Frenchman who in 1999 achieved the supremely counterintuitive feat of simultaneously winning the *lanterne rouge* and the official award for Most Aggressive Rider (which paid 100,000 euros). "I don't mind being beaten," Durand said to reporters that year. "What I hate is being beaten when I haven't tried."

I love the *lanterne rouge,* I think, because its best recipients understand not merely how to lose with honor, which is a cliché, but something deeper: that absolute loss must be honored.

"Wim," I say when I walk up to him. "I wrote about you—"

"Yes. No, I remember," he says. His face is all sharp angles, from cheekbones to nose to chin to teeth, and his sentences come out chopped apart from each other. He's exactly my height but when racing he'd been twenty pounds lighter. Now we're about the same weight.

"Did you become a farmer?" I ask. "That's what you said you wanted to do."

"I am."

"Do you still ride?"

"Cycling? It was already too hard for me when I was a professional." He's joking.

"What about Kenny van Hummel, man? Can he hang on?"

He smiles. "I think he's got what it takes. He suffers much and well. You can see that."

Van Hummel is the Dutch rider in his first Tour de France who fell into last place in the treacherous Stage 6 and has been consolidating his lead on the bottom spot since. He's finishing so far behind the other riders that there's a chance he'll get kicked out of the Tour one day for missing the time cut (the maximum daily gap allowed by organizers, which depending on the stage and the average speed ranges from 4–25 percent of the winner's time). I want him to stick. He was the first rider to start this year's Tour—the initial racer off the start ramp for the time trial in Monaco—so if he wins the *lanterne rouge* he'll bring some poetry to the title. It was born of such odd fates: Arsène Millocheau finished nearly 65 hours behind the winner in the inaugural Tour, in 1903, then vanished into history, never to race the Tour de France again. Van Hummel is just a shade under two hours behind Nocentini.

"So, Wim," I say. "What do you think of Contador versus Armstrong?"

"Armstrong?" he says. He blows a huge breath out of his mouth, a common Belgian expression. "Are you kidding me? He's going to win."

The Tour barrels on toward the Alps. The roadside crowds shame those in the United States, Spain, even Italy. The French people make a picnic of the day, enjoying a five-hour meal to watch thirty seconds of racing. They take a month's vacation and drive their campers from stage to stage, so you see the same characters over and over. The girls wear bikinis, the women go topless sometimes or paint letters on their butts and line up backside to the peloton to spell words, and the men flaunt bellies that gush up out of swim thongs and spill over onto their thighs. There is the German Didi Senft, who dresses like the devil and runs beside the riders waving his pitchfork at them. There are antiquarians on late-nineteenth-century penny-farthings, bicycle postmen in full vintage uniform, costumed milkmaids, and, of course, sauced men in fright wigs. There are clowns, Teletubbies, SpongeBob SquarePants. A herd of seven Hereford cow costumes. Santa Claus. It's as if the Tour incites people to run to their attics and dig through their trunks. Superman. A tomato. A chicken. A bunny. Babar the Elephant. I pass Dore Holte, the American who has become almost as well known as Didi the Devil. Dore rides a bike nearly to the top of a mountain stage before the race comes, then sprints on foot beside the riders when they pass—all while wearing a football helmet with the horns of a real longhorn-steer sticking out about 3 feet on each side. He takes vacation time from his job at Boeing to attend most of the Grand Tours. "It's cycling! It's religion! Texas!" he helpfully explained one day when I asked him why he does such a thing.

And Nocentini stays in yellow.

On the fifth day of the easy week, Stage 12, Levi and Cadel Evans get caught in a crash just a few kilometers from the finish. They get up and straggle in at the end of the long pack. Evans has dirt all over his shorts, looks stunned, slack-jawed, and is blowing spit out of his mouth. Levi's shoulder is scraped and dirty. That night he finds out his wrist is broken. His Tour is over.

The next morning at the bus Levi stops by to wish the team good luck before he leaves for home. Until he gets back to his doctor in the United States and figures out what to do, his arm is temporarily bound up with a makeshift cast of padded gauze, gauze strips, and gauze wrap held together with zip ties.

Armstrong sees it and says, "Did the mechanics make that?" and cracks up.

Ryszard, the *soigneur,* is standing near me. He says, "He is keeping morale." He reaches out and stretches the corners of my mouth up into a smile. "*C'est la vie,* eh? You must keep morale morale morale, this one knows it."

In his good hand Levi is carrying his helmet, bubble-wrapped for the flight home and with his name written on it in marker. "I would ride with the pain," he says. "I would. Leaving the Tour hurts worse than the wrist ever could. But I can't hold the handlebar. It's just a physical impossibility." His right shoe is coming untied, and the lace drags on the ground.

"Hey," Armstrong says to me, "nice jacket." I'm wearing Rapha, the cycling equivalent of a designer label, which Armstrong knows because his bike shop is one of the few in the United States that stocks the clothing. The zipper is offset to one side, a styling detail. Armstrong points at me and says, "But you should return it. The zipper's crooked."

He's not a naturally funny person. Even his close friends say his humor tends to be corny and repetitive. He's best described not as clever or smart but as cunning. And for as moneyed and as cultured as he has become, he is still in essence, as I was told by a person who was employed by one of Armstrong's sponsoring companies and worked closely with him on several projects, "the kind of guy who would be happy putting his car in a ditch every weekend." He became exposed to the idea of appreciating art (and architecture) during his first trips to Europe in his pre-cancer era, but he didn't seriously pursue his interest until he retired in 2005. Today, he likes to reference artists in his Twitter posts—Sebastião Salgado, Mark Ryden, Eric White, James Jean, Rosson Crow, Takashi Murakami, Ed Ruscha, Tomoo Gokita. For the 2009 season, he asked Kenny

Scharf, Shepard Fairey, Damien Hirst, and other artists to create designs for his race bikes. (At the end of the season, he would auction them through Sotheby's for $1.2 million, which he donated to his cancer-fighting foundation.) The walls of his home have displayed Michael Gregory, Bettie Ward, Barry McGee, Tony Berlant, Andres Serrano, and others. (Of the Serrano work, titled *Piss and Blood VII*, Armstrong has noted that he's given a lot of both to earn the money to buy it.)

It's an impressive collection, yet there's a dissonantly competitive spirit to Armstrong's pursuit of it all, as if when he understood that art was something sophisticated people should enjoy, he set out to be the best at enjoying it. Someone who worked with him on an extended commercial project told me that "when Lance found out I was a visual person, he took me around his house to see his art collection, and we had to stand before each one and dutifully appreciate it. And we couldn't move on until he felt he'd accomplished the appreciation." A comment in an interview he gave to *Architectural Digest* in 2008 hints at his win-or-lose approach to even the arts: "When I go to an exhibit, people's first reaction is usually, 'What the hell is he doing here?' But when you ask questions, start buying, they concede, 'Maybe he does know what he's doing.'"

During the Tour, he said that his motto is:

WIN LOSE
LIVE DIE

It's more like the interwoven strands of his DNA. Every decision Armstrong makes can seem to be based on the idea of a winner and a loser. "When I was on the team with him," says Michael Barry, who rode for U.S. Postal Service from 2002 to 2006, "he'd tell us one week that we had to try a restaurant because it was his favorite, then the next week he'd tell us we had to go to a different one, because it beat the other one. He never really had that deep-seated, long-lasting affection for one restaurant or one musical group or . . . or many other things most people form attachments to."

After Armstrong walks away from me, an Astana team member comes over and stands beside me and we talk a while. Eventually he points at Armstrong's yellow-and-black bike, custom-painted in Livestrong colors to stand out from the blue-and-white team issue. "You could paint six more bikes these colors," he says.

"What?"

"That's how many ride for Lance now in their hearts," he says. It's not until later that I realize that with Levi gone, there are only eight riders left on the team, and once Contador and Armstrong are accounted for, that leaves just six.

It would not be wrong by much to call the people who surround the Astana bus the morning before Stage 14 a mob. Middle-aged men climb onto the team cars to try to get a clear view over the crowd that is pushing against the riot fencing that marks off the narrow, safe space for Astana's riders and their bikes. Voices shout, "Lance! Lance!" Arms sticking up above head height blindly snap digital pictures, the flashes at times so unrelenting they resemble a strobe against the light blue paint of the bus. A woman staggers out of the melee holding her nose with a blood-tinged hand and crying.

A little bit down the block, outside the AG2R bus, the leader of the Tour de France, Rinaldo Nocentini, signs hats for some teenage fans. He poses for five, six, seven pictures, puts his arm around a pretty French girl who speaks no Italian, shakes the hand of an American. A man with a gray moustache and a gourmand's potbelly under a black-and-white three-piece suit flicks his open hand upward several times once he catches the attention of the yellow jersey. Nocentini understands and lifts his sunglasses up onto the top of his dark brown hair. His eyes are bright, showing blue and green in the camera flashes, and his smile is not something he comes up with just for the photo.

No Italian had been in yellow since Alberto Elli had it for four days in 2000. Nocentini's streak will end up being longer by one day than that of Italian legend Marco Pantani, who had it for seven straight days on his way to winning the 1998 Tour de France. To find the equal of Nocentini's ownership in Italy, you have to go back to Claudio Chiappucci's eight days in yellow in 1990. But one reason Nocentini remains free enough from the crush of media and mobs of fans to flirt with pretty girls and accommodate the stage directions of old men is that his reign has been dimmed by the perception that, though he won yellow fairly, he's been kept in the color by Astana. Throughout the week, Astana has controlled the pace when AG2R ran out of firepower or endurance.

Today, as Stage 14 winds to an end, it will seem as if Nocentini's time in yellow has, too. And the rider set to inherit it is the popular George Hincapie, who gets into an early break that at times will have more than 12 minutes on the pack and maintains as much as 8 minutes late into the race. He's the best-placed rider in the break, 5:25 behind Nocentini, and for much of the day he is the virtual yellow jersey—the leader on the road if everything were stopped at that moment. Bruyneel and Armstrong will each later, and separately, tell me they tried to help Hincapie get his second yellow jersey (he had it for one day in 2006, the year after Armstrong retired) because the three of them are still close friends. What happens with the jersey becomes one of this Tour's biggest public dramas.

But there's also a private Astana conflict going on at the same time. At one point Astana goes to the front to manage the gap, as it wavers between 6 and 9 minutes. Ideally, Bruyneel and Armstrong would like Hincapie to take yellow with a lead of no more than 2 to 3 minutes—a difference Astana can easily take back in the mountains. But, Bruyneel tells me later, Contador disagrees and wants to chase the break down. Bruyneel's account is supported by raw footage of an Armstrong documentary that is being shot by Academy Award–winning director Alex Gibney, who later shares the material with me.

Contador drifts back to the car so he can argue with Bruyneel without broadcasting it over the team radio. Bruyneel tells him that if Hincapie gets the jersey by at least 2 minutes, Columbia will work to control the race the whole next day. "This is the deal I have made with them," Bruyneel says.

Contador says, "Fucking two minutes? Two minutes and a half?"

Bruyneel says, "Alberto, Hincapie will lose six or seven minutes on Mont Ventoux. Don't worry. This is the best for the team."

Contador leaves, Astana tempers the chase, and with just a few kilometers to go, the break appears as if it might beat the pack by 6 minutes. Hincapie will be in yellow. Desperate, Nocentini's AG2R team tries to chase but doesn't have the firepower to close the gap. This is when the public drama explodes.

Garmin joins AG2R at the front and hacks away at the time difference. The tactic could be interpreted as a way to keep Wiggins and Vande Velde up front and out of trouble in the closing kilometers. Or it could be seen as the American-based and so far winless Garmin team's attempt to keep the jersey from Hincapie—so his American-based team doesn't get any more publicity than the bounty that Cavendish's wins have already generated. Though the motive is difficult for me and most everyone else to discern at the time, afterward Bruyneel tells me that Garmin's chase was intended not to win any advantage but to make Hincapie lose. Gibney shares more pre-release footage with me that appears to prove this to be accurate as well.

The Astana car pulls alongside Garmin's. Bruyneel, who this day is riding in the passenger seat, rolls down his window and says to Garmin's Matt Johnson and Matt White, "You don't want George to have the jersey?"

The reply is indistinct to others in the car, but Bruyneel says, "Okay." Then he explains to those in the car, "They don't want George to have the jersey. It is in the book. We will remember that."

Columbia—Hincapie's own team—adds to the confusion by setting up at the front to lead Cavendish to the head of the pack sprint (to earn at least some points toward the green jersey) while also seemingly trying to blockade the peloton to slow the race. The tactic almost certainly backfires and increases the pack's speed, further reducing the gap to Hincapie. By now, though, the action is so helter-skelter no one is sure what is happening. (In fact, during the chaotic finish, Cavendish will be the first of the main pack across the line but relegated by officials to last place for the stage after his rival for the green jersey, Thor Hushovd, protests that Cavendish rode too dangerously and blocked him.)

The final gap between break and pack: 5:20. Hincapie is out of yellow by 5 seconds. Stories about who chased when and how hard circulate wildly. Columbia and Garmin feud. Garmin and Astana feud. Columbia and Astana feud, then Columbia and Garmin and Astana feud. All of Hincapie's teammates reportedly take off their yellow Livestrong bracelets because, a source on Columbia tells me, the team heard that during the race Armstrong had said, "I like George, but I don't like him enough to give him yellow."

Outwardly, Hincapie handles the disappointment with class. "It's devastating," he says the next day before the start. "And I have intense feelings about it, but I will keep those to myself. It's a bike race." In private, Hincapie tells Bruyneel and Armstrong that he is "frustrated with and pissed off at the two most powerful men in cycling."

Armstrong tells me, "His feelings were upset. He felt like he had the yellow jersey, that he deserved it and earned it. Trying to reach out to him that night was like chasing a girl who won't pick up the phone. I didn't sleep that night. I was distraught."

For Nocentini, those controversial 5 seconds mean twenty-four more hours in yellow. On the podium, he takes his yellow flowers. He is kissed on each cheek by beautiful women. He is cheered, photographed. Maybe he's gotten used to some of that by now. But he seems to take a deep breath up there, and hold it in a little. The Tour de France's easy week is over.

GENERAL CLASSIFICATION AFTER STAGE 14

1.	Rinaldo Nocentini, AG2R	58:3:52
2.	George Hincapie, Columbia	+0:00:05
3.	Alberto Contador, Astana	+0:00:06
4.	Lance Armstrong, Astana	+0:00:08
6.	Bradley Wiggins, Garmin	+0:00:46
7.	Andreas Kloden, Astana	+0:00:54
9.	Christian Vande Velde, Garmin	+0:01:24
10.	Andy Schleck, Saxo Bank	+0:01:49
17.	Carlos Sastre, Cervélo	+0:02:52
19.	Cadel Evans, Silence-Lotto	+0:03:07
29.	Denis Menchov, Rabobank	+0:05:02

I Have Kept the Faith

The plaza in Pontarlier seems to ripple and flow, it is so thick with people and vehicles—twenty team buses, forty team cars, another twenty-five or so support cars that haven't yet left for the feed zones where they'll sit for hours and await the arrival of the famished racers. There are also all the riders on their way to the morning's sign-in, with one foot clipped into a pedal and the opposite leg free and dabbing the ground so that they dart about this odd pool in starts and stops like minnows. And the square is thick as well with a tension composed of anticipation, relief, anxiety, and impatience all made more potent than usual because, as Levi Leipheimer said before he left the race, "The real Tour de France is just about to start."

The closing week begins with today's 207.5-kilometer Stage 15. The route goes from this plaza in France into Switzerland, then, after five intermediate smaller climbs, ends with a relatively short ascent that has a reputation among the racers that exceeds its objective numbers. Verbier is 8.8 kilometers from base to crest, with an average grade of 7.5 percent and no kilometer on it steeper than 8.5 percent. The great climbs of the Tour are usually longer, steeper, or both. The Tourmalet, for comparison, is almost identically steep but nearly twice as long. Yet the riders who have previewed Verbier warn that it could explode the race.

From Verbier, the riders will take a rest day, then face two more stages in the Alps followed by the time trial in Annecy. After an easier stage designed to do nothing more than get the race closer to Provence, the riders will confront Mont Ventoux. The monolithic mountain rises 21.1 kilometers, with long, nasty stretches of 9 and 10 percent just after the base and in the middle. The final kilometers climb an exposed, windswept, sun-baked lunar-like landscape. A long evening transfer by high-speed train will take the racers near Paris. The next day the remnants of the pack will pedal at a largely ceremonial pace into the city (toasting one another with champagne as they ride), where the stage will at last become a race and the 2009 Tour de France will wind down in laps of the Champs-Élysées.

I am waiting for an Astana rider to come out of the bus and maybe talk a little about the tension when I hear a voice shouting from outside the team barrier: "Bill! Hey, Bill!"

Chris the mechanic is standing amid the crowd, holding a black-and-yellow bike over his head. "I can't climb over," he yells when we make eye contact. "Come get this."

I walk to the edge of the riot fencing. He's holding the bike flat over his head, horizontally instead of upright, and though the density of the crowd prevents him from even leaning in toward me, he angles his arms down so the bike moves my way a foot or two, the pedal on its bottom side nearly grazing heads. People reach up to touch the bike as if it's a relic. I put one hand around each wheel and lift as I step backward, and I am holding Lance Armstrong's bike.

In my life as a cyclist I have held so many bikes I could not even pretend to guess the number. I have carried them on stairs, through doors that open out, doors that open in, double doors, automatic doors, weighted doors. I have handled bikes stood up on one wheel in elevators to accommodate other passengers, through revolving doors, up and down escalators, through the aisles of offices. I have lifted and lowered bikes from pickup trucks, box trucks, car roof racks, van roof racks, truck roof racks, two-story lofts, display windows, storage hooks screwed into roof beams, bridges, scaffolding, porches, and fire escapes. When I have a bike in my grasp, I no more have to think about where it is or what to do with it than I have to worry about the whereabouts of the toes on my feet. I have become a natural.

I freeze. What if I drop Lance Armstrong's bike?

"Over here," says Chris, who's climbed or walked around the barrier and is already messing with something on the saddle of one of the other bikes. I set Lance's bike down and, holding it by the seat, from behind I wheel it over toward the bus. Then I grab the stem right where it meets the handlebar and pull the bike up in a wheelie so I can flip it around and back its rear wheel in against the bus at an angle, just the way the mechanics had already done with Muravyev's and Paulinho's. I am sweating as I do this.

I let out a short but immense breath when I let go of Lance's bike, and I say, "Damn."

Chris looks up from his fiddling on another bike. "For sure. Big day," he says.

When Lance comes out of the bus a hundred people or more call his name. He is kind of jumpy, juking his shoulders around, bobbing his head a little. He rubs his hands together. He is smiling, and his eyes are operating with a kind of long-running focus. They seize on something and concentrate on it, and even swivel a bit to remain fixed after he's started turning his head to look at something else.

"Here we go," he says to me.

I tell him that it's a big day. In case he doesn't know, I guess.

He stops all the incidental motion and I become the subject of his focus, that intense vision that lingers as if it isn't quite satisfied with its evaluation but has to leave to follow wherever Armstrong is taking it next.

"This one," he says, "is for all the fucking marbles."

That's the moment I become convinced Armstrong is going to win the Tour de France.

Not many people who are in a position to make an informed decision would agree with me. I know Bruyneel wants him to win but isn't sure that he can. Even Chris Carmichael has been hedging, saying that the numbers are encouraging but that "he definitely doesn't fall into the category of favorite." The fucking marbles and my dumb admiration of the *lanterne rouge*, which makes me think that no one knows more about heart than Wim Vansevenant, and the way the entire team wants Armstrong to win instead of Contador, and other indistinct things all fuse in that instant and, embarrassingly, I believe in the guy as much as I did in 1994.

The pack rides as if the mountains between Pontarlier and Verbier are nothing but a minor annoyance. They keep the speed high and chase down attacks until finally, around 60 kilometers into the day, a break of 15 is permitted to form out of several small escapes and chases. Cancellara has made it in there, thinking not of a stage victory but that when the climbers have dropped the pack and catch the break on Verbier he might be around to help Andy Schleck. David Millar is in the break as well, to do the same for Wiggins and Vande Velde. It's a great move by their teams. Astana spends much of the day at the front. Popovych keeps dropping back to the car for bottles, stuffing six or seven in his jersey, then riding to the front of the pack again. Nocentini in yellow rides behind Astana. There is nothing he can do to keep his jersey today. The gap from pack to break rises over and dips back under four minutes then jumps over again.

Roadside flags and banners snap in the wind rather than flutter, and from the cars with their maps and GPS and smartphones with Internet search capabilities comes the news that there will be a tailwind when the pack climbs Verbier. Some of the older riders knew this already.

The fans who have ascended Verbier to watch the race have parked at the base and walked or taken the lifts up, and their cars have spread out from the mountain to such a degree that, in the 10 kilometers preceding it, the roadside, every field, and every parking lot of every shop is jammed. The lift operators say they sent up 100,000 people.

At the top, just past the finish line, standing against the temporary chain-link fence that keeps fans off the course, I ask Ryszard what he thinks will happen today. He pretends to not understand me.

"Today," I say. "What do you think of today?"

"Ah, today." There is a pause of several seconds. Behind us, a projection screen as big as a billboard is showing the breakaway about to make the left that marks the start of the climb. Two riders have jumped out about 50 seconds ahead of the break and, last time I heard a time check, the pack was about a minute behind. "What I think," says Ryszard. "I think it is a beautiful sunny day and what should happen—"

The giant television screams as the pack careens through the left turn and onto the first slope of Verbier. Garmin is at the front with Millar, who must have dropped back from the break just for this reason, and Wiggins and Vande Velde are behind him. Then Saxo swarms around the Garmin jerseys and passes them, and converges on the front. Behind them, the peloton starts to go single file on a hill—the kind of high-speed formation normally seen on flat roads or descents. Saxo is lining the race out. They are taking the Tour de France to full speed in the Alps.

"What should happen," says Ryszard as if he's seen it all before, "is that we should have more beautiful sunny days. Okay?" He turns and looks down the mountain road. All business. I study him for a bit in profile, his big gray moustache and the forearms lean and muscled from all the massages he gives. He is deliberately looking down the road now. I've seen him at finishes all over the world all through the year, and though he kept his tone even just now, this is the first time he's ever paused while deflecting one of my questions.

"You think Lance is going to win," I say to Ryszard, not expecting a response and not getting one. "So do I."

Then I turn and look at the screen. Jens Voigt is on the front for Saxo. His quadriceps pop and heave with every pedal stroke and his arms push forward against the handlebar as if he is trying to bully his bike uphill. Wiggins is behind him, Vande Velde, then Kloden, Schleck, Contador, and Armstrong. Behind them the field is crumpling. The polka-dot jersey—the best climber so far, Franco Pellizotti—cannot hold the pace. The world champion Ballan is off. Nocentini is fighting to honor his jersey in his last few sentient seconds in it.

Voigt swings off the front by yanking his bike to the left, and when he does so he crosses almost all the way over to the far shoulder of the other lane like a drunk stumbling across a street. He's blown. Nicki Sørensen takes over for Saxo. Suddenly there's Cancellara—Spartacus—who has drifted back from the breakaway and is just in front of Sørensen waiting, waiting, waiting. When the group reaches Cancellara, he begins to churn the pedals and his head bobs loose on his shoulders, and he looks up at the sky as if the effort has broken some central thing inside him. But he keeps going and this, finally, is the move that cracks the race apart.

Armstrong leaps sideways into the left lane and forward, and Contador follows him. Frank Schleck rides between Armstrong and Cancellara, who has seized up and is dropping back. Contador catches on to Frank Schleck's wheel, and Armstrong gets behind him with Andy Schleck and Wiggins trailing, and that is the whole race. Everyone else is in pieces. They have been climbing less than 3 kilometers.

They are getting near their absolute limits, these five, and by any measure of what most people would consider the boundaries of human endurance or the ability of the body to function under duress, they should slow down. Wiggins hangs on only by thinking, *If this is what it's doing to me, maybe it also feels this way to them.*

As the five of them swoop around a banked right turn, Contador drifts left. He looks over at Lance on his right, who is now almost even with him. He stands and pedals out of the saddle, glances behind him, drifts a little farther to the left, and watches Armstrong again.

Contador's movements are little, precise, contained and perfect motions, like the action of an expensive clockworks. He does the same things over and over and over in the same space, never wavering in how much he bends his elbow or how far his bike ticks to the side or the angle of his knee at the top of the stroke. And when he attacks there on Verbier, it is not with force but with frequency that he changes what we know about the farthest edges of a human's ability to propel a bicycle up a mountain.

Up top, when Contador accelerates and in seconds rides himself so clear of the group only he occupies the great space of the screen, there is a kind of communal gasp before the cheers and shouts and moans and curses erupt. There has never been an ascent like this in the Tour de France. That is not hyperbole, nor supposition. It is the fact of Alberto Contador's ride.

Much later, the perhaps evil but assuredly genius Michele Ferrari will calculate Contador's VAM—*velocità ascensionale media,* the formula that converts a rider's climb into a universal measurement that allows comparison across different slopes and speeds— at 1,852. Other sources come up with slightly different numbers. Ross Tucker and Jonathan Dugas, two South African exercise physiologists who run an analytical website called SportsScientists .com, come up with 1,900. Either number is the fastest rate of ascent ever measured. The closest is 1,848, clocked by Bjarne Riis on Hautacam in the 1996 Tour de France, for which, he confessed in May of 2007, he had doped with EPO. Armstrong's highest was 1,790, on Alpe d'Huez in 2004.

In one kilometer of riding, Contador opens a gap of 17 seconds on Andy Schleck, who was the only rider who could even try to match the acceleration, and 30 seconds on the rest. Schleck's tongue hangs out. Contador opens his mouth slightly, licks his lips, ticks away at the mountain. Behind both of them the group is fracturing. Kloden will ride up to it and pace Armstrong. Sastre will catch them. Wiggins and Frank Schleck will open a small gap. Armstrong's sunglasses are up on his helmet, the earpieces stuck into the vent holes, and so hang over his brow like the miniature brim of a hat. He peers out at the mountain rising in front of him. His body erupts into sweat, shines in the sunlight Ryszard praised. His jersey is zippered open nearly to his navel and he is tossing his bike from side to side. The two medallions he wears on a chain swing wildly, bumping against his biceps. One is a cross given to him by someone who died of cancer. The other, given to him by his ex-wife, Kristin, carries a Bible verse from Second Timothy:

I have fought the good fight,
I have finished the race,
I have kept the faith.

When Contador crosses the line he thumps his chest twice with a fist made by his right hand, then fashions the hand into a pistol and fires off an imaginary shot. He is 43 seconds ahead of Schleck, 1:06 ahead of Wiggins and Sastre, 1:26 ahead of Evans, 1:29 ahead of Kloden, and 1:35 ahead of Armstrong. The yellow jersey is 2:36 down the mountain road.

In the bedlam beyond the finish line, I run into David Millar and ask him if what it looks like is true—that the Contador-or-Armstrong question has been answered. He is haggard and dry-mouthed and he blinks and without hesitation says, "Contador's the best in the world, isn't he, at three-week stage races?" He rides off. I make my way to dope control, where I assume Armstrong will be caged until he can pee for a test. He is standing inside the fencing there, tipped back on his cleats, drinking a bottle of water. The veins of his legs throb against the skin. He says something unbelievable. He says, "I'm content."

He takes a swig of water and leans back farther on his heels, his demeanor that of a man enjoying his favorite lounger, and he says, "Saxo Bank hit the bottom full gas. Everybody was on the limit and Alberto was still able to accelerate. That's what days like today are for: they tell you who's the best. I gave it everything I had. Days like this, you can't deny that. It would be bad form, bad cycling form. I'm going to . . . "I'm a *domestique*."

Forty-five minutes and forty-three seconds after Contador crosses the line, the *lanterne rouge*, Kenny van Hummel, does the same. "They have a dream of winning the Tour de France," he tells me. "I have the dream of making it to Paris. I want to sprint on the Champs-Élysées. We have different dreams, but they are all dreams."

STAGE 15 RESULTS

1. Alberto Contador, Astana	5:03:58
2. Andy Schleck, Saxo Bank	+0:00:43
5. Bradley Wiggins, Garmin	+0:01:06
6. Carlos Sastre, Cervélo	
7. Cadel Evans, Silence-Lotto	+0:01:26
8. Andreas Kloden, Astana	+0:01:29
9. Lance Armstrong, Astana	+0:01:35
19. Rinaldo Nocentini, AG2R	+0:02:36
22. Christian Vande Velde, Garmin	+0:02:41
65. Denis Menchov, Rabobank	+0:06:27

GENERAL CLASSIFICATION

1. Alberto Contador, Astana	63:17:56
2. Lance Armstrong, Astana	+0:01:37

3. Bradley Wiggins, Garmin		+0:01:46
4. Andreas Kloden, Astana		+0:02:17
5. Andy Schleck, Saxo Bank		+0:02:26
11. Carlos Sastre, Cervélo		+0:03:52
12. Christian Vande Velde, Garmin		+0:03:59
14. Cadel Evans, Silence-Lotto		+0:04:27
29. Denis Menchov, Rabobank		+0:11:23

Miracles in Cycling

Bruyneel is eating a sandwich when the first break goes.

We are just a few kilometers out of the start in Martigny, and he has a towel tucked into his collar like a bib to keep crumbs and stains off his shirt. The foil the sandwich had been wrapped in is spread on his lap.

"They go before the climb," says Alain Gallopin from the front passenger's seat, picking up the GC sheet from his lap and getting ready to write down numbers. In the Tour de France there are always two directors in each car. (Eki and Dirk Demol, a Belgian director, are in car 2.) Chris is jammed against the right rear door, and I'm plastered against the left. I only got in here because Chris agreed to stack all the wheels and gear between us on the seat and pretend he doesn't mind being squashed for four and a half hours.

The first climb of Stage 16, a two-mountain day, is the 24.4-kilometer Col du Grand-Saint-Bernard, rated *Hors Catégorie* thanks to its length and steepness. It doesn't officially start until 16 kilometers into the stage, but already the road is rising to its base. Bruyneel reaches for the radio mic, which is tethered to the roof of the car with an elastic cord. "Okay, boys," he says, "attacks immediately. We see Cervélo is in there. Stay caaaaalllllmm. We are getting numbers."

We're the first team car, courtesy of Contador's yellow jersey, and through the windshield we can look past the pack and see two or three Cervélo jerseys going up the hill amid a break that could be as big as twenty riders.

"There goes Cancellara," says Lance over the radio.

"It's okay," says Bruyneel. "Let him go, let him go."

The Schleck brothers have vowed to never stop attacking Contador. "We will try until we die," Andy Schleck said on top of Verbier. "In Paris-Nice he was as strong as he is now and he lost it all. That could happen again." Wiggins has been less outspoken, saying only, as he has the whole Tour, that he wants to take each day as it comes. But he is so ethereally gaunt, so nearly ghost-like in his leanness, that his physique is more frightening than any vow he might make. Such a man might haunt Contador all the way into Paris.

Armstrong, for his part, has repeated that he will work for Contador all the way to Paris. Bruyneel never had any question it would be this way. "Lance is realistic," Bruyneel tells me. "He respects what a team must do. And he respects the way of cycling. You've heard this for many years. Now you will see it." Contador still seems to need proof of this. He rides up beside Armstrong and taps him on the butt, then signals for Armstrong to open a space in the line for his leader. Armstrong smiles, though it looks a little like Horner's race face. He makes room and Contador slips into the group.

"I couldn't dislike the guy any more," Armstrong tells me afterward. "But, like any of us are going to be *that guy*—the dick that disrespects cycling tradition and Johan's orders? If anybody, it would be me, but I never could. I would do whatever I was told to do. It's what you do. It's how cycling works."

Gallopin, who's been listening to the race radio, shows his scribblings to Bruyneel, who then says into the team radio: "Okay, boys, so twenty, twenty-one riders in the front. Greg and Dmitriy, you set the pace. Do not kill the team for this. Best guy in the break is Karpets at six minutes. Two guys from Saxo: Voigt and Cancellara. Three for Cervélo: Marchante, Haussler, Roulston. So we know what that means."

Armstrong says, "Three from Cervélo?"

"Yes."

"Two from Saxo?"

"Yes."

"Fuck."

In the team meeting this morning, they'd anticipated this: Saxo, Cervélo, and Garmin would probably try to get some riders into whatever early break got away. Those riders would then sit in, doing as little work as possible. At the top of the first or second mountain, Schleck, Sastre, or Wiggins would attack, and when they reached the break they'd have teammates with fresh legs to help them.

"We're going to be okay," says Bruyneel to the team. He hits the button that rolls down his window, then he balls up the towel and holds it fluttering out in the wind. The crumbs are whisked away.

We are just onto the Grand-Saint-Bernard's early slope, a long section of easy grades that range from 4.5 percent to 6. Bruyneel keeps a near-steady stream of patter going into the ears of his riders. In the car, the mood is tenser than any of the other times I've been in it, but to hear Bruyneel's tone, you might think we're back at the Giro and he's ribbing Eki about gold medals again. Again and again he refocuses the racers as their concentration fails. Rast and Muravyev keep speeding up, and Bruyneel keeps saying things like, "No need to go fast. Don't worry about the breakaway. It doesn't matter. We only worry about the attacks that will come. Take it easy. Set a pace to stay together and wait for the attacks."

In the third week of the Tour de France, the riders' bodies are beginning to eat themselves; they simply can't take in enough calories or liquid to match what is being depleted, which is a key reason that racers such as Contador, Schleck, and Armstrong—whose physiologies through some yet-to-be-defined quirk adapt to this stress and don't fall apart to the extent that others do—are able to assume such complete dominion over athletes who are in most ways equally gifted. (Whether or not Wiggins possesses this freakish quality is still to be discovered, since this is his first time riding as a leader in the third week of the Tour.) One result of this automastication is that the body begins to shut down functions not essential to pedaling or steering through a corner at 50 mph—such as the ability to perform an ordinary thought process. "You become stupider and stupider and stupider," Zabriskie explains to me one day. "You start to do things like leave your riding shoes behind in the hotel room, which is bad enough, but then you can also barely understand why your director is upset with you for doing it. You're not suffering. It's way past that. You're disappearing."

On the radio, Armstrong says, "For the guys who don't know the top of this climb, it is very, very hard—9.5 percent in the last kilometers."

The map and elevation profiles of today's route have been cut out of the book and taped to the dash. Every kilometer of the climb is color-coded and the last four are almost solid black—"percentage superior to 9 percent," as the key explains. Riders are already dropping out of the pack and past our car, mostly the sprinters assembling into a survival group they call "the autobus," an ad hoc, all-teams cooperative they form to make sure they all get to the finish within the time cut. We pass through them in knots of three and four, then six and eight, then twelve and sixteen as the bus takes shape. These men who would bash into each other at 45 mph to win a sprint are talking to each other, gesturing, putting hands on one another's shoulders, eating, sitting up with one hand on the bar, and staring skyward hoping to see the summit. Then we pass into the ragged ones and twos of the riders who have been ejected from the group against their will, and they are slump-shouldered, looking only roadward, at the pavement between their failed legs. Sometimes one will creak his head over sideways to look at us, and I feel as if I am watching some kind of refugee evacuation. There is a sense of desolate and absolute loss to them.

"Hey, Johan," says Armstrong. "Bottles."

We honk at the com car and drive past while Chris performs

the contortions necessary to extract bottles from the cooler buried somewhere under wheels and jackets and *musettes* and tools. Popo has fallen to the back of the peloton to be the water carrier. Chris hands the bottles one by one to Bruyneel, and as Bruyneel hands them out the open window, Popo says, "I want to do some shit over the last steep."

Bruyneel says, "For the moment you wait."

Six bottles go down the back of Popo's jersey. Two go in his jersey pockets and one in his cage. He's carrying nine pounds of water uphill.

Over the radio, Armstrong says, "Klodi, how are you?"

Kloden says, "I'm good. I'm with Schleck."

"I don't think we have anything to worry about, Johan," says Lance.

"No," says Bruyneel. "No, no, no, we are not worried. Steady pace. Wait for the attacks is all."

Chris says, "Lance sounds good. He sounds like he's sitting in the car with us."

Bruyneel says, "Yeah. Are we even going uphill?"

Gallopin nods.

But the most notable thing for me is not Armstrong's fitness. It's his demeanor. Being freed from the struggle for Tour leadership seems also to have freed him to openly become the team's leader on the road, using and exerting his experience to its fullest extent.

We drive past number 76, and Bruyneel picks up the mic and says, "Tony Martin is dropped. Tony Martin is dropped now."

"That's because he's young," jokes Armstrong over the radio.

Martin, a twenty-four-year-old German riding for Team Columbia, had been having an impressive debut and at the start of the day was sitting eighth, just 3:07 behind Contador. Today, he is finding out that his body might be one that eats itself in the third week of the Tour de France. He will lose more than 16 minutes.

We drive past snowy fields. The riders are in the steep final kilometer and Bruyneel reminds them to put on their jackets before they start downhill, and to eat and drink. Then he says to me, "Did you bring Haribo?"

I pass up an opened bag, and he pinches out a fingerful before offering it to Gallopin. "Ah, no," says Gallopin. He rubs his stomach. "When I worked with Fignon he loved them and always had some and asked me to eat them, so I did. So much I can't like them anymore."

Gallopin is talking about two-time winner Laurent Fignon, one of LeMond's rivals. Bruyneel says, "Yeah?" and seems to be filing the information into his long-term memory. Maybe it will come in useful at some point, who knows. Gallopin shakes his head and rubs his stomach. As this is happening the car is plunging down the mountain road at about 130 kph, and the tires squeal as if terrified or in great pain every time we corner.

The race goes through a valley after the descent, and though most of this road ascends steadily to the base of the Col du Petit-Saint-Bernard, the slope is gradual and the peloton regroups. The break is around four minutes ahead of them. Kloden comes back to the car, and as Bruyneel hands bottles out he says to Kloden, "It would be nice to be one-two-three, eh?"

Kloden smiles and does a little twitch of his head that is a one-gesture nod, and says, "Wiggins is so fffffucking fast in the time trial. And they are strong in the mountains."

"Second to our strength," says Bruyneel. "We can take the whole podium, Andreas."

We have crossed from Switzerland into Italy and will end the day in France. The Astana team truck, which like other supply vehicles is following the off-course route to get to the finish before the riders do, will be stopped at the French border today and searched for three hours. Nothing illegal will be found.

The break still has seventeen riders in it when it hits the start of Petit-Saint-Bernard, a Category 1. There are 22 kilometers of climbing left, then 31 down and the stage is over. The pack is around 5 minutes back. The autobus is 11 behind.

In Spanish, Contador asks if they should start to chase.

"No, no, it's okay," says Bruyneel. "Leave the gap at five minutes. Keep it there so other teams get nervous. At five minutes they are a threat first to the other guys in podium positions. We only watch for attacks. Don't chase. Stay fresh for attacks."

Contador says something else in Spanish, and Bruyneel replies, "We do not chase. Alberto, Velits is in the break. He is five minutes thirty-two behind Andy Schleck, so you see he is a threat for Andy Schleck's white jersey. Velits, the guy from Milram. Karpets is three minutes thirty behind Schleck. Astarloza three minutes eleven. They are threats for the podium. Stay calm."

We drive for a little in silence. Later, Bruyneel will say, "Always, Contador has doubts. He doubts my plan for the race, my tactics while we race. He doubts his teammates—that they know what to do. For his benefit he needs someone he can trust besides himself. That is not me, so it's good that we will split." In a few days, I know, Bruyneel will formally announce that he is leaving Astana at the end of the year, and Armstrong will announce the formation of RadioShack, his new team for 2010.

The quiet is broken when Lance says, "Any word on the conditions up there, the wind, et cetera?"

Dirk in car 2 has it: "At k one-twenty-five we come into a town and there it's crosswind from the left. Crosswind from the left. Headwind at the top of the climb. Headwind at top."

We pass Menchov, who's been dropped. Bruyneel looks out at him and says, "Menchov." A pause. "That's Menchov there." There's both awe and regret in his voice, as if we're driving by a dying lion our safari party shot.

Saxo goes to the front and jumps the pace, and the gap to the break comes down to about 3 minutes. Up ahead, the break is splintering under its own attacks. Mikel Astarloza will eventually get away with four others and go on for the win—which will lose its luster five days after the race ends, when anti-doping officials announce that he failed a drug test for EPO while training for the Tour. (His will be the only positive doping result associated with the Tour in 2009.)

About 9 kilometers from the top, Bruyneel says, "Be ready, boys. Be ready, be ready. Be ready for the attack of the Schlecks. Alberto, Lance, Andreas, be ready. They're going to go." And in the next switchback, Schleck accelerates. Contador, Wiggins, Kloden, and Frank Schleck follow him, along with a Liquigas rider named Vincenzo Nibali.

Armstrong can't.

"Stay on the wheel, Andreas. Stay on the wheel," Bruyneel says. "Good, Klodi. Stay on that wheel. Come on, man, hang in there on that wheel."

We pass Armstrong. Bruyneel looks out at him for a heartbeat. We continue up the hill.

Later, Bruyneel tells me what he was thinking: "He wanted to win the Tour de France. And he believed he could. But you can't suddenly ride away from the best if you were unable to keep up with them a month earlier. Everyone called Lance's win in '99 a miracle. But it was a long, steady progression that looked like a miracle because only he and I saw the work. I anticipated the most he could hope for this year was to keep up with the best. Knowing that, I still signed on to do the comeback, though I'm not sure he would have. Miracles in cycling? There are none."

A blue figure flashes forward past our windows. Then through the windshield, in front of us, we see Lance Armstrong pounding away at his bicycle.

"Lance attack! Lance attack!" Bruyneel screams into the radio. Then: "Stay on the wheel, Andreas, very good. Very good, Alberto."

Armstrong is hurtling across the gap.

"Come on, Lance," says Bruyneel. "You're almost there. Catch that wheel. Catch that wheel."

And he does. Contador, Kloden, and Armstrong go over the crest with Schleck and Wiggins, and Astana's hopes for a podium sweep are still alive. When Contador is asked about the moment later that day, he says, "Lance did a lot of work today. But I didn't really need his help."

STAGE 16 RESULTS

1. Mikel Astarloza, Euskaltel	4:14:20
10. Alberto Contador, Astana	+0:00:59
12. Lance Armstrong, Astana	
13. Bradley Wiggins, Garmin	
14. Andreas Kloden, Astana	
16. Christian Vande Velde, Garmin	
19. Andy Schleck, Saxo Bank	
24. Carlos Sastre, Cervélo	
46. Cadel Evans, Silence-Lotto	+0:03:55
85. Denis Menchov, Rabobank	+0:16:40

GENERAL CLASSIFICATION

1. Alberto Contador, Astana	67:33:15
2. Lance Armstrong, Astana	+0:01:37
3. Bradley Wiggins, Garmin	+0:01:46
4. Andreas Kloden, Astana	+0:02:17
5. Andy Schleck, Saxo Bank	+0:02:26
9. Carlos Sastre, Cervélo	+0:03:52
10. Christian Vande Velde, Garmin	+0:03:59
17. Cadel Evans, Silence-Lotto	+0:07:23
42. Denis Menchov, Rabobank	+0:27:04

It Is Not a Dream to Quit

I am standing a little less than 2 kilometers from the top of the final climb of Stage 17, the Col de la Colombière. It's separated from the penultimate mountain, the Col de Romme, by only a 5-kilometer descent, so the pair effectively form one monster slog.

From the Tourmalet to Alpe d'Huez, I have ridden many of the classic mountains of the Tour de France myself, so as the racers ascend these fabled roads I know something of what they must feel—the ordinary human's approximation, to be sure, but close enough to imagine the sensations and emotions coursing through the champions. I have pedaled in a blinding fog and against a stream of liquefied sheep shit flowing down the road in the Pyrenees. I've descended roads so hot the melting tar shifted beneath the wheels in turns, and roads so cold my steering settled back to a safe level only after my gloved hands stopped shivering and froze motionless on the handlebar. I have had my little triumphs: I've twice gotten finisher's medals in the Etape du Tour, the event that gives amateurs a chance to race a real stage of the Tour de France a few days before or after the pros; on the famed climb of Hautacam, where in 2000 Armstrong in one of the all-time great rides of the Tour took the yellow jersey by flying away from Ullrich and Pantani, I once beat an Olympic athlete (a figure skater, but still). And I have had my failures: in 2002, fat, out of shape, and enduring a job I hated, I was the last by 20 minutes in my group of friends to the top of Ventoux. To stand beside a mountain road and, as the racers pass, to peer into their eyes—that is my favorite way to experience the Tour de France.

Madness is upon this mountain. The helicopters that first came into view far below as hornets swarming the skinny roads rose to eye level like special effects in a war movie as the race ascended beneath them, and now they hover directly overhead, roaring and swatting air down upon us. Far down the mountain, I can see the crowd clotting the road until forced to scatter by an assault of sirens, lights, and horns. But even then, the fans stand thick and close, leaning into the path wedged open by the vehicles. A great bawl travels up through the crowd as if we are a telephone line. We begin shouting in our turn as the racers come.

Contador is leading, with the Schlecks on his wheel and bare road behind them. I am at the apex of a right turn, and they pass literal inches from me—so close that afterward I will look down and see that someone's sweat has dripped onto my shoe. Contador's eyes are without bottom, and he is looking back into them instead of out at the world. Andy Schleck's eyes look as if he has just hit a classmate with a spitball while the teacher was writing on the blackboard. Then they are past, up the hill.

I know what it was like to see into Contador and Schleck, and the moment will last as one of my great memories of any Tour de France. But because I am standing on an isolated Alpine road there are some things I don't know just then. I don't know that Schleck initiated this break by attacking 5 kilometers from the top of the Romme. And I don't know that only his brother Frank, Contador, and Kloden could catch his wheel. I don't know that Armstrong, Wiggins, Vande Velde, and Nibali formed a chase group that was 1:20 back at the base of this climb, the Colombière, with another group nearly 3½ minutes back and the rest of the peloton in pieces. I don't know that in the team car Bruyneel and Gallopin figured out that the attack and the makeup of the groups improved the chance of Astana's podium sweep: all Kloden has to do to move into third is finish 31 seconds ahead of Wiggins, and to remain in second, Armstrong has to stay with Wiggins and finish within 49 seconds of Schleck. I don't know that on the Colombière, Contador peeled off Schleck's wheel and temporarily faded back to Kloden, who was visibly struggling and shook his head to whatever Contador had asked. I don't know that Bruyneel figured out that Contador wanted to attack the Schlecks and, sensing that Kloden would be dropped if that happened, said three times into the radio, "Alberto, don't go. Don't go. Don't go." I don't know that just before I saw him, Contador attacked anyway. I don't know that Kloden was dropped, that he was watching his chance for a podium disappear up the narrow road of the Colombière, and that in the Astana car Bruyneel was screaming, cursing, beating the steering wheel so hard with his fist that he damaged it. And I don't know that as Contador and the Schleck brothers will go on to approach the finish, Contador will tap Frank Schleck on the butt and go through the motions of doing a sprint but clearly gift the stage to the elder brother—a not-uncommon practice in cycling but one that's unexpected in this instance because the reward of a stage win is usually granted by one rider to another only when they have cooperated to leave a rival behind.

Kloden rides by me in a palsy, and because I think he's jumped out of a group below and is chasing instead of having just been dropped, I yell, "Good job, Klodi!" He hears nothing. His eyes are a void. He is gone.

Armstrong is coming. It's not that I can't stop myself but that I have no idea I'm going to yell what I do, or feel what I do. When Armstrong cuts the corner, shiny with sweat and blowing spit from his mouth and with his blue eyes like an ice cave, I run a few steps with him and scream into his ear, "Ride that fucker down!"

I want Contador to win. That is clear to me even at that moment. I want him to win because he should. He is, as Armstrong said, "the biggest and best talent on the bike—maybe the best ever." But that is, maybe, why I also want Armstrong to win: because he can't. This is not an exclusive revelation. Driving the Tour's early stages, it was common to see hand-lettered or spray-painted messages taped to parked campers, or held high roadside by the fans themselves, that were critical of Armstrong: LA DOPE! And AVEC LANCE ARMSTRONG LE TOUR ES DOPE. Or: PHARMSTRONG. Lately the frequency of the signs had increased but the tenor had changed: WELCOME BACK LANCE. HOPE RIDES! ALLEZ ARMSTRONG. LUTTEZ AVEC NOUS CONTRE LE CANCER.

And, earlier today, scrawled in four-foot yellow chalk letters on a rocky mountainside:

GO
F**K
EM
LANCE

I was in the car today with my expat friend Jim, a photojournalist who has covered the Tour for twenty years. We'd begun stopping along the route to talk to the fans. Though the longtime, pop-culture consensus is that the French despise Armstrong because of his unemotional, American-big-business style of dominating their Tour, and because he was never caught doping, seven out of ten people we talked to told us they like Lance now. They said he is a hero even when he struggles, that he has become a symbol of the Tour de France, that he has shown he believes in fair play. Jim, who's lived in Paris so long he wears a beret daily without irony and plays in a French jazzy funk band, tried to explain the shift in their mentality. "They think he's beginning to *assumer*," he said, pronouncing the word *ah-sue-may*. "It is difficult to translate, but he's inhabiting fully who he is. When you do that you find truth and you become . . . you become . . . you become inherently beautiful. He's like Henry Miller's one-legged whore."

"I'll be sure to let him know that," I said.

There is something else I can't know as I stand there on the mountain watching Contador and the Schlecks and Kloden and Armstrong race: the Tour continues its random and relentless decimation of those who dare to try finishing it. Yesterday, Jens Voigt had smashed into the road at around 50 mph on the final descent. Bruyneel had to squeal the brakes and jerk the team car up against the vertical mountainside on our left to avoid running into the accident. Voigt, who was still rolling and flopping on the pavement as we passed, lost consciousness for about four minutes, was bleeding profusely from his mouth and nose, broke his jaw and cheekbones, and suffered a concussion. Today, riding alone, trailing the entire Tour de France after being dropped on the first of the day's five climbs, Kenny van Hummel lost control of his bike in a wet corner while descending the second mountain.

I'd spent some time with him that morning before the start. He seemed bemused that he had achieved a bit of fame. "Even among the Dutch, not many knew me before," he said. "I win five races in May and the team puts me in the Tour and . . ."

"And what?" I asked. There was a television crew from his home country waiting to interview him for a nationwide show called *The Heart of Holland* that was following his progress every day.

"And I am still here," Kenny said. He had dark, curly hair and a sprinter's solid build on his five-foot-nine body. He seemed to always have stubble on his chin and ringing his mouth, though he never looked deliberately unkempt. The hairs of this stubborn hero may just refuse to be shaved away. His manner was goofy but intent, like that kid in high school who wasn't very smart but tried hard and had a good heart, and because of his sincerity could be taken advantage of by the true juvies.

The Skil-Shimano team's press agent reminded me that the television crew was waiting and, having overheard Kenny's answer and found it wanting, also alerted me that the correct follow-up was, "And his website received ten million hits a few days ago."

That morning, in a report in *L'Equipe*, one of the Tour's directors had called Kenny "the worst climber in the history of the Tour." I asked him if he'd seen the story. He said no. He said, "Every day I am fighting. And I will keep fighting until I crash off my bike or someone shoots me off my bike. It is not a dream to quit."

The crash ripped open Kenny van Hummel's knee. He was transported to a hospital, where he underwent nine hours of surgery.

The new *lanterne rouge*, starting tomorrow, is Yauheni Huta-

rovich, who'd been more than 45 minutes out of last place. He
didn't deserve to lose.

STAGE 17 RESULTS

1. Frank Schleck, Saxo Bank	4:53:54
2. Alberto Contador, Astana	Same time
3. Andy Schleck, Saxo Bank	
5. Lance Armstrong, Astana	+0:02:18
6. Andreas Kloden, Astana	+0:02:27
7. Bradley Wiggins, Garmin	+0:03:07
9. Christian Vande Velde, Garmin	+0:04:09
25. Carlos Sastre, Cervélo	+0:07:47
63. Denis Menchov, Rabobank	+0:21:31
81. Cadel Evans, Silence-Lotto	+0:29:43

GENERAL CLASSIFICATION

1. Alberto Contador, Astana	72:27:09
2. Andy Schleck, Saxo Bank	+0:02:26
3. Frank Schleck, Saxo Bank	+0:03:25
4. Lance Armstrong, Astana	+0:03:55
5. Andreas Kloden, Astana	+0:04:44
6. Bradley Wiggins, Garmin	+0:04:53
8. Christian Vande Velde, Garmin	+0:08:08
13. Carlos Sastre, Cervélo	+0:11:39
32. Cadel Evans, Silence-Lotto	+0:37:06
44. Denis Menchov, Rabobank	+0:48:35

A Guy I Idolized

Armstrong is warming up when his kids arrive. It is a little after
3 p.m. on a cloudy day in Annecy and already 123 riders have set off

one at a time on the 40.5-kilometer loop around the clear, narrow lake that shares the city's name. The best effort so far belongs to Fabian Cancellara, who about an hour ago finished in 48:34, with an average speed of a little over 31 mph. That seems fast enough to win Stage 18.

Armstrong doesn't start until 4:38 p.m., three minutes after Kloden (who follows Wiggins) and three in front of Frank Schleck. Andy goes next, and Contador last. Cancellara could win the day, but these last six rides are the ones that will decide who has a chance to fight for the overall win on the last day of real racing, the climb up Mont Ventoux in Stage 20.

"Daddy!" screams Grace, one of Armstrong's seven-year-old twin girls. Luke, who is nine and wearing a Hurley shirt, simply runs forward, trusting as boys often do that when he reaches his destination his father will be ready to be tackled. And, indeed, Armstrong locks his son in a hug. Luke's hands can barely touch across the width of Armstrong's back. Someone has given Astana cycling caps to Grace and Bella. After they hug their father, then let Armstrong's girlfriend, Anna, move in for a kiss carrying the baby, Max, the two girls begin pulling up grass strands and tossing them into the air like confetti as they twirl around and shout, "Ahhhh-stana!"

After just about three minutes of this, someone has given the girls Livestrong caps instead. Though the official press conference to announce the RadioShack deal isn't until six o'clock tonight, the news has leaked. And Bruyneel has confirmed to the press that when he leaves the team at the end of the year it will be to begin the new one with Armstrong. But the girls are seven and, in full possession of their age's shared giggliness, they continue their whirling grassy cheers for the team Armstrong wishes he wasn't on.

He is on the trainer now, the earpieces of his iPod plugged in. A sleeveless Livestrong vest exposes the sharp lines where his dark biceps turn to pale white—what most of the public would call a farmer's tan but in his profession is only one part of what is known as the cyclist's tan. The rest: white hands from wearing gloves and, from the three-quarter length of the bib shorts on the thigh, and hours spent in socks and shoes, an otherwise tan leg bookended by pale panels that are impossible to hide on a beach. It is an unglamorous, even ridiculous side effect of the profession.

The bike he is warming up on is his Yoshitomo Nara art bike. It will sell for $200,000 at the Sotheby's auction at the end of the season, but, because it is predominantly yellow, when he takes to the course today the bike will draw some boos from fans who feel he is being disrespectful of the jersey and its current owner. The spinning of the rear disc wheel, which is painted light blue with white cartoon heads, attracts the attention of Grace and Bella. They settle in to watch their father do his job. Luke is off somewhere hunting for some of the helium balloons that are being sold in the area open to spectators.

Astana has cordoned off a big section in the park beside the lake by using its team bus and its bike-carrying tractor-trailer as the two sides of a square. Tape, fencing, and police officers keep the crowd at bay on the other two sides. Several hundred people are out there, many of them rotating in to see if they can spot Armstrong or Contador, then leaving to find more accessible racers, but the first couple rows of people are sitting on the grass to take in the whole show. Kloden has come out at some point and is warming up next to Armstrong, wearing a sleeveless white T-shirt that shows the red devil tattoo high on his right arm. They are under the truck's retractable awning, which has been put out to keep off the day's spattering of rain. Armstrong is spinning at ease, fluid and without much force, listening to music, and for the most part staring straight ahead. But sometimes he pulls a face at the girls, and once he squirts his water bottle at Anna and teases her. Sometimes he looks down and sees a message the artist Nara has handwritten in a spot on the frame that Armstrong will be able to read when he drops into his aero tuck: NEVER FORGET YOUR BEGINNER'S SPIRIT.

Contador comes out of the team bus.

Armstrong happens to be stretched forward rehearsing his aero tuck at that moment, and he keeps his head straight and unmoving but averts his eyes down and to the right, as if he cannot bear to see Contador. He flushes and his jaw sets up hard and tight, and his tongue pushes out against his chin. Then he pulls his vision back and, still without moving his head, looks down at the frame of his bike, and something seems to let loose inside him. He sits up, and sighs and rolls his shoulders, and picks up the brown towel that is draped across his unmoving front wheel (only the rear spins when a bike is mounted in these trainers) and wipes his face, then looks at his daughters, at Anna, and back over his left shoulder, where a friend from Aspen sits on the steps of the trailer, holding Max. There is no sense in trying to determine if this is another strategic performance or a burst of true emotion. After a year of following Armstrong, I have concluded that with him such events are both. He is a man who uses his genuine emotions as weapons, as tools. He wastes no feeling.

Contador is on his bike now, on the other side of Kloden, his ears plugged with his own iPod buds, Astana-blue glasses hiding his eyes. His spin is so sprightly it seems almost a little showily so. He sits light upon his bike and his legs flash in their motion. Four days from the end of the Tour de France he seems as a fresh as a sliver of ripe fruit. Like the team's riders, I've found my loyalty drawn to Armstrong almost completely—and against my determination to remain objective—but there is also no denying Contador's strength. In emotional isolation, he has withstood the physical and psychological attacks of all of his rivals, including the one on his team.

Off to his right, the people sitting there sing the Contador chant. After a few rounds, three other people sitting nearby insert a coda. When the song ends with the longest iteration of the racer's name—"Conta-dooorrrorrrorr"—the other group interjects, "Lance!"

The night before, at the hotel, Contador apologized to the team for his attack, Bruyneel told me. "But it was more the kind of statement only to get us to go away and leave him alone," he says. Contador is not the first Tour de France champion to ride his own race. One of the greatest in the history of the sport was a bullying and selfish leader. The Badger, Bernard Hinault, was known for not granting other riders a stage in exchange for helping him gain time on rivals, for verbally humiliating and intimidating riders who questioned his leadership, and for abusing his status as the peloton's *patron* by announcing directives that included bans on attacking (to allow the contenders to rest for upcoming mountain stages). Hinault also instigated an intrateam rivalry that makes Contador-Armstrong look like a couple of schoolkids tussling. In 1985, Hinault was going for his fifth Tour win but his new teammate, Greg LeMond, was clearly superior. Their team director ordered LeMond to hold back and ride in support of Hinault, and in return Hinault promised to help the American win the next year. But in 1986, in the first mountain stage, Hinault attacked LeMond for a gain of more than 4 minutes and took the yellow jersey from Jørgen Pedersen, who'd been expected to lose it—to LeMond. The next day when Hinault attacked again in the mountains, LeMond disobeyed team orders and counterattacked. Hinault hung on to the jersey, but LeMond gained back most of the time and won the stage. In the Alps four days later LeMond rode into yellow, then the next day Hinault launched a vicious attack at the base of Alpe d'Huez that LeMond eventually chased down. (He was the only one who could manage to stay with his teammate.) The two crossed the line holding hands and LeMond would go on to win. Hinault claimed his tactics were designed to wear down LeMond's rivals and to let LeMond prove to the world he deserved to win the Tour. LeMond, in a 1998 interview with Bryan Malessa that appeared in *Bicyclist Online*, said, "It was like being burned by your brother. The thing is that Hinault wasn't your typical teammate. He was a guy I idolized."

Armstrong starts out too fast. At the first checkpoint, at kilometer 18, he is 10 seconds faster than Cancellara. At the second he is 11 seconds slower than Cancellara, at the third 26 behind, and by the fourth, at kilometer 37, he has lost 1:11. In the final 3.5 kilometers he loses 15 more seconds. His time is decent enough to put him back into third in the General Classification, and it seems possible he will be able to defend his now-11-second gap over Wiggins on Ventoux. They have split in the four crucial mountain stages: they finished twice together; once Wiggins beat Armstrong by 29 seconds over the 8 kilometers up Verbier; and once Armstrong beat Wiggins by 49 seconds over the 16.3 kilometers up the combination of Romme and Colombière.

But conversely, Armstrong's time is poor enough that defending his position against Frank Schleck now looks nearly impossible. The two finished together at Andorre-Arcalis and over the two Saint-Bernards in Stage 16. But on Verbier, Frank Schleck was 29 seconds faster than Armstrong, and 2:18 faster over Romme and Colombière—that's a 2:47 gap over 24 kilometers. Ventoux is 21 kilometers long, and after today Frank Schleck is in sixth place overall but only 34 seconds behind Armstrong.

Kloden rides slightly better, but not as well as he needed to take a shot at the podium on Ventoux. When he returns to the Astana bus, he hurls his bike to the ground and disappears inside.

It is Contador who defeats Cancellara. He has ridden away from his rivals in the mountains and in the time trials, and now in this last test against the clock he outspeeds the world's greatest time trialist. He is shimmering in yellow as he talks afterward, his teeth are white and his smile is wide, and he can make a joke now about the lack of connection with his team. His radio earpiece stopped working less than halfway through the trial. "But it's okay," says Contador. "I'm used to it. I raced without the radio not so long ago."

Armstrong looks old and tired. He came into the Tour de France as lean as his younger competitors. But instead of riding himself into that silvery, translucent spectral state in which everything is stripped from the body except the resilience at its core, he somewhere slipped into the plain state of being tired. He's had a horrible day at work and his kids are running around screaming, and for the first time since I've known him he seems just flat worn out the way I sometimes am, the way sometimes all of my friends are. He seems like one of us.

STAGE 18 RESULTS

1. Alberto Contador, Astana	0:48:31
6. Bradley Wiggins, Garmin	+0:00:42
9. Andreas Kloden, Astana	+0:00:53
12. Cadel Evans, Silence-Lotto	+0:01:14
16. Lance Armstrong, Astana	+0:01:29
21. Andy Schleck, Saxo Bank	+0:01:44
24. Christian Vande Velde, Garmin	+0:02:00
70. Carlos Sastre, Cervélo	+0:03:47
79. Denis Menchov, Rabobank	+0:04:11

GENERAL CLASSIFICATION

1. Alberto Contador, Astana	73:15:39
2. Andy Schleck, Saxo Bank	+0:04:11
3. Lance Armstrong, Astana	+0:05:25
4. Bradley Wiggins, Garmin	+0:05:36
5. Andreas Kloden, Astana	+0:05:38
8. Christian Vande Velde, Garmin	+0:10:08
14. Carlos Sastre, Cervélo	+0:15:26
29. Cadel Evans, Silence-Lotto	+0:38:20
43. Denis Menchov, Rabobank	+0:52:47

True Enough

Ventoux looms.

That is not a metaphorical description. Like Mount Rainier seen from Seattle, the 1,912-meter mountain towers above the landscape. The sole geographic mass of significant height and bulk in all of Provence, in just over 21 kilometers Ventoux rises a little less than 1,600 meters—measured straight up, nearly a full mile higher than the town at its base. Looked at from that town, Bedoin, that faraway peak seems perennially and beautifully snow-capped. In reality the mountain's cap is naked limestone devoid of trees, bushes, or any notable vegetation.

Ventoux looms. That is a fact of its stature in the race's history. In the Tour's fourteen trips to the top, the mountain has laid waste to human ambition, and human life. In 1955, the Tour de France winner of five years earlier, Ferdi Kübler, was reduced to a wobbly zigzag to reach the finish and that night announced his withdrawal by saying, "Ferdi has killed himself on the Ventoux." In 1967, an amphetamine-laced racer, Tom Simpson, actually did collapse and die. He was just 2 kilometers from the summit, and his desperate last words—"Put me back on the bike"—haunt the road still. The great Eddy Merckx desired a victory here so badly he rode to exhaustion in 1970. He collapsed senseless after he crossed the finish, and had to be revived with oxygen.

Ventoux looms particularly for Lance Armstrong. He characterizes his relationship with the mountain as uneasy. Others call it cursed. He's never won on this road, and often found only trouble at its terminus. In the 2000 Tour, he consolidated his hold on the yellow jersey by matching Marco Pantani pedal stroke for pedal stroke up the climb. Just before the finish, Armstrong eased off, gifting the stage to the Italian. That was the honorable move, the right thing to do. But Armstrong, in his second year as Tour champ and still awkward when it came to the mores of leadership, afterward openly admitted he'd given the win to Pantani. That was an insult. Pantani repaid the slight a few days later by launching a mountain attack on Joux-Plane that caused Armstrong to bonk and nearly lose the Tour. In 2001, the Frenchman Richard Virenque, fresh off his suspension for doping and eager to win back the hearts of his country, promised an early attack on Ventoux and delivered on his word. He rode all the way to victory while Armstrong chased him through the deafening boos of the rabid, partisan crowd, which would have heaped abuse on whoever happened to be chasing Virenque. In a time trial up the mountain in the 2004 Dauphiné Libéré, an eight-stage race in June popular as a warm-up for Tour de France contenders, Iban Mayo rode 55:51, a new record for the ascent. (He broke the 56:50 mark set in 1990 by Jonathan Vaughters, now the Garmin director.) Mayo was being touted as a major threat to Armstrong's Tour hopes that year. Intent on demoralizing him, Armstrong dug so deep trying to match the pace that, according to some inside his circle, he derailed his training program and harmed his preparation for the Tour. "Maybe it's not possible for me to win on this climb," he told the media after chasing Virenque in 2001.

And Ventoux looms for me as I hurtle toward it in a car with Jim again, after spending the previous day on a moto following the race. In a minor repeat of Stage 3, yesterday Armstrong had slipped into a split toward the end of the race. Tucked into a twelve-man group that Cavendish led across the line for a fifth stage win, Armstrong finished 4 seconds ahead of all the other podium contenders, turning a day that was supposed to be nothing but a transition to Ventoux into another reminder that he understood the Tour better than anyone. But it had also served as a reminder of the vanity of his struggle. Even with the additional 4 seconds, he was still just 38 ahead of Frank Schleck. I had accepted that the gap wasn't enough to keep Armstrong on the podium—especially since Andy had hinted that on Ventoux he chiefly was going to attack not to beat Contador (whom he'd more or less realized he couldn't crack) but to help his brother beat Lance.

In failing to win, Armstrong had become somewhat like one of us. But when he'd still seemed likely to stand on the podium, even if on its lowest step, he was a better version of us—the us we try to be, or at least think about being someday. To see him finish in fourth, however, going down in history as just one more rider in the pack of the 2009 Tour de France—that is no comeback I want any part of.

We pass through fields of purple lavender, and of gnarled and whitely green olive trees, and apricot and cherry orchards, and stands of lemon trees, and we drive between immense fields of low waving cereal. Today's 178-kilometer route cruelly exacerbates the suffering the riders will experience once they reach Ventoux. For much of the day they roller-coaster up and down from the start in Bourgoin-Jallieu, gradually gaining height the whole time until they reach an elevation of 996 meters after around 120 kilometers. Then they waste their gain in just 17 kilometers by descending to a low point of 244 meters before beginning a steady upward crawl toward the turn that marks the start of the climb. Once the race slams into the mythic mountain, says Bjarne Riis, Saxo Bank has a three-point plan: "We will attack, attack, and attack again."

A big breakaway is out in front after 65 kilometers, sixteen men seesawing a gap between eight and nine minutes, but the pack is barely chasing. The best-placed racer in the break is Tony Martin, who is 55:39 behind Contador.

In the car, we skirt a raging forest fire and drive under a throat-scratching ceiling of its smoke. We pass the yellow-and-red van of Yvette Horner, the accordionist who used to play on the podium of every Tour stage until being replaced in 1964 by canned music, and who still follows the race on her own. We drive into the little town of Bedoin, the last point on the map before the climb starts. The course proceeds through town on streets solid with fans, then doubles back and softly rises past a farm or two, then makes a left turn familiar to cycling fans worldwide and smacks into Ventoux.

From here, the ascent is unrelenting: The grade averages 7.6

percent overall, but there is a horrible 7-kilometer stretch in the middle when the slope never dips below 9 percent and 3 of its kilometers buck up at a 10 percent rate. "It never lets up, you never recover," Vaughters had told me. In 1999, when he rode his sub-hour record ascent, the previous mark of 1:02:09 had stood since 1958. "You pin it at the turn. You stay pinned. You hope you reach the top before you fall off your bike."

There are 1 million people on the mountain today. And, as I tell a sports radio program that calls me from the United States for a color commentary (exaggerating for laughs, but just a little), half of those million people are drunk, and the other half are really drunk. We drive honking through a bacchanalia. The car is assaulted, doused with beer, blocked by what appears to be a rave. Sometimes when we are forced to a stop, we get pushed in rocking motions from the back, as if friendly Samaritans are trying to help us gun out of a snowbank. Among the creatures we pass are two Elvises, a herd of Smurfs, the Pope, a boatful of Vikings, two chickens, a kangaroo riding a man, Barney Rubble, several sumo, two prisoners (chained together at the legs), two spacemen (tethered), and four cross-dressed cavewomen who are, sadly, separated from Barney by a few cruel kilometers of 7 percent slope.

There are cycling fans, too, holding signs that beseech various racers for miracles, or even now still covering the pavement with painted tributes and pictographs. And some people up here are simply devotees of the Tour de France, similar to the way that back in the United States there are people at the races who are followers not of cycling competition but of Lance Armstrong. But most of Ventoux's temporary residents appear to be fans neither of cycling nor of the Tour but of excess. They are here because there is a celebration here. For them, this could be Mardi Gras. Or a Dionysian Mystery rite three thousand years ago. There is no madder scene in sports anywhere in the world at any time, not a World Cup soccer final, not the Super Bowl, not the Olympics. It seems the mountain might collapse under the weight of its party.

With about 7 kilometers to go, we drive past the tree line. The road ahead wafts through a nightmarish and disorienting, wind-wracked lunarscape. This part of the mountain is often closed to traffic not only for snow, like any high-altitude peak, but. also, because of its bare exposure and Ventoux's solitary position on the landscape, for winds. Weather gauges at the top record ongoing gusts of 50 mph about 240 days out of the year and have measured extended bursts up to 200 mph. Gusts up to 65 mph have been reported today. We nose the car into the crowd, aiming for a service road about 5 kilometers from the top. Jim knows some people who have organized a party in a big tent here. The race is still more than 20 kilometers from the base of Ventoux. The break has more than 6 minutes, and the pack is doing nothing more yet than suffering the usual amount they would after nineteen days and 3,128 kilometers of racing.

When we get out of the car, the wind slaps us, howls, throws dust in our eyes. Sunlight ricochets off the white of the rocks around us. We lean into the wind and make our way to the party tent. It's a big white structure that's tethered down like a circus tent in a tornado belt, reserved for a few groups running deluxe cycling vacations—for people who pay lots of money to have companies pamper them while they ride their bikes and follow the race. One of the groups is Marty Jemison Cycling Tours, and there, standing right inside the tent watching the race on a big plasma TV angled across a corner in front of some couches, is Marty Jemison.

He'd ridden the Tour de France for the U.S. Postal Service team in 1997 and 1998, and the next year won the stars-and-stripes jersey in the U.S. national road championship. But when Bruyneel took over the team in 1999 and put together his first Tour squad—the one that would go on to capture the first of Armstrong's seven victories—he left Jemison off. The racer became one of the first, and for a long time the most visible, of the casualties inflicted by Armstrong and Bruyneel on their way to greatness. In his disrespected stars-and-stripes jersey, Jemison was a symbol of what it takes to win the Tour Armstrong-style and, I suppose, of what it takes to be the best at anything.

I walk over and shake Jemison's hand, and he asks me if I want a cold beer. I take one and drink it and we watch the race and we talk about the Tour and Ventoux, and his business, and his homes in Girona, Spain, and Salt Lake City. It was a long time ago, 1999, and Jemison is not a mere memory of that year. He is not, after all, a symbol. He's a guy whose life has turned out okay.

The break is on the mountain, and we have to go.

On the way to the car, we walk by two men with rainbow hair, a swarthy man in a pink bikini and a platinum Marilyn Monroe wig, and a middle-aged man who is bent over, hands on thighs, making heaving noises while an elderly woman holding a bottle of wine pats his back. We also pass a resting pack of young amateur cyclists in matching red uniforms and as thin as pros, sitting casually on the top tubes of their bicycles with a general air about them that says, desperately, that they are not fatigued but no longer deign to ride a road so crowded with jokesters, mythic peak just 5 kilometers away or not. You can lose yourself to the Tour de France in drink, or inside costumes, or through the pure blanking power of the effort it takes to ascend the mountain. In the losing, you become a part of the Tour de France. The line between spectator and participant dissolves, and you become, even if in a small way, a player in the show. But all I've lost here on Ventoux is hope. Or, I suppose, it could be said that I've gained something: knowledge. I accept now that there really are no miracles in cycling. What's worse, in a way, is that denied our miracles, we go right on living: after 1999, Marty Jemison never got another shot at riding the Tour, the dream of every cyclist, yet here he was on the mountain today, enjoying the race, happy with his life.

We drive past the Tom Simpson memorial 2 kilometers from the top, up on the scrabbly rocks to the right. I turn my head to stare at it as we go by. Earlier, David Millar told me he was going to unbuckle his helmet and tip it to Tom in tribute as he passes. Other racers do the same, and just about any amateur who summits Ventoux stops on the way back down to contemplate the memorial, or slip one of the surrounding stones in a jersey pocket to take home. Simpson will be a part of the Tour as long as it exists, because he lost himself to it in the most complete way. I don't want Armstrong to become Tom Simpson today, but I don't want him to become Marty Jemison, either.

At the finish, I wander around for a while. There's one accessible television, hidden behind the VIP platform, and I stand there and stare at the screen but I don't want to watch what is happening. The break started the climb with about a 5-minute lead, but the gap is now barely 3 minutes. There's a chase group that includes Contador, the Schlecks, Armstrong, Wiggins, and Kloden, and the attacks have begun. Frank Schleck launches an exploratory jump, and when Armstrong covers him immediately, Andy leaps up the road. In three brutal minutes, Andy attacks four times. Each time the group that pulls itself back to him is smaller. I watch Contador lead Wiggins, Lance, and Frank up to Andy once again, and as soon as they all regroup, Frank attacks.

I walk away. I can't watch it. I go out on the road and stand about 50 feet past the finish line, against the chain-link fence that keeps spectators out. I can look down the mountain and see the road weaving all the way back to the trees. I stand there, staring.

When I look around the finish again, most of the team *soigneurs* have taken up a post around me, preparing for their riders to come through. I see Ryszard standing a little closer to the finish line than I am, with his square red cooler, and his *musettes* full of towels and jackets, and his backpack full of whatever it is full of. I walk over and say hi.

He considers me, frowning. He looks down the rock-strewn slope at the road I'd been looking at. He looks back at me and says, "Are you going to stand here the whole time?"

"Whatever," I say. I'm about to walk away.

Ryszard says, "Because I am wondering if you could help me. I must go there for Lance." He points closer to the finish line. "And it is such a lot of people around him the next rider comes and pass me and it is too late to give them. See? So could you?" He motions to the bags, some jackets.

I nod. It is the only response I can form.

"You will watch for Kloden."

I nod again.

"Here they come," says Ryszard. He motions at the road below us with his chin. I look, and see the race out in the open. Two survivors of the breakaway are, against all odds, still out front. One of them is Juan Manuel Gárate, who in about 20 minutes is going to arc up around the final hard right-hand bend and sprint straight into the mouth of the final 10 percent grade for the win that salvages the Tour for Menchov's Rabobank team. The other is Tony Martin, the kid from Columbia who fell apart on the Saint-Bernards but found a way to put himself back together today. A big length of road behind them, I see the yellow jersey of Contador and recognize the particular style of Andy Schleck, who rides like a kid running through a grass field after school. I watch them pedal between the wild riots on each side and the sirens and lights in front of them and behind, these monastic men who so incomprehensibly suffer so quietly.

"Okay," says Ryszard as he gathers half the material. "They will bring Lance to me."

"How is he?" I ask.

"Ah, good." And he walks off, casual, just like that, as if the answer barely needed to be given.

And I see it, then: Armstrong and Frank Schleck are out on the bare road together. They have dropped Wiggins. Later, Bruyneel will describe for me how Armstrong stayed with Frank through his three attacks and Andy's seven. "He was riding like . . . like . . . He was riding like Lance Armstrong."

The crest of Ventoux erupts. The race is here. I see Kloden coming through the cars and motos and bikes and faces and TV cameras and I scream, "Andreas! Andreas!" I wave my arms and jump but he is about to ride past me. As loud as I can I shout, "Klodi!" He veers over to me, a little puzzled, but I point at the bag hanging on my shoulder. He reaches over and opens it and pulls out a jacket and puts it on.

"Thank you," he says.

One more time, the best response I can summon is a nod. I have become a small but real part of the comeback of Lance Armstrong.

"Way to go," I say to Kloden, but he is already riding off, descending the backside of Ventoux to find the team bus parked somewhere down there. "Way to go," I say to all the riders descending the road before me, but like Klodi, none of them will hear me.

I am walking down the road looking for Jim when I glance over to my left and see Frank Schleck on his bike, braking down to walking speed, rubbing his nose.

"Frank," I say, and he looks over at me.

"Way to go," I repeat myself. He gives a little, tired nod. He is about to pass by me when I say, "Man, are you disappointed?"

He tilts his head as he looks over at me. He rubs his nose and coughs and coasts at my speed and looks at me as if he is deciding something of which I am only a small part. He laughs. He says, "Not at all. It's nothing."

"Nothing?" I say. When he and Andy were kids in Luxembourg, I know, they used to pretend the street out in front of their house was the Champs-Élysées. "What about your dream, you and Andy, of winning the Tour together—"

"Ah, no," he says. "When we dreamed about doing the Tour it was only that we finish together in Paris. I won a stage and he is on the podium, so it is actually more than we ever expected." He takes his left hand off the bar and reaches over across his body and shakes my hand, as if we are sealing some kind of deal. I thank him, not to be polite but because I mean it. There are no miracles in cycling, or in comebacks, but there are plenty of dreams. And some of those come true, or at least true enough.

STAGE 20 RESULTS

1. Juan Manuel Gárate, Rabobank	4:39:21
3. Andy Schleck, Saxo Bank	+0:00:38
4. Alberto Contador, Astana	
5. Lance Armstrong, Astana	+0:00:41
6. Frank Schleck, Saxo Bank	+0:00:43
10. Bradley Wiggins, Garmin	+0:01:03
12. Andreas Kloden, Astana	+0:01:42
16. Christian Vande Velde, Garmin	+0:02:34
32. Cadel Evans, Silence-Lotto	+0:05:45
71. Carlos Sastre, Cervélo	+0:09:36
98. Denis Menchov, Rabobank	+0:19:18

GENERAL CLASSIFICATION

1. Alberto Contador, Astana	81:46:17
2. Andy Schleck, Saxo Bank	+0:04:11
3. Lance Armstrong, Astana	+0:05:24
4. Bradley Wiggins, Garmin	+0:06:01
5. Frank Schleck, Saxo Bank	+0:06:04
6. Andreas Kloden, Astana	+0:06:42
8. Christian Vande Velde, Garmin	+0:12:04
17. Carlos Sastre, Cervélo	+0:26:21
30. Cadel Evans, Silence-Lotto	+0:45:24
51. Denis Menchov, Rabobank	+1:16:28

Lots to Learn

Like any single day of the Tour de France beheld on its own, the ride of the Champs-Élysées is a marvel. The survivors of the three-week crucifixion rumble over the famous cobbled street, whoosh along the Seine, then dash around the Place de la Concorde (where, not irrelevant to the current spectacle, the public used to gather to revel in beheadings and dismemberments). They storm past the Tuileries Palace and leave the Louvre behind as they head back to the Champs-Élysées to barrel toward the Arc d'Triomphe, only to dive through a hairpin turn at the last instant and complete the whole revolution again. Seven times they do this, with sirens splitting the air and the wheels of the team cars as loud as locomotives on the cobbles. The riders, who for most of the long day into Paris have been tootling along at parade pace, hoisting champagne glasses for the cameras, saying goodbye to friends in the pack, and riding in front of the peloton to pose for pictures, are now racing for real—showing off for the crowd a little but mostly in exaltation burning themselves down one final time simply because they find themselves strong enough to do so. There is always a doomed but courageous break-away that lasts until there's one lap to go. And in that final lap witnessing the sprinters' teams close on the break is an irreconcilable heartbreak—you pray for the escapists to defy the odds and stay away for the win, but you also lust for the carnivorous bringing down of the hunted by the pack. (And this year, Cavendish satisfies our hunger by ravaging the peloton for his sixth and final stage win.)

But the day always feels anticlimactic to me. There is something too formal about it, something too far removed from the raw emotions of the road. Dignitaries observe the proceedings—barely—from the most exclusive, invite-only tribunes erected at the finish, while the moneyed and the tenuously connected buy access to tribunes such as the Rive Gauche, which in packages for up to 500 euros offers "a personal welcome by Tour de France hostesses, a welcoming cocktail, a gastronomic lunch located close to the Champs-Élysées, grandstand seats just at the finish line, refreshments served in the tribune, a VIP Tour de France gift." The wealthiest teams rent suites in the hotels overlooking the course, and from the balconies, wives, CEOs, and important clients holding gilt-edged glasses of Campari and champagne remark on the bravery of the racers. The Tour de France is suddenly made to feel too much like mere entertainment, like just one more event in one more busy day in Paris.

The end of the stage marks the beginning of a glacial two-hour processional called "the protocol." Politicians are introduced and speak at length about the lessons they will take from the Tour and apply to their governance. With the street population reduced to a mere tenth of that which watched the race, the winners mount the podium. Then the teams in order of finish take a victory lap around the Champs-Élysées. In its rhythm and length and motion and unpredictability, the Tour de France may be, as many of its admirers have noted, the sporting event that most closely mimics life. I go back and forth on that one. But if the metaphor is accurate, then the protocol in Paris is that part of life we endure not through strength, will, cunning, or even luck but through our puzzling slavishness to the human need for boring ceremony.

But this year was different. There he was on the lowest step, with his kids watching him watch someone else rise above him and hoist the trophy and wear the yellow jersey. He was not even the oldest rider to ever get on the podium. Raymond Poulidor was forty when he got third in 1976. This was no miracle. This had not ever been his dream, third place.

Andy Schleck, on step two, was in the white of the best young rider, the second year in a row he'd worn it. He'd pulled a wheelie, laughing, when his team crossed the finish line during their protocol lap, and Frank had been shaking his head and smiling. Alberto Contador was in yellow shorts and a yellow jersey and wore a black cap decorated with an embroidered yellow hand firing a pistol shot. He was twenty-six years old and he'd won the last two Tours de France he'd entered and the last four Grand Tours. And in a decade's worth of Tour de France racers he had been the only one who could bring down Armstrong, and that in a race when Armstrong was racing eight hearts to his one.

In a few minutes things will go to hell—the organizers will insult Contador by mistakenly queuing up the Danish national anthem instead of his own—and will keep going that way for a while. Tomorrow at a press conference in Madrid Contador will say, "My relationship with Lance Armstrong is zero. He is a great rider and has completed a great race, but it is another thing on a personal level, where I have never had great admiration for him and never will." Armstrong will retort via Twitter: "If I were him I'd drop this drivel and start thanking his team. W/o them he doesn't win," and in another message, "Hey pistolero, there is no 'I' in team. What did I say in March? Lots to learn. Restated."

The next day, Contador will meet with the Spanish prime minister, José Luis Rodríguez Zapatero, who will clarify a national position on the issue of his country's hero: "He has no rival, even if that is hard to accept for some."

Over the next few months, Contador will leak unverifiable stories about the Tour: Armstrong had red, puffy eyes at the breakfast table the morning after Andorre-Arcalis; the morning before the time trial at Annecy, the whole team left without Contador, and because Armstrong sent a team car to pick up his family, Contador was forced to ride to the race in his brother's car; he had to go to a bike shop himself to buy the time trial wheels he wanted, because he couldn't get any from the team, although they'd been supplied to Lance.

"Fairy tales," Armstrong tells me. "It's like, which bike race was he at? You know how my family got from the airport to the race start? The camper. We had to shove them in the camper. They didn't take a team car."

Some blame for Contador's perceptions can be attributed to the lunacy the Tour imposes upon its practitioners. Armstrong ventured some batty suppositions of his own under the stress of the race. At one point, convinced someone was tampering with his bike, he kept it in his hotel room while he slept, and asked Chris to work on it there, too. But Contador certainly had a reason to see things differently than the rest of his team; by the end of the year, all the other Astana riders on the Tour roster will defect to Armstrong's new RadioShack team.

I will end up not minding the ugliness of it all—the two of them combined don't even get close to Hinault alone—but the pettiness will feel wrong. Champions should not squabble. I will ignore as much of the sniping melodrama as I can, because I won't want that to be my final memory of the comeback of Lance Armstrong.

I'll stay right here on the Champs-Élysées instead. Contador is holding the trophy bowl aloft with his left hand and with his right flashing his number of Tour victories, which is also in a wonderful coincidence the victory sign but which someone hoping for a happy ending might mistake for the peace sign. Andy Schleck is looking away, off to the right, his expression once again that of a kid enthralled by what lies outside the walls of wherever he happens to be, and maybe he is looking at Frank or maybe he is seeing two boys sprint down a lane in Luxembourg. Lance Armstrong is looking up at Alberto Contador, at his trophy or his victory sign or both. It doesn't matter because he has neither. His expression balances dismay and desire. His children are watching him. His mother. His friends. His fans and his enemies. He worked so hard to lose in front of them. If he could become a little like us when he needed to, maybe we can be a little like him next time we need to.

STAGE 21 RESULTS

1. Mark Cavendish, Columbia	4:02:18
26. Andreas Kloden, Astana	
44. Christian Vande Velde, Garmin	
55. Bradley Wiggins, Garmin	
56. Frank Schleck, Saxo Bank	
59. Cadel Evans, Silence-Lotto	
62. Lance Armstrong, Astana	
63. Andy Schleck, Saxo Bank	
97. Alberto Contador, Astana	
109. Carlos Sastre, Cervélo	
146. Denis Menchov, Rabobank	+0:00:36

GENERAL CLASSIFICATION

1. Alberto Contador, Astana	85:48:35
2. Andy Schleck, Saxo Bank	+0:04:11
3. Lance Armstrong, Astana	+0:05:24
4. Bradley Wiggins, Garmin	+0:06:01
5. Frank Schleck, Saxo Bank	+0:06:04
6. Andreas Kloden, Astana	+0:06:42
8. Christian Vande Velde, Garmin	+0:12:04
17. Carlos Sastre, Cervélo	+0:26:21
30. Cadel Evans, Silence-Lotto	+0:45:24
51. Denis Menchov, Rabobank	+1:17:04

EPILOGUE
JANUARY 9, 2010

I need to get out for a ride," says Lance Armstrong. "So can I ask you a favor—can I call you back later?"

"Sure," I say. "I don't want you to come up one training ride short of winning the twenty-ten Tour and blame it on me."

When I got home from the Tour de France, everyone I knew asked me what it had been like. I told them some great stories— about Armstrong blowing past the car that day on the climb up Petit-Saint-Bernard, and about being up on the top of Verbier on the day of the fastest climb in history, and I ham up the story about being scared of dropping Lance's bike, and I even tell everyone about my fateful talk with Kenny van Hummel. I could tell stories about the 2009 Tour all day. But I couldn't seem to tell anyone what it was like.

What it was like was like seeing a solar eclipse in the Stone Age. Something that felt momentous had happened, but afterward nothing seemed to have changed and I was left guessing about the origins and implications of what had passed.

I realized that if I wanted to hold on to whatever it was that had seemed so important about the comeback, whatever it was that made Lance Armstrong's ride at the Tour so vital and raw, I was going to have to talk to him about it. I'd done exactly the right thing by not formally interviewing him during the season. At the final time trial in Annecy, for instance, while I could sit on the steps of the team bus, then later sprawl out in the grass behind Armstrong's kids, a journalist who'd finagled his way past the security at the velvet rope was observed taking notes and got thrown out. I just hung around, hour after hour and day after day of race after race, and I learned more than I would have even if I'd coaxed Armstrong to sit down for a formal interview in which he'd have given me the formal answers. But now I needed to, as his friend had said, interview the shark.

At the press conferences he'd been doing since the Tour, and at the RadioShack winter training camp in Tucson, and in scheduled interviews with the cycling media, he would promote his new team and feed his bickering feud with Contador, but that was not what I wanted.

The phone rings again, and I tap the answer button.

Armstrong is in Hawaii, training with Carmichael and the newly hired Allen Lim, a quirky and innovative physiologist who previously worked for the pro peloton's most strident anti-doping team, Garmin. (And in the traditional Armstrong memes, his supporters see Lim's willingness to go to RadioShack as proof that Lance is clean, while his detractors cite it as an indication of his depravity. In a December 7, 2009, post, the popular cycling website NYVelocity .com, one of the most frequent critics and accusers of Armstrong, says the hiring is "a deliberate corruption of one of the champions of Garmin's mission. It's akin to Al Capone buying off one of the Untouchables just to prove that money can trump principle.") Lim has Armstrong swallowing pill-size, wireless thermometers so they can study changes in his core temperature as he rides. Armstrong is also riding with streamers of red and white yarn stuck to his skinsuit and helmet so Lim can conduct a real-world aerodynamic analysis of his slipstream (instead of in a wind tunnel, the way everyone else does it).

Lance and I talk for a little about training and racing and the rudiments of swallowing thermometers ("We don't reuse them," he says, "which everyone asks") and at some point it comes up that he wouldn't be going through all this if he didn't really believe he could win the Tour in 2010. And I say, "You really believed you were going to win the 2009 Tour, too, didn't you?"

"Oh, yeah," he says. "Even before the start. Even after the first stage, getting tenth and being a fair ways down and clearly out-classed, I believed, 'That's okay—we're still just getting into this thing, I'm still going to win. I'm going to *find* a way to win the way I've always done.' After Grande-Motte, when I was in that split in Stage 3 and gained forty-one seconds, I was even more sure that I was going to win. I didn't change my mind, I didn't realize I wasn't going to win, until Verbier."

I say, "When I was standing up there that day, and you'd just lost the Tour and we all knew it, you said you were content. That blew me away."

"Well," he says, "there was nothing more I could do. Alberto was spectacular on Verbier. We were close to the end of the Tour, too. When you think about the Tour, Verbier feels like it was half-way through because so much happened after that. But there were only four or five days left of the Tour after that. The damn thing was almost over. So part of me was like, 'I did what I could. I tried my best.' What they teach you at the YMCA when you're playing soccer. Do your best. What your mama tells you. I did what I could, but Alberto is a great bike rider and he rode away from us all."

I ask Armstrong why he thinks he can beat Contador next year.

"I know what I need to address," he says. He's talking about the ability to accelerate over and over from already high speeds, and absolute top-end climbing speed. He and Lim will also no doubt look for some kind of edge in what Lim calls thermoregulation, or a way to create a personal microclimate that lets one rider race in cooler conditions than everyone else on the hottest days—an inno-vation that could be implemented by a highly technical piece of gear such as a body-cooling vest, helmet, or skinsuit, or by some-thing as simple but logistically challenging as continually reducing body heat by dumping water over Armstrong's head. "It's interest-ing to be in the same place—literally, physically the same place that

I was twelve months ago today," Armstrong says. "I'm riding on the same terrain, covering the same climbs. Chris is here with all the data we had last year, so we can just overlay it. Allen's here and we're working with his stuff. I got a good chance. If Alberto rides a perfect race—if he rides physically as good as he did in 2009 and can be controlled by a team director who makes the decisions instead of him—he'll be almost impossible to beat. But he's very uncoachable. I respect Johan a lot for dealing with it for so long, and even more than Johan, the staff and riders. That total disrespect for the work people do—I've never done that and never understood it. I'll never get it. In this game, there's one guy that wins the Tour and he gets rich and famous, and if you're that guy and you don't hook up your brothers, man, it comes back. He always had a lot of handy excuses: *his earpiece fell out, he didn't understand the instructions in English.* . . . I can't wait for July. I'm serious. I'm . . . man . . . I want to fucking . . . I want to beat him. The whole world will be watching."

Armstrong's seven-year win streak was remarkable. But now that he's faced Contador and lost, he needs to defeat Contador to keep his achievement from being diminished. One thing the 2009 Tour made clear was that not only was Armstrong dominant from 1999 to 2005, but his competition was weak relative to Contador. The eight racers who in those seven years stood on the podium with Armstrong have, combined, just six Grand Tour victories. In the past three years alone, Contador has four all by himself. And, unlike those eight riders, he took one of those wins head-to-head against Armstrong. Contador is the only person who ever stood on a Tour de France podium with Armstrong who managed to win *any* Grand Tour with Armstrong in the race.

"He's the guy who brought Lance Armstrong down," I say.

He laughs. "Yeah. Well, the story is . . . don't write your final chapter."

"But the comeback part of the story is over," I say. "You're back." And I tell him that what I hope to know is something I suspect might have no simple, definitive answer: why he came back. Not an accumulation of reasons. Not a list of entities that benefited.

I'm asking, really, why all of us ever try to stage our own comeback, and why comebacks fascinate us so much.

He can't answer the question, though he tries. "I had spent basically three years not exercising much. On a regular basis but very little—I went from five or six hours a day down to thirty minutes a day. And I wasn't happy with that lifestyle. My personal life was a little rocky. My business dealings became very serious and almost all of them became very successful. With that came the stress and the responsibility of managing a lot more money than I had when I retired and a lot more money than I damn sure ever thought I'd have. And the foundation continued to grow and grow and grow, and I put myself out there more from a cancer advocacy standpoint—not wearing a bike jersey and saying a few words about cancer support, but wearing a suit and a tie and testifying on Capitol Hill."

He was a hero who tried living as a celebrity, and a competitor who tried living as a philanthropist. Bike racing might have been nothing more than the quickest and simplest retreat back to what he knew. But maybe, I suggest, bicycles give him something that nothing else can.

"Butterflies," he says, and when I laugh he does. It is such a simple and direct response it has to be an unfiltered truth. And he opens up.

"Balance," he says. "My life—keep in mind, for twenty-five years—had been for four, five, six hours I'm riding a bike. Cycling, it's one of those sports you can do eight hours a day. You're going to be tired at the end, but if you did an eight-hour run you wouldn't run again for a week. I think people are better, smarter, more present, and more patient when they've done some type of exercise—that goes for an eight-year-old and a sixty-eight-year-old—and I need more, perhaps more than most people, to get the results I want. Bike racing is the thing that provides me with the most balance."

This is not some idiosyncratic theory of the good life Armstrong has cooked up as justification. There are some scientific indications that because cycling combines sustained aerobic exercise with complex brain functions such as balance, timing, and spatial awareness, it might be ideally suited to soothe the brain. In a 2008 study of 115 students at the Humboldt University of Berlin's Institute of Sport Science, students who engaged in ten minutes of exercise that required complex, highly coordinated movements performed better on a test measuring attention and concentration than students who did simpler aerobic exercise. (And both groups tested better than when they hadn't exercised.) Another study at Vanderbilt University found that after performing short, complex exercises that emphasized balance and quick reaction and decision making—all descriptors of what it takes to navigate a race peloton—adults were 40 percent more successful at solving a puzzle than when trying to do so after being idle. In a 2005 survey of clinical trials and research held at a conference in Washington, D.C., among the presentations from scientists from Georgetown University, Johns Hopkins, the University of Wisconsin, and Duke University Medical School were findings that the changes in the brain activity of meditating monks are directly comparable to the changes that occur during the act of pedaling a bicycle.

"It's a simpler existence," Armstrong says, "the life—not of an athlete—but that of a big-time endurance athlete. I train, I sleep, I get a massage, I eat, I take a nap. I have four kids, so I balance them in, and some work with the foundation. And I also want to be able to have some fun, to sit down and have two or three glasses of wine at dinner if I want. But things like this—talking on the phone with you right now—that's a bump in the road of my day, so to be a bike racer I have to do less of all the extra stuff I used to do. The past four years, there were a lot of times when I'd be doing stuff but saying to myself, 'What I really wish is that I was on a bike ride right now.'" He pauses and says, "What I have to get back to this year—I'm just talking to myself—is doing long rides alone. I did long rides in 2009 but very few alone. I'm always around people—teammates, fans, sponsors, donors—always surrounded by people. That time, a two-hour ride or a four-hour ride, a six-, eight-hour ride, that time alone is invaluable. In the old days I did most of my training alone. And that is probably the single most important thing I missed."

Being alone on a bike on an empty road is one of the best things about the sport, I tell him, and he agrees and for a few seconds we're quiet. I ask him what's going to happen when he no longer can ride the way he needs to. He pulled off the comeback this time, but when he retires again he really will be too old to consider having another shot at winning the Tour. He's going to lose the simplicity, the balance, and the butterflies.

"I won't," he says. "I won't get back to that place where I wasn't . . . I was really not an athlete. I won't get back to that place. There's a lot of guys—they're not the best in their sport anymore, but they still do it and they're still competitive at their own level—a guy like Ned Overend." Overend, who was the first-ever world champion in the nascent sport of mountain biking in 1990, retired from full-time professional racing in 1996. In 2009, he finished second at the Mount Washington Hill Climb, the hardest uphill race in the world. The New Hampshire mountain road climbs 4,650 feet in just 7.6 miles for an average grade of 12 percent—nearly the same elevation gain as Ventoux in about half the distance. It has slopes as high as 22 percent and sections of dirt road, and near the top the winds are so high that riders are regularly blown off the road and crash. Overend finished 16 seconds behind Phil Gaimon, a six-foot-one, 148-pound pro with a resting heart rate near 35 beats per minute and a body fat percentage of 4.2. Gaimon was twenty-three years old, Overend fifty-one.

"Go out and ride with Ned," Armstrong says, "and he'll kick your ass seven days a week because he's Ned Overend and he rides every day and he cares about his lifestyle and his game. I lost sight of that for a while."

Back at the Tour, when I asked Wim Vansevenant if he was happy being retired from bike racing, he said, "You find your rhythm."

The greatest *lanterne rouge* ever became a farmer. Fausto Coppi gave up the love of a nation to be with the love of his life. Don Giacomazzi dug a spoon into the Superior Dairy's rocky road ice cream, death be damned.

Lance Armstrong had to come back to the Tour de France. With his own victory over cancer and his ongoing worldwide crusade against the disease, with his four children, with friendships that range from Bono to Bill Clinton, Armstrong is accurate in his famous assessment that his life is not about the bike. But without the bike, he loses sight of what his life is about. It is on a bicycle, chasing and being chased, attacking and attacked, winning and losing, that he finds the rhythm for the rest of his life.

ACKNOWLEDGMENTS

The kid hung in there through a tough year and was always able to give me whatever I needed to get the story right, so my premier offering of gratitude goes to Natalie. My manuscript readers Peter Flax and David Howard influenced every page. Loren Mooney, editor in chief of *Bicycling* magazine, gave me support and freedom without which I couldn't have pursued the story, and also allowed me to report and write about Armstrong for the magazine and book simultaneously. (Several sections of this story were originally researched for and appeared in slightly different forms in *Bicycling* and at Bicycling.com, and the material was used in these pages only with Loren and *Bicycling*'s consent.) Andrew Hood was a great help in talking through the context and particulars of the story. Bruce Hildenbrand conducted ancillary interviews and provided background material. I followed the Tour of California with the assistance of Bill Gifford, who also helped by expressing critical opinions that pushed me to balance the story. At the Tour de France, I followed the race with the assistance of James Startt and Luti DeOliveira, and the book is significantly richer in text and images thanks to the immeasurable cycling knowledge and photographic skills of James. Deb Cosgrove helped with logistics throughout the race season. South Mountain Cycles and Coffee Bar, to which I periodically escaped to structure and write portions of the book, provided continual inspiration by reminding me why so many love the sport so much. Alex Gibney got the book pointed in the right direction with a late-night phone call that talked me out of a quagmire. My editor, John Glusman, saw many things in the story I could not. Domenica Alioto, Antonella Iannarino, and Susan Raihofer kept chaos at bay while I wrote and revised. And none of this would work at all without my agent, David Black.

Finally, I am indebted to the LMYA Socceroos U-11 girls travel soccer team (Abby, Brooke, Colleen, Julia, Julianna, Katie, Kira, Kristen, Lauren, Madison, Mackie, Madalyn, Natalie, Rachel, Reese, and Rileigh), who welcomed their assistant coach back even though, during his frequent absences, they dominated their division in the 2009 spring and fall seasons.

INDEX

ABOUT THE AUTHOR

BILL STRICKLAND is the editor-at-large for *Bicycling* magazine, the world's largest cycling publication, and the author of the cycling-related books *Ten Points: A Memoir, We Might as Well Win* (coauthored with Johan Bruyneel), and *The Quotable Cyclist*. With the world's number-one cycling race commentator, Phil Liggett, Strickland has provided narration and instruction for Tour de France and other race videos for World Cycling Productions. He has ridden and raced throughout the United States, Europe, Australia, and Africa and currently races for the amateur cycling team Hup United.

www.TrueBS.net